# The Sound of Sight

## The Neil Halford Story

This is the story of a young boy, his family and the small town in which he lives. It is a story of tragedy. It is a story of love. It is the story of an incredible boy, born out of catastrophe, nourished by the love of his family and the concern of his community.

Our country's foundation is the American family. What makes the United States a great nation is the strength of the family. The Halfords are your "average" American family: a mother, Linda, a father, Larry, and two children, Ryan and Neil. Though many are statistically average, there is no typical family. Each one is distinct and unique. On most days, a family's life is routine, normal, even boring. Yet, there are times when every one experiences joy and faces tragedy, each to a different degree and in a different way. A family, strengthened by its mutual love and support, can overcome its challenges, survive its tragedies and prosper.

Like millions of others in this country, the Halfords have experienced the agonies and ecstasies of life. However, unlike most, their challenges have been extreme and their lives have been extraordinary.

# The Sound of Sight

## THE NEIL HALFORD STORY

Neil R. Halford

PRESTIGE PUBLISHING COMPANY

*For further information, you can contact the author at:*

The Sound of Sight, LLC
P.O. Box 547
Fort Calhoun, Nebraska 68023

*or call:*

(402) 306-6756

*or e-mail:*

www. thesoundofsight.com

*Book design by The Floating Gallery*
*www.thefloatinggallery.com*

Printed in the United States of America

Library of Congress Control Number  2004098077
ISBN  0-9762830-0-X

*With love and respect, I dedicate this book to my parents. I thank you for having the courage to allow me to succeed, and for the years of unending sacrifice. To Nelson, Jay, Biz, Husk and Billy, I've heard it said that most people are lucky to have one good friend over the course of their life. I've been blessed with five. Finally, to the community of Fort Calhoun, thank you for so many years of unwavering support. I couldn't think of a better place to have been raised and to raise my family.*

# Contents

# Chapter One

## INTRODUCTION

*On June 27, 1969 I married my high school sweetheart and officially became Linda Halford. We were a young couple, struggling financially. However, every year our lot improved. In early 1970, we bought our first house in Fort Calhoun. Our first son, Ryan Wayne Halford, was born on May 19, 1971. Three years later, on September 26, 1974, Neil Raymon Halford was born. These early years were happy years. I had two beautiful, healthy boys and was married to a wonderful man, who was an exceptional father.*

*We were both raised in Fort Calhoun, Nebraska. Though a small town, with a population of 800, it was only thirty minutes from downtown Omaha. Thus, we had the best of both worlds. We had the quiet serenity of a small town and all the modern advantages of a metropolitan area. My parents, my older brother, my younger sister and their families all lived in Fort Calhoun. The people in the town, our neighbors, were like an extended family. Like any family, there were always minor disagreements. However, whenever a member of the Fort Calhoun family faced a crisis, the town rallied to their support. It is a characteristic unique to small towns. Larry and I took it for granted; until one day, when tragedy struck our family. I truly believe if we had not lived in Fort Calhoun, this story, our family and our lives would have been much different, would have been much more tragic.*

*Wednesday, July 20, 1977, was a beautiful summer day. That morning, I went to work at the local bank. Larry had the day off and planned to spend it with the boys. He worked long, hard hours. Any free time he had, he spent with his sons. Ryan and Neil cherished the time they spent with their father. None of us realized the events of this day would change our lives forever.*

# The Accident

"Daddy! Daddy! Help!"

Larry had heard Ryan, his oldest son, call for help many times before. This was different. This was a scream of fear, a scream filled with terror. In an instant, he was running toward the anguished cries.

He was a veteran of the Vietnam War. Wounded in action, he was a decorated war hero, who had seen many men die. Yet, in spite of the death and tragedy he had witnessed, he was not prepared for what he saw upon exiting the stall. Neil, Larry's two-year old son, was standing at the entrance to the barn. His face was unrecognizable, crushed and entirely covered in blood.

Rushing to Neil, he took him in one arm and Ryan in the other, and sprinted to the truck. Larry knew that every second counted. Laying Neil on the front seat, he sped toward town. Ryan was huddled against the passenger door, silently crying, frozen in fear. He had never seen his Dad move so fast, drive so fast. Larry held a towel over Neil's face, trying to stop the bleeding. It wasn't working. Blood was rapidly covering the entire seat.

Larry was faced with a critical decision. The hospital was 15 minutes away. Should he drive to the hospital or, upon reaching town, should he call the EMT's. Fort Calhoun had a volunteer fire department, whose members were his friends and neighbors. They were well trained and capable. He knew they would try everything they could to save Neil. However, his major concern was how long it would take them to respond to the emergency call.

As he approached town, seeing Neil covered in blood, Larry decided he could not take the chance. He must take Neil directly to the hospital. Passing by the Fort Atkinson State Park, he saw his good friend, who was the park ranger, Steve Kemper. Coming to a screeching stop, Larry ordered Ryan to run to Steve, "Ryan, tell Steve that I've taken Neil to the hospital. Have him call your Mom."

Upon hearing Larry's tires screech to a stop, Steve turned toward the road. For just a moment, his eyes met Larry's. Steve saw the fear in his eyes. He knew something terrible had happened. Ryan ran, crying to Steve, as Larry sped away. Larry couldn't wait to talk to Steve; life was draining from Neil's body with every drop of blood.

Clutching the hysterical boy in his arms, Steve tried to make sense of Ryan's frantic cries. The only words Steve could understand were, "Neil! Blood! Hospital!" After several minutes, Steve managed to calm Ryan. It was then that he learned the terrible truth. He immediately made two telephone calls.

The first was to Immanuel Hospital to give notice that Larry was en route. Then he called Linda, informing her that Larry had taken Neil to the hospital. Not knowing the extent of Neil's injuries and not wanting to alarm her, based upon the frightened ranting of Ryan, Steve told her nothing more, than that she should go to the hospital.

Racing through the narrow streets of town, Larry quickly reached the primary intersection. Ignoring the stop sign, he turned south on Highway 75. Tires squealing, he cut in front of a semi-truck. Ignoring the trucks blaring horn, he floored the gas pedal. By the time he reached the edge of town, he had broken the speedometer. The speedometer had a maximum speed of 120 mph.

Highway 75 was the major north thoroughfare for Omaha. The traffic was always heavy. Over the noon hour, it was especially busy. With his emergency lights flashing and his horn blaring, Larry recklessly passed cars. Refusing to slow down, he sped down the centerline of the highway, forcing cars in both lanes to the side of the road. Larry knew that he was risking their lives, but he had no choice. His son was dying.

Neil was lying on the seat, in a pool of blood. The gurgling sound, which Larry felt was Neil breathing, had stopped. Larry could not afford to take his eyes off the road, so he began to talk to Neil, hoping it would help keep him alive. "Hang in there, Doot. We're almost to the hospital. They will make you better. I love you, Doot."

Larry didn't think about the accident. He didn't feel any guilt. In fact, he didn't feel anything. It was much like Vietnam, when he was under attack. His every movement was instinctive. The only difference was that this time he wasn't fighting for his survival. He was fighting for his son's life. His every sense was heightened. Fueled by adrenalin and fear, his only thought was to save Neil.

Normally a ten-minute drive, he reached the interstate in three minutes. Barely slowing to turn onto the entrance ramp, he saw an Omaha policeman in the opposite lanes. The policeman, seeing how recklessly Larry was driving, turned on his lights and siren, crossed the median, and started the pursuit.

Seeing the police car, he knew he couldn't stop. His son would die. No matter how many police tried to stop him, he was determined to get Neil to the hospital. Then, he would deal with the police.

Immanuel Hospital was located in Northwest Omaha. When the hospital came into view, Larry's hope was renewed. It had taken him seven minutes. To his surprise, as he pulled up to the emergency entrance, a team of doctors and nurses were waiting. Skidding to a stop, the medical team immediately took Neil and rushed him inside.

The policeman reached the hospital just as the nurses were placing Neil on the gurney. He saw a little boy covered in blood, laying lifelessly on the gurney. What he thought had been a madman at the wheel, he now realized was a father trying to save his son. He returned to his car, said a prayer for the boy, and quietly drove away.

Holding Neil's hand, while the nurses wheeled the gurney to the emergency room, Larry repeatedly whispered, "I love you, Doot." Stopped at the doors of the emergency room, he watched Neil disappear amid a throng of nurses and doctors. Unconsciously, Larry slowly backed away, until he hit a wall. Then, suddenly exhausted and overcome with grief, he slowly dropped to the floor, leaving a trail of blood on the wall. He began to sob uncontrollably, silently, repeatedly admonishing himself, "How could this happen? What have I done?"

Sitting on the floor, his thoughts reverted back to the events of that Wednesday morning. It was a typical Nebraska summer day. The intense heat and humidity of the early morning signaled the forecasted temperature of one hundred degrees. Larry had the day off from work and he planned to spend it with his sons.

Linda awoke to the radio alarm with Alan O'Dey singing "Undercover Angel." Six a.m. was too early to get up. She hit the snooze button, instantly silencing Alan. Embracing Larry, her husband of eight years, she whispered, "Larry, I don't want to go to work. Let's take the boys and spend the day at the river."

He knew she was daydreaming. Linda worked as a teller at the local bank. Except for Neil's birth, she had not missed a day of work, since the bank had opened in 1974. No matter how tired or sick she was, she always went to work.

"That's a great idea. Get up. Prepare the food. Get the boys up and ready. Then wake me," he jokingly ordered, as he rolled over, planning to go back to sleep. Hitting him in the arm, Linda responded sarcastically, "If I have to do everything myself, I might as well go to work." Interrupted by the return of music on the radio, she silenced the alarm and rose from the bed, knowing that she would go to the bank.

Rolling over, Larry looked at the clock radio. It was 8:30 and the house was silent. After the verbal repartee with Linda, he had fallen back to sleep. Then, he heard the patter of little feet and muffled giggles coming from the hall. He knew the sound of his precious boys. Ryan was the elder at six years of age and Neil was almost three.

Whenever their father stayed home, they had a routine. The boys would sneak into the bedroom, believing that their father was asleep. They would then jump on him, waking him up. Larry closed his eyes, pretending to be asleep.

"When I say go, we both jump on him," Ryan whispered to Neil as they stood next to the bed. Neil responded with a nervous giggle, ready to move on Ryan's command. "Go!" Ryan yelled.

In an instant they were on Larry. They wrestled. Larry would gently throw them off the bed. They would return, attacking from all sides, determined to be "King of the Bed" by pushing their Dad off the bed. Eventually, after a long struggle, they won. Their Dad ended up lying on the floor. The boys bounced on the bed, celebrating their victory.

Still lying on the floor, Larry ordered, "Hey, McGoo and Doot, time to get dressed." These were his nicknames for Ryan and Neil. No one knew why, but when Neil first learned to talk he called Ryan, "Ian McGoo." So Larry started calling Ryan, "McGoo." Larry called Neil "Duke" after John Wayne. However, when Neil first said the name, it came out as "Doot". Hence, Neil became known as "Doot."

Their Dad's order having signaled the end of the celebration, the boys stopped bouncing. Standing on the bed, towering over their father, they looked at each other. Instinctively, without saying a word, they made one last jump. After landing on their Dad, they escaped. Ryan grabbed Neil's hand and they scampered to the safety of their bedroom.

As was his habit, after the bedroom brawl, Larry took the boys to the Midway Café for breakfast. It was a gathering place for many of the local farmers and townspeople. When Larry and the boys entered the café, they were greeted to a round of "good mornings". It was like having breakfast with one big family.

Breakfast was always a challenge. Neil wanted to be treated like Ryan. This meant no high chair, pancakes with syrup, and a big glass of milk. Inevitably, something would spill. By the time the meal was done, Neil's shirt had become a mixture of milk, syrup and butter. Larry was a man with a short temper. However, when it came to his boys, he had the patience of Job. Nothing they did upset him. A messy breakfast was a time for fun, not discipline. Clothes could always be washed.

"Daddy, can we go see Hank?" Neil asked, as Larry was washing his face.

"Do you really want to go to the farm?" Larry replied, knowing what their answer would be.

"Yes! Please! Please! Please!" the boys pleaded in unison.

"Okay, Hank will be our next stop."

Raymon, Larry's father, was a horse trainer. Larry was raised around horses. For the last few years, Raymon had worked for a wealthy banker, training prize appaloosa horses. Larry and a good friend, Frank Starr, had purchased an appaloosa colt. Bred by two champions, he stood fifteen hands and was well muscled. Their intent was to train it and sell it within two years. The colt's name was Hank.

Hank was housed on a farm owned by a friend of Larry's. Larry paid rent and was responsible for the food and care of the colt. On his days off, Larry would take the boys to the farm, clean the stall, brush down Hank and ensure that he had enough food and water. Hank was gentle with the boys and loved their attention. Larry, knowing that a horse can change its mood at any moment, was always very careful. He did not allow the boys near the horse, unless they were with him.

Before the Corps of Engineers had harnessed the Missouri River, this great river cut a swath several miles wide, separating Iowa and Nebraska. The construction of a series of dams, which had harnessed the power and controlled the course of the river, had created a two-mile wide strip of some of the flattest, richest soil in the world. The farm was located on this Missouri river bottom, one mile east of the Halfords' home. Once the pride of the valley, the farmstead was now abandoned. The barn was white, with a red roof. It was structurally sound, but dilapidated. The paint was chipped and faded and the roof was missing many tiles. The corral was large and secure. Hank had the barn and corral to himself.

Upon arriving, they immediately settled into their routine. Larry ordered

Neil to play in the field next to the barn, while Larry and Ryan tended to Hank. Neil knew that once the chores had been completed, his Dad would let him ride Hank.

As Larry and Ryan approached the stall, Hank recognized them and stood by the gate, hoping for a treat and some special attention. After a few minutes of affection, they entered the stall and began cleaning it. Hank, who was normally very calm, seemed unusually agitated that day, making it difficult for Larry.

While they were struggling with Hank, Neil heard the commotion inside the barn. Curious, he climbed through the fence and began to walk toward the corral entrance of the barn.

"Ryan, take Hank to the corral," Larry ordered, frustrated with the colt's behavior. Ryan opened the stall gate, intending to lead Hank to the corral. Hank, seeing his chance for freedom, bolted from Ryan's hold and trotted toward the corral. Confident that Hank would remain in the corral, Ryan returned to help Larry.

Neil turned the corner to enter the barn, unaware that he was on a collision course with destiny. He took one step into the barn and saw Hank bearing down on him. There was no time. Hank was on him before he could move. Instinctively, Hank jumped, trying to miss Neil, but he was too close. Hank's front legs cleared Neil, but the hoof of his right hind leg hit Neil in the face, knocking him back into the corral. Laying face up on the ground, Neil was stunned, in shock. Somehow he managed to stand and move toward the barn, whimpering as he walked.

Hearing Neil's cries, Ryan left the stall to see what was wrong. Larry, intent on the job at hand, was oblivious to what had happened. Suddenly he was frozen by the sound every father fears. The loud, shrill scream of his son calling for help.

Still sitting on the floor of the hospital, Larry's thoughts were abruptly interrupted. He was jolted back to reality, by the anguished cries of his son coming from the emergency room.

"Mommy! Daddy!"

There was nothing he could do. Earlier, he had tried to enter the emergency room and was blocked by the nurses. All he could do was listen to Neil's agonizing cries of pain. Those cries would haunt him for many years. Now, sitting alone, Larry wrestled with his thoughts and anxieties, while his beloved son struggled for his life.

Driving to the hospital, Linda's mind was racing. She wasn't sure what had happened. Steve said he didn't know how badly Neil had been injured. She assumed it was a normal childhood injury, such as a broken arm or a cut that would require a cast or some stitches. However, deep inside, her natural instinct as a mother told her that it was much worse.

Arriving at the hospital, Linda rushed to the emergency room. Upon entering the hospital, she immediately saw the blood on the wall. Following it down, she saw Larry slumped over, sitting on the floor. Their eyes met. Immediately, she knew that this was much more than just a broken arm. Larry's eyes were lifeless, void of any feeling. His clothes were covered in blood. Instantly, she knew it was Neil's blood. A sense of panic and fear suddenly engulfed her entire body. She wanted to know what had happened. There were so many questions, but seeing Larry, blood covered and sobbing, she knew that this was not the time. She quietly helped him to a bench. Linda sat beside him and took him into her arms. Together, they sat, crying, praying.

# Life or Death

When Neil was rolled into the emergency room, everyone leaped into action. One look at Neil and they all knew that this was a life-threatening situation. In reality, there was not one person in the room who believed he would survive.

The members of the emergency room staff were a team, well trained and specialized. They dealt with life and death daily. Each person had assigned duties. No matter how critical the patient, the routine was consistent. Initially, a quick, basic examination was performed to determine the status of the patient and the extent of his injuries.

The first concern was Neil's ability to breathe. Did he have a clear airway? This was complicated by the damage to Neil's face. Thus, his only airway was through his mouth. A quick check showed that it was clear. He was breathing. Then, they placed him on oxygen.

Simultaneously, they measured his pulse rate and blood pressure. Typically, a child has lower blood pressure and a more rapid pulse rate than an adult. Neil's pulse was 85 and his blood pressure was 110/60. Considering the amount of blood Neil had lost, surprisingly, both were within the normal ranges.

Since Neil had been born at this hospital, they had a record of his blood type. He was Type O, Positive. They immediately started giving him a blood transfusion. This continued for the next eight hours.

At this point, they could not give him any pain medication. They needed him conscious and awake for the CAT scan. A CAT scan of the brain would help them determine if there was any damage or swelling of the brain. Unfortunately, there was some swelling in his brain. Once the CAT scan was completed, Neil was medicated, though always conscious.

As his face was being cleaned, the damage became apparent. It was extensive. In effect, his entire face had been crushed and flattened, as if it had been ironed. It looked like the face of a rubber doll, when you push the face inward. There was no contour left to his face. He had no nose. The most extensive damage was to the eyes. This was another indication of potential brain damage.

The attending physician examined him in total disbelief. He knew that there was no way this boy should be alive. If Neil had been two years older, with a more mature, brittle bone structure, he would have died. His bones would have broken and been pushed into his brain, causing instant death. At his age, his bones were much smaller and more pliable. Thus, they either bent or were completely shattered. Once Neil had been stabilized, the doctor determined his most immediate needs. An ophthalmologist was first. Neil's eyes were the most critical concern. Then would come the neural surgeon, who would determine the extent of the brain damage. Last would be a plastic surgeon. Neil's entire face would have to be reconstructed.

The name on her hospital identification card read Jill. That was all that was required. Everyone knew her. She had been the supervising trauma nurse for six years. Before today, she thought she had seen everything. She was wrong. Never had she seen a small child with such extensive injuries. Jill thought this little boy would never survive. She knew it was a miracle that he was still alive.

As the senior attending nurse, Jill was responsible for supervising the other nurses. Her training and experience had taught her to never become emotionally involved, to never become attached to any patient. Looking around the room, she saw that many of the other nurses were crying. Jill knew this would be a long night. She also knew many of her associates would not be able to endure the extensive and severe surgery, which Neil required. Many of the young nurses were mothers with small children. Neil's injuries and probable death made them all realize how fragile their own children's lives were. In anticipation of what lay ahead, Jill ordered two other teams of nurses be placed on standby.

After Neil had been stabilized and she had taken time to comfort and encourage each of the nurses, she reviewed the patient's chart. Jill read the patient's name, "Neil Halford." "Oh, my God!" she whispered, with tears swelling in her eyes.

For the last two hours, she had been operating on the son of one of her closest friends, Linda Halford. When Linda and Larry were first married, they lived in an apartment in Florence, a suburb of Omaha. Jill and her husband were their next-door neighbors for two years. During that time, Linda and Jill became close friends. Though they had not seen each other in over two years, she immediately wanted to run to Linda. She knew she couldn't. The best way to help her friend was to stay with Neil. Wiping her tears away, she returned to the operating table, determined to save this special little boy's life.

Upon Neil's arrival, the hospital called Dr. Wallace Engdahl. He had been the Halfords' family doctor for ten years. Hearing of the tragedy, he immediately rushed to the hospital, where he consulted with the attending physician. Dr. Engdahl insisted that the hospital call Dr. Truelson, the premier ophthalmologist in Omaha.

"Raymond, I just got a call from Immanuel Hospital. They need one of us in the emergency room." Dr. Truelson explained, "I think it's pretty routine. Would you mind taking the call?"

Raymond Crossman had just completed his residency. He had joined Dr. Truelson's practice three weeks earlier. Being the junior doctor, he had no choice but to accept the assignment.

"No problem. I can leave immediately."

"Great. I'll call the hospital and confirm that you are en route."

Fifteen minutes later, Dr. Crossman arrived at the hospital. The moment he entered the emergency room, he knew there was nothing routine about this patient. He was alarmed by the amount of attention and the urgency of the attention directed toward the young patient. Several nurses were crying and the room was deathly quiet. A disturbing signal was in the eyes of the nurses. Their eyes reflected the pall of death.

The attending physician quickly briefed Dr. Crossman on Neil's condition. Then, Dr. Crossman began his examination. It was difficult. Due to the severity of Neil's trauma, and in spite of the efforts of the staff, Neil's face was seriously swollen. The swelling prevented a complete examination. Initially, the doctor examined the right eye. All of the contents of the eye, the iris, the lens, and the optic nerve were gone. There was no saving Neil's right eye.

To examine the left eye, Dr. Crossman had to make several small cuts, in an effort to see through the swollen tissue. The left eye was also seriously damaged, though most of the contents of the eye were still intact. Neil would never see out of this eye, but there was some hope that he might be able to detect light and shadows.

The left eye raised some serious issues. The fact that the injury was inflicted by an animal in a corral combined with the extent of the damage created a major threat of infection. If Neil acquired an infection in his eye, it could quickly migrate to his brain, causing death. The surest way to prevent infection was to remove the entire eye. It was Dr. Crossman's decision. Should he run the risk of infection to give Neil the chance to have some light vision?

Though confident in his abilities, he wanted the second opinion of his senior partner, Dr. Truelson. He had performed many operations during his internship and residency. In all of his years of training, he had never seen such total devastation. He did not know it at the time, but he would never have another patient as critical as Neil Halford. The situation was further complicated by Neil's young age. Even though he had been taught to approach each patient in a clinical, analytical, emotionless manner, in this case he couldn't. He felt so helpless. There was so little he could do. The most likely prognosis was that Neil would die. Even in the best case, he was going to be totally blind. Like so many of the nurses, Dr. Crossman struggled to hold back his tears. After a lengthy telephone conference, they agreed that the left eye should be saved.

For the next three hours, Dr. Crossman operated on Neil. He completely removed the right eye. Thoroughly washing the eye cavity with antibiotics, he then sewed it shut. As part of the surgery, he placed a temporary orb in the eye cavity. This would enable Neil to obtain a false eye in later years.

The left eye was the focus of most of the operation. Dr. Crossman had to restore all of the eye's contents to their correct position and carefully stitch them in place. He used a microscopic lens to accomplish this surgery. After completing the surgery, he carefully washed the left eye with antibiotics, in hopes of preventing any infection. Over the next few weeks, Dr. Crossman performed two additional surgical operations on the left eye.

Immediately after the surgery, Dr. Crossman left the hospital, anxious to return to the sanctuary of his family. Though he tried to forget, the sight of Neil would haunt him that night and for many, many years to come.

During this period, the neural surgeon had examined Neil's CAT scan and determined that until the swelling receded, he could not determine if there was any actual brain damage. Only time would tell.

After completing the eye surgery, the plastic surgeon, Dr. Edward Bacari, commenced reconstructing Neil's face. This would be the first of four surgeries over the next five years. At this point, Dr. Bacari was not concerned about Neil's appearance. His major concern was removing the residue of the crushed bones, cleaning all of the wounds, and rebuilding Neil's basic facial structures, such as his jaws, his nasal cavities and airways, and his eye sockets. This surgery took more than four hours. It required more than 300 stitches and three feet of wire to hold his face in place.

During the surgery, which lasted eight hours, nurses were constantly being substituted, shuttling in and out of the emergency room. Just as Jill had anticipated, many of the younger nurses could not emotionally deal with the case. Crying nurses were frequently escorted from the emergency room. Jill remained with Neil until all of the surgery had been completed. No one, including Jill, believed that Neil would live. It went unspoken, but it was in everyone's eyes.

Each time a doctor or nurse would leave the emergency room, Linda and Larry would anxiously ask about Neil's condition. Each time they would get the same reply, "The doctors will talk to you when they are finished."

The more time that passed, the more helpless they felt. Hopeless not in any routine sense, but as a deep, dark despair that visits families only occasionally and threatens unthinkable destruction.

Oblivious to time, Linda and Larry were lost in their sorrow. It seemed like one moment they were alone and the next the hospital was filled with family and friends. News spreads like wild fire through a small town, especially when it is about a native; one of their own. Linda's mother, brother and sister lived in Fort Calhoun and Larry's brother lived in a neighboring town. They were all there. Others also came. The waiting room was overwhelmed with people.

Finally, at 9:00 p.m., two doctors emerged from the operating room; Dr. Bacari, the plastic surgeon, and Dr. Engdahl. Seeing the doctors approaching, Larry and Linda stood. Looking exhausted and very somber, Dr. Engdahl asked if they wanted to meet privately, away from the throng of people.

"These people are our family. They all love Neil. We'll talk here." Larry replied.

Motioning for them to sit, Dr. Engdahl knelt by them and took Linda's hand. Larry put his arm around Linda, holding her tightly. Holding their breath, they expected the worst. They feared that Neil was dead. With Dr. Bacari standing next to him, Dr. Engdahl quietly, almost reverently, gave his report, "Neil had extensive damage to his face. Essentially, every bone in his face was either broken or crushed. He lost a tremendous amount of blood." Turning toward Larry, he said, "You did the right thing driving him to the hospital. Another few minutes and he would have died. That's how close it was."

Linda and Larry both sighed, releasing their breath. Neil was alive! Their newfound hope was quickly dashed, as Dr. Engdahl continued, "Neil is alive, but in very critical condition. He has lost his right eye and his left eye was severely damaged. His nose and nasal cavity were destroyed. There is some swelling in the brain, which means there may be some damage to the brain. In addition, with extensive eye injuries, there is a heightened level of concern about infection. We don't know and won't know for some time the extent of the damage. We had to reconstruct his entire face. He has more than three hundred stitches and three feet of wire holding his face together."

During the doctor's report, there were moans and sobs coming from the crowd of family and friends. Linda and Larry were in shock. The joy of learning that Neil was alive had turned to despair. Their son was still near death, and if he lived he could be blind and brain damaged. Linda began to cry, Larry holding her even tighter.

"He will be transferred to the Intensive Care Unit in about two hours, at which time you will be able to see him. I will be back in the morning to check on him and will meet with you again at that time."

Dr. Engdahl finished his report by trying to offer some encouragement, "I know it sounds bad, but there is always hope."

At the same time Neil was moved to the recovery room, his life hanging in the balance, fifteen miles away, Dr. Crossman rocked his two-month old daughter to sleep. Tearfully, he held her that entire night, keeping her safe from the cruel realities of life.

Across town, Jill returned home. Falling into her husband Archie's arms, she spent the night in his loving grasp, crying and praying for Neil.

# Never Ask "Why?"

Larry and Linda nervously sat in the waiting room of the Intensive Care Unit. Even though surrounded by family and friends, they seemed to be alone. Larry blankly stared at the floor. The Kempers had brought him some clean clothes. He had taken the time to clean up and change.

Linda suddenly arose, walked to the nurse's station, and asked, "What's taking so long? He should be here by now. Nothing's wrong, is there?"

The nurse patiently answered Linda, giving her the same answer as she had five minutes earlier, "Everything is okay, Mrs. Halford. He should arrive at any moment. The doctor has to release him from the recovery room, before he is brought to his room. I will let you know the moment Neil arrives."

She tried to be as understanding and sympathetic as possible. Everyone in the hospital knew about Neil Halford. Immanuel Hospital had only been open three years. In the short history of the hospital, Neil Halford was the most traumatic, most devastating case it had ever experienced. Word of his condition rapidly spread throughout the hospital. Everyone knew that Neil was fighting for his life. Several of her closest friends were in the emergency room, when Neil arrived. Although they were experienced, they were devastated. The entire staff was praying for Neil's recovery.

Before returning to her seat, Linda looked at the clock. It was 11:30 p.m. She realized Neil had been at the hospital for almost twelve hours. After several short conversations, followed by the obligatory hug, Linda sat next to Larry. She laid her head on his shoulder. He responded by putting his arm around her and giving her a reassuring hug.

Shortly thereafter, Linda abruptly sat up. Through the window of the door, which was the entrance to the Intensive Care rooms, she saw two nurses rolling a hospital bed into the room assigned for Neil. Shaking Larry back to reality, she excitedly whispered, "Larry, I think it's Neil! I just saw a bed rolled into his room."

They arose in unison and hurried to the nurses' station. Before they could ask, a nurse opened the door. Though, from their appearance, she immediately knew that the couple at the station must be Neil's parents, as a courtesy she reverently asked, "Are you Neil's parents?"

"Yes. Can we see him?" Linda anxiously asked.

The nurse understood they were anxious to see Neil, but she did not want them to enter the room unprepared for what they were about to see. Balancing the need for an explanation with their desire to be with their son, she tried to be precise, yet compassionate.

"My name is Ms. Wilson. I will be Neil's attending nurse tonight. He is still under the influence of the anesthesia. In addition, he is receiving pain medication through an I.V. His jaws are wired closed to allow his facial bones to set. His face is bandaged to protect the wounds. It will be several hours before he regains consciousness. When he does, it will be very difficult for him to talk."

"Is he in any pain?" Larry asked. Linda was startled. These were the first words Larry had spoken in four hours.

"No. He is resting comfortably."

Linda wrapped her arms around Larry, anticipating that she would need him for support. They quietly followed Ms. Wilson to Neil's room. At the door, Linda hesitated. Larry, feeling her fear, hugged her. He was also apprehensive. His last memory of Neil had haunted him all night. He could not forget that horrible sight. The image of Neil standing in the barn entrance, his face crushed and covered with blood, was vividly imbedded in his mind. He knew it would be there for the rest of his life. Larry was so glad that Linda did not see Neil like that. He thought it was better that she remember Neil as her beautiful, precocious, little boy. Slowly, Larry coaxed her into the room.

Breathlessly, they edged toward the crib, which held their son. Upon first sight of Neil, Linda immediately buried her head in Larry's chest, uncontrollably sobbing. Larry, his eyes not leaving Neil, tightened his hold on Linda. Neil lay still, unaware of their presence. The scene was surreal. Tubes were protruding from Neil's leg and mouth. His head, from just above the mouth was completely wrapped in a bandage. Uncovered, he seemed so frail. It was as if he had lost twenty pounds in only hours. Though it went unsaid, Larry knew that Neil was near death, that the next few hours were critical.

"He looks so fragile, so weak, so helpless." Linda whispered, tears streaming down her face. Larry helped Linda to a large chair in a corner of the room. Wrapped in each other's arms, they silently wept for their son's life. Nurses constantly entered the room. Carefully monitoring Neil's condition, they also changed his bandages every hour.

The first time the nurses changed Neil's bandages, Linda did not want to watch. Larry did. He wanted to know everything. However, as the nurse slowly and carefully unwrapped the bandages, Larry was not prepared for what he saw. Neil's face was badly swollen. His right eye was gone, replaced by a white orb. There were stitches everywhere. Below each jaw, a wire was tied in a knot. The only analogy Larry could think of was Frankenstein. Based upon what he saw, he did not believe that Neil would ever look normal.

Failing to control his emotions, Larry tearfully returned to Linda, where they sat in a tight embrace. Linda, emotionally exhausted, quickly fell to sleep. Larry could not sleep. He was living in hell. It was a hell created by agonizing grief, excruciating guilt, and despairing doubts. Question after unanswerable question raced through his mind. "Why Neil? How could I let this happen? What happens now? If he lives, what will Neil's life be like? How will he grow up? What do I do? How does he feel? What do I say to my wife? What do I say to Neil? How will Ryan be affected?"

Larry could not answer any of these questions. Though Neil lay in a crib next to him, Larry could still not believe it had really happened. Unconsciously, he hoped it was nothing but a bad dream. As the hours painfully and slowly passed, Larry gradually accepted the reality of Neil's condition.

Then, the moment arrived. The nurses were absent and Linda was sleeping. It was time for a father to be alone with his son, for Larry to be alone with Neil. Leaning over the side of the crib, looking at his frail, helpless son, fighting for his life, Larry was filled with a new resolve. He knew that there were no answers to his questions, which had haunted him for most of the night. In fact, those questions were not important. The only thing that mattered was Neil. Larry marshaled his emotions and vowed to accept the situation, whatever it may be, and to make the best of it. He would never dwell on the negative again. He would never ask why, again.

Kissing Neil on his chin, he whispered, "Hey Doot, it's me. I hope you can hear me. I am so sorry, son. I promise you that no matter how tough, how difficult, you will have the same opportunities as any other boy. This is my solemn pledge to you, son."

# The Miracle

Neil had been in the hospital for seven days when another tragedy struck the Fort Calhoun community. Frank Schafer and his wife, Lana, were both born and raised in Fort Calhoun. They had been married for five years with two sons, seven and three, and a third on the way. Lana was expecting another son in four months. They were devout Christians and members of the local Baptist church.

In his spare time, Frank was building a garage attached to their house. It was a beautiful, late summer Saturday, an unusual reprieve from the sweltering July heat. Frank, with the help of some family and friends, had just finished setting the main steel support beam, which weighed 500 pounds. He was alone. His helpers had left and his wife was in the house.

Frank was shoring up the beam when disaster struck. The beam slipped loose from the wall pocket. Collapsing the wooden supports, it fell, striking Frank in the head. Fifteen minutes later, after calling Frank's name several times with no response, Lana went to the garage.

Turning the corner to the garage, she saw Frank. He was lying motionless on the floor, his head resting in a pool of blood. Calling his name she ran to him, kneeling at his side. After unsuccessfully trying to revive him, she rushed to the house and called the Fort Calhoun Rescue Squad.

Linda and Larry, like the previous seven days, were sitting in Neil's hospital room. Everyday, Neil showed dramatic improvement. He was becoming very active and animated. His energetic, bubbly personality was returning.

Neil was taking a late afternoon nap and his parents were also resting. The noise of a new patient being moved into the room across the hall awoke Linda. Suddenly, she sat upright. Linda recognized the woman trailing behind the gurney. It was Lana Schafer.

Gently nudging Larry, Linda whispered, "Larry, is that Lana Schafer across the hall? Something must have happened to Frank."

Startled by Linda's words, Larry glanced into the room. "You're right", Larry replied. "That is Lana."

Larry and Linda had known Frank and Lana since they first started elementary school. Arm in arm, they quietly exited Neil's room. Seeing the couple approach, Lana met them at the door. Tearfully, she explained what had happened. Then she repeated the doctor's prognosis. Frank had experienced severe trauma to the head, resulting in major swelling of the brain. A shunt had been put in place to help alleviate the pressure on the brain. Then Lana further explained his condition by quoting the doctors, repeating the same words that Larry and Linda had heard, "Only time will tell. There is always hope."

After discussing Neil's and Frank's conditions for several minutes, they each returned to their critically injured loved ones.

Everyday Linda struggled to control her emotions, to maintain a positive attitude. Each day, as Neil improved, it became a little easier. Then, she would see Frank, lying helpless in his hospital bed. Sitting by Larry in Neil's room, once again she would be overcome with a sudden rush of emotions. First her son, and now one of the nicest people she had ever known, was face to face with death. Larry pressed her head against his shoulder, to quietly comfort her, and whispered, "I know Linda, I know."

As the next few days passed, Neil slowly continued to improve, Frank did not. Each day, several members of the Schafer's church would hold vigil with Lana. They would pray, sing hymns and meditate. Several times the hospital staff had to request that they keep quiet.

Ten days after Frank had been admitted, the doctor told Lana that he would not come out of his coma and would eventually die. Lana became hysterical, loudly exclaiming that the doctor was wrong, that God would heal her husband. From that moment on, the religious vigil became more intense and louder, with more people participating and supporting the Schafers.

Larry and Linda both believed in God. However, they did not attend church regularly and were not fervent worshippers. In stark contrast to the Schafer family, they worshipped God quietly and privately.

Then one day, unexpectedly, Frank suddenly awoke and began speaking to his wife. Instantly a celebration erupted. Joyous "hallelujahs" and praises could be heard throughout the hospital.

Hearing the celebration, Larry and Linda left Neil to see what had happened. To their joy and private dismay, Frank was sitting up in bed. Later that day, the doctors examined Frank and declared him completely healed. They couldn't explain how, they could only attest to his condition. Two days later, Frank was released from the hospital.

After Frank had left, sitting in Neil's room, Linda was filled with mixed emotions. She was elated that Frank had completely recovered, yet disappointed that Neil, while recovering, would never be the same.

With tears running down her face, she whispered to Larry, "Maybe we should have been more religious. If only we had gone to church more, maybe this wouldn't have happened to Neil. Why would God save Frank, yet let a little boy like Neil suffer so much?"

Over the last two weeks, Linda had been gradually accepting Neil's condition. Occasionally, she would lapse into a period of regret and despair. As she once more laid her head on Larry's shoulder, she knew what he was about to say, "Linda, don't look back. We need to deal with today. We must make the best of our situation and never ask why."

# *Coming Home*

It was August 27, 1977, the day Larry and Linda had long anticipated. After five weeks of hospital food, sleepless nights, and a roller coaster of emotions, their two-year old son was being released from the hospital. Excited, yet apprehensive, they couldn't wait to take Neil home. They yearned for a return to the life they had enjoyed before that fateful day in July.

Their older son, Ryan, had bounced around between family and friends. They spent very little time with Ryan. The stress of the extended stay in the hospital had begun to take its toll. Though they were thankful that the day had finally arrived, Larry and Linda were still riddled with doubt. They did not know how their son would adjust to the life long challenge that lay ominously ahead.

While Larry dressed Neil, Linda gathered up the last of the gifts. People had been so kind and generous. Larry had already transported a load home the day before. Now, it looked as though they would have another full carload on this trip. For a moment, she paused, and looked upon the face of her son. The bandages were now removed and the scars of his recent operations stood out, in strong contrast to his smiling face. Linda was choked with emotion. She remembered the chubby cheeked little boy who had kissed her good night a mere month and a half before. Though he displayed an astounding mental vitality, his struggles were evident in his ravaged body. His arms and legs, once strong and vibrant, were now thin and weak from the long stint of hospital inactivity.

The time at the hospital had been both inspiring and depressing. The nurses told them that due to his medication, Neil would be semiconscious for days. That was not the case. The day after the accident, Neil woke up and immediately started talking. It was difficult, because his jaws were wired. That did not deter Neil. It was a blessing. Almost immediately, Linda and Larry knew that there was no brain damage.

Dr. Crossman had indicated that, because of his age, Neil would never remember being able to see. He was right. Neil never once questioned his inability to see. Though weak and blind, Neil's personality quickly returned, both good and bad. Neil was his talkative, enthusiastic, cheerful self. He was also his stubborn self. Neil had been potty trained at a very young age. While in the hospital, the nurses wanted him to go in a bedpan. He emphatically refused. He demanded, tubes and all, that he be lifted from the bed and carried to the stool. The nurses viewed this as an inconvenience. Linda and Larry were encouraged. Unconsciously, Neil was making a statement. He would not let this accident change his life.

The stay had been difficult, filled with moments of encouraging triumphs and disappointing setbacks. Neil underwent several minor eye surgeries. Just as Neil was regaining his strength, an operation would set him back for days. Neil would always bounce back, without ever complaining.

"How is he going to do it?" she asked herself. "How will he get around without running into things?"

Her mind was full of insecurity and doubt. She imagined their home. Once filled with the sounds of laughing children, she feared there would never again be any laughter or joy. Linda tried to be strong, for Neil's sake. Though, sometimes, without warning, she would be consumed with despair and fear.

"Is it time to go yet?" Neil asked, struggling to talk through his jaws, which were still wired shut.

"Its almost time, Doot," Linda said, trying to sound as excited as Neil. Like Larry earlier, she had vowed to never let Neil know of her doubts and fears.

An hour later, they pulled into their driveway. Linda and Larry were anxious, consumed by a sense of anticipation and nervous tension. Ryan and Neil were chattering away in the back seat. Neil's excitement was contagious. Larry parked the car and lifted Neil from the back seat. He carried him up the stairs to the front door. Larry opened the front door and set Neil on his feet.

Holding their breath with apprehension, they carefully watched Neil's every step. Neil, on shaky legs, without assistance, slowly made his way. With his arms outstretched, serving as his radar, he cautiously navigated through the living room and down the hall to his room. Occasionally, his arms would make contact with a wall or piece of furniture. Without hesitation or help, Neil would alter his course and continue. Watching from a distance, Larry and Linda were heartened by the fact that Neil obviously remembered everything about the house, from the floor plan to the location of the furniture. Ryan followed close behind, keeping a watchful eye on his brother's progress. Upon reaching Neil's room, Ryan began showing Neil where his different toys were located.

After a few minutes of inspection, Linda hurried in and ushered Neil into bed. "You'll have plenty of time to play with your toys later. Now, you need to rest." She said, tucking Neil beneath the covers.

Neil took her face in his little hands. He pulled her face down, gave her a kiss and said, "I love you, Mommy."

"I love you, too." Linda said, fighting back the tears.

Over the next few weeks, Linda discovered that many of her fears had been groundless. Neil quickly adapted to his new situation. As the days passed, she realized just how wrong she had been. The father-son wrestling matches soon returned. She was constantly stopping the wrestling matches between Larry and Neil, for fear that Neil would break the wires holding his jaws. She watched as his cautious steps of insecurity soon changed to a confident walk and finally to a run. She recognized that Neil had quickly returned to his normal reckless and fearless self.

Neil's strength constantly amazed Linda and Larry. When they left the hospital, they both were concerned about caring for Neil. While in the hospital, Neil had twenty-four hour, hands on care. Larry and Linda hoped they would be able to provide the same at home. They quickly learned that their concern was unnecessary. Neil rarely complained about his condition and attempted to do most things for himself.

Though Neil's strength and spirits improved daily, Larry and Linda both knew that overwhelming challenges lay ahead.

# Baking Day

The Fitzgerald family lived next door to the Halfords. Margaret and John Fitzgerald had five children, Robert, 16, Kathy, 15, Bill, 14, Jeannie, 13, and John, 8. John and Ryan were inseparable. The two girls were the Halford's regular babysitters. Between babysitting and playing, the two Halford boys spent most of their free time at the Fitzgerald house. They were like part of the Fitzgerald family.

Margaret, called Margie, was a registered nurse. She worked at the county hospital, with Thursday and Sunday as her days off. Thursday was Margie's baking day. Ever since Neil's accident, Thursday had not been the same. Before the accident, every Thursday morning was her special time with Neil.

Her children were all older, involved with their friends, their athletics and their school activities. Even Ryan was now in school. Neil had been like another baby in the family. Once again, she had someone to hold, someone to rock, and someone who loved to have her read books. Neil had been such a precocious, talkative and inquisitive little boy.

Every Thursday morning, like clockwork, Neil would appear in her kitchen. He would arrive shortly after she had started baking the first batch of his favorite cookies, chocolate chip. The sweet smell of baking chocolate would slowly float out her kitchen window, across the fence, which separated their back yards, and through Neil's bedroom window. Neil would be playing, anxiously awaiting the aromatic announcement that it was "Baking Day."

Without hesitation, Neil would immediately rise, leave his house through the front door, walk up the street, enter the garage, open the squeaky door to the house and stomp up the stairs to the kitchen. When Neil opened the squeaking door, it signaled his entrance. It was then followed by eight very loud, purposeful stomps, as Neil climbed the steps to the kitchen. Her children all called Neil "L'il Big Foot." Upon entering the kitchen, he would announce himself with the words, "Good morning "Mar-kie." She smiled. He struggled to pronounce her name.

Upon entering the kitchen, he would assume his usual position on the stool next to the kitchen counter. There he would spend the morning, helping bake the cookies. He loved to roll the dough and cut out the cookies. More than making the cookies, he loved to eat the dough. Without fail, in the end, there was always more flour on him than on the counter.

Standing in the kitchen, she began to recall that terrible day and the many sad days that followed. It had been ten weeks since Neil's accident. The news devastated her entire family. They were a devout Catholic family. Neil's accident put their faith to the test. They all loved him and considered him to be part of their family. Even her husband, John, who was a very strict disciplinarian, had cried upon hearing the news. She had spent many nights holding her children, as they cried for Neil.

A nurse, she had attended to many patients with serious injuries. With Neil, her experience and her knowledge didn't help. The first time she visited Neil in the hospital and saw this tiny, frail little boy lying in his crib, all swollen, with tubes everywhere, she felt helpless. There was nothing she could do for her favorite little boy. She couldn't stay. She did the only thing she could do. Crying, she found the hospital's chapel, where she prayed, asking God, "Why Neil?" She then prayed for Neil's recovery.

It had been three weeks since Neil returned home. Most of the time he remained in his house, playing with his toys. At first, it was difficult for her girls to baby sit. They were nervous, not knowing what to expect, what to do, or how to act. The first few days had been very emotional. Each night her girls would cry themselves to sleep. She was afraid that this could not continue. Margie feared her daughters could not deal with the emotional stress of taking care of Neil. But, slowly, things improved. As Neil became stronger, his enthusiasm and energy returned.

Preparing to continue with her baking chores, suddenly, unexpectedly, she heard the creak of the garage door. Every Thursday, since Neil's return home, she had left the garage door open, hoping, but never believing, that one day Neil would return. Holding her breath, she anxiously waited. Hoping, yet knowing it couldn't possibly be true. Then came the familiar sound of "L'il Big Foot,' clomp, clomp, clomp, clomp, clomp, clomp, clomp, clomp. With the last step, she was greeted with the words she thought she would never hear again, "Good Morning, Mar-kie."

Margie stood in total amazement. Neil had made the walk by himself. She didn't care how he had done it. She was elated. Her Neil was back. As she hugged him, fighting back the tears, she looked skyward, and whispered, "Thank you, God." At that moment, she knew that Neil would make it, that he would be just fine.

# *Shopping*

"Mommy, can I go with you? Pleeease?" Neil begged.

It had been two months since Neil returned home from the hospital. Linda was not just surprised, but was amazed at how well he was doing. Though still weak and frail, he acted like nothing had happened. Ryan immediately took Neil in tow, allowing Neil to follow him everywhere and helping him whenever needed. Linda wondered how long the honeymoon would last, before they returned to the normal antagonistic relationship of two brothers. "So far, so good," she thought.

Today Linda was going to the grocery store. Before the accident, Neil always enjoyed shopping with his Mom. Linda did too. It was their quiet time together. Neil especially loved going to the grocery store. His Mom always let him get a treat.

Since his return home, Linda was hesitant to take him shopping. She was concerned about his strength, but more so about the frustration he would have, not being able to see what she was buying. Over the last two weeks, this fear had diminished. Neil had readily accepted his blindness and seemed to have no recollection of being able to see. With this in mind, Linda responded to Neil's request, trying to make it sound exciting for him.

"Sure you can, Neil. It'll be like old times, just you and me. If you're good, I'll even let you get a special treat."

Neil, remembering their fun trips of the past, excitedly ordered, "Let's go Mom! Let's go!"

A short time later, Linda pulled into the parking lot of the Bakers Supermarket on North 90th Street, in Omaha. It was her favorite grocery store. Neil and she had been there many times. The trip was short but fun. One thing about Neil hadn't changed. He loved to talk. For the entire trip, he carried on a conversation with his Mom. Entering the store, she lifted Neil into the seat of the cart and proceeded to the produce section.

Pushing the cart and conversing with Neil, she suddenly became aware of the stares. As she passed by, people would turn and stare at Neil, often whispering to their companions. Neil's face was heavily scarred from his stitches, his nose was only partially rebuilt and he had two, small wire knots, one under each side of his chin. They were the knots securing the three feet of wire, which held his face together. She knew he looked grotesque to a stranger.

This was in stark contrast to her shopping experiences before the accident. Neil was a beautiful baby, with chubby cheeks, a cute little nose and bright, blue eyes. Many times, people would compliment her, telling her that Neil was "so cute." Several people told her that Neil looked like the Gerber Food Baby.

Fighting back her tears, she was determined not to let this deter her. She knew Neil was oblivious to the stares. Linda continued to talk and play with Neil, as they searched for the items on her list. That day, Neil got two treats.

Upon arriving home, Neil ran to play with Ryan while Linda put the groceries away. Then, she could no longer hold back her emotions. With her tears beginning to flow, she walked down the hall to her bedroom. On the way, she stopped and took down the picture, which hung on the hall wall. It was a picture of Neil, which was taken just before the accident.

Hugging the picture, she sat on her bed, slowly rocking and crying. She cried for herself. She wanted to turn back time, to once again be able to look into her son's beautiful blue eyes. Her tears were also for Neil. She relived the stares, the silent whispers and the looks of distain. Linda feared people would never accept Neil; that they would never look past his scars to find the real Neil, the Neil she loved.

"Mommy, Mommy, where are you?" Neil called.

Wiping away her tears, so Neil would not know she had been crying, she replied, "In my bedroom."

She could hear the pat of Neil's little feet on the wood floor running down the hall. Taking him into her arms, she hugged him, refusing to let go. At least for this day, he was safe in her arms.

## POSTSCRIPT — CHAPTER ONE

*I am Larry Halford, Neil's father. He asked me to write the postscript to this chapter. Obviously, his accident was the singular most significant event of our family's lives.*

*When the accident first occurred, I truly feared that my youngest son was dying. After the doctors gave us the news that he would be blind and likely brain damaged, I initially thought it would be best if he did die. Little did I know at the time, but Neil would not only recover, not just endure, but also excel.*

*People often ask me if I blamed myself for Neil's injuries, if I felt any guilt. At the hospital, as I sat there, listening to Neil's agonizing cries coming from the emergency room, I was besieged with emotion. Feeling responsible, I was overcome with a smothering sense of dread, a depression that drained me of my strength. I was emotionally and physically exhausted.*

*The first time I saw Neil in the hospital room, heavily bandaged and tubes running everywhere, I was once again overwhelmed. It was not guilt. It was not grief. It was a sense of tremendous responsibility and the birth of an unwavering determination. I decided at that moment that I would do everything in my power to ensure that Neil lived a happy, satisfying life. No matter what it took, I would make it happen.*

*Initially, I wanted to kill Hank. I wanted the personal satisfaction of shooting him. Then, as reason conquered emotion, I realized that it was not his fault. Even so, I knew I could not see him again. I had my father sell the horse.*

*At first, my wife Linda struggled. She was devastated. When the day started, she had two beautiful children. When the day ended, one son was near death. To her credit, she never once blamed me. Linda was angry. She didn't understand how God would let this happen. She kept asking, "Why God? Why Neil?"*

*That first night, in the quiet of Neil's dark hospital room, after the initial shock had disappeared, we agreed that we could not look back, that we could not dwell on the past. We had to accept the situation and make the best of it. It would be a daunting task. It was a mission that would take years. At that moment we agreed to never ask why.*

*Our mission started the next day. Initially, we had to ensure that Neil was receiving the best medical care possible. With the help of our friends, we checked on the qualifications and reputations of Neil's doctors. We required second opinions on any major medical decision.*

*For the next five weeks, while Neil was in the hospital, we were there all of the time. We never wanted Neil to be alone, while he was recovering, while he began the difficult adjustment to being blind. But to his credit and my amazement, Neil immediately accepted his condition and went on with his life. He quickly returned to the high energy, happy child we had always known.*

*When Neil returned home, there was a natural period of adjustment.*

*His older brother, Ryan, immediately became Neil's guide and protector. He was constantly with Neil and always let Neil play with him and his friends.*

*We were very fortunate to live in a small town. Many people in the town came to Neil's aid. This was true, not only in the early days of Neil's return, but throughout his entire life. Our next-door neighbors, the Fitzgerald family, were a great support. Their children were our baby sitters and became our sons' best friends. Margie was like a grandmother to Neil. Our best friends, the Kempers and their two boys helped us in many ways. At first, Linda and I were hesitant about leaving Neil. Steve and Jeanine Kemper would literally drag us out of the house. They knew we needed an occasional break from the stress of Neil's condition. They were always there, whenever we needed help.*

*Once Neil was home, Linda and I continued to be besieged with responsibilities and decisions. Neil had four subsequent operations during that first year. We searched for the most prominent eye doctor in the country to explore all options with Neil's remaining eye. Neil struggled to get acclimated. He was constantly running into walls and doors, resulting in cuts and bruises, which often times required trips to the hospital for stitches. Neil's jaw remained wired shut for six months. This required special preparation of all of his meals and someone to feed him.*

*We contacted the social services administration for the state, to learn about what programs were available to help Neil with the challenges of being blind. Although he was only three, we were very concerned about his education. The local school district superintendent helped us contact the Nebraska School for the Visually Handicapped. Over that next year, we developed a plan for Neil's education. Our goal was always to eventually have him return to the local public school. As I had vowed that horrible night, Neil would have the same opportunities as any other child. An important step was for Neil to mainstream into the public schools.*

*Linda and I, through a friend, contacted St. Joseph Hospital, in Omaha. For several months, we met weekly with a counselor who was a specialist in working with families, who had experienced a traumatic tragedy. This counselor helped us to confront our fears, our frustrations and our emotions. He helped us to understand what Neil and Ryan were feeling.*

*Although our main concern was Neil, Linda and I were also concerned about Ryan. He had witnessed the terrible accident. In addition, for five weeks, he was without his parents, moving from one relative to another. Unfortunately, even after Neil came home, most of our attention was focused on Neil.*

*One of our greatest regrets is how we neglected Ryan. At that time, Ryan was entering the first grade. To this day, Linda and I have no recollection of any of Ryan's first and second grade achievements. Ryan always struggled with school, especially reading. I believe his problems stem from our lack of attention and support during those very formative grades, where reading basics are taught. Through it all, even though he was only seven years old, he was an incredible big brother for Neil.*

*As I look back on those years, there were so many people who helped us. Linda and I would like to take this time, without naming anyone, to thank everyone who came to our aid and for all the prayers that were offered for Neil. We could not have done it without you. Neil would not be the man he is today, if you hadn't helped. We were blessed to know each of you.*

# Chapter Two

## Introduction

*It was August 26, 1979. The beginning of what I feel was the second chapter of my life. I was one month shy of my fifth birthday. My favorite song was "You Light Up My Life" by Debby Boone. "The Super Friends" on Saturday morning and "Dallas" on Friday night were my favorite television shows. My very best friend was my fifteen-year-old, next-door neighbor and babysitter, Jeannie Fitzgerald. We were inseparable. The few hours a day when I was not with Jeannie, I spent tagging along after my eight-year-old brother, Ryan.*

*Our house was a small, three-bedroom ranch. It was located on Madison Street, a narrow, quiet small town road. There was a creek and a large wooded lot behind the house. One block away was a city park, with a large playground. It was paradise for a small boy. My whole world was within walking distance. In my bedroom, the tinker toys and "See and Say" books were slowly giving way to Star Wars and toy guns. I had developed a love for story records and would spend hours in my room, lost in the world of the Lone Ranger and Davy Crockett.*

*My childhood, with all of its innocence and security, was about to change. I was as unsuspecting as only a four-year-old boy could be. Many of the events and experiences which occurred over the next three years of my life would play a large role in shaping me into the man I have become.*

# The First Day

It was Sunday, August 26, 1979, a day Linda hoped would never come. After she awoke, she lay silently crying. This was the day they would take Neil to his school.

It would not be as she had imagined. Waking Neil each morning, preparing him breakfast, making his lunch, sending him off with a hug and kiss, and watching him walk to school hand in hand with his older brother. Reality for most families, it was only a distant dream for Linda.

She knew this day was inevitable and necessary. It was Neil's only hope. For the past week, she had been struggling with the decision. Her mind told her yes, her heart cried out "NO!"

As she turned to Larry, he was still asleep. The night before, they were all up very late. The boys were excited. It was the first time they had been allowed to stay awake past midnight. They watched some of Neil's favorite movies and ate popcorn. Of course, the night would not be complete without the obligatory wrestling match between the boys and Larry. It was a typical Saturday night at the Halford's. Although it went unspoken, everyone, even the boys, knew that this night was special. They knew that on Sunday, the life they had known would change.

Sunday was the day Neil would begin school at the Nebraska School for the Visually Handicapped.

After dressing, Linda went looking for her boys. It was 10 a.m. Usually they were up at the crack of dawn, playing and fighting. Not hearing a sound, she opened the door to Neil's bedroom. The bed, to which Larry had carried him at 1:30 this morning, was empty. Her next stop was Ryan's room. She carefully opened the door, not wanting to wake them if they were still sleeping. Neil lay on the bed, cradled in Ryan's arms, both still sound asleep. She stood quietly, relishing the moment, tears once again streaming down her cheeks.

She wanted to wake Larry, but decided against it. The boys loved to wake their Dad. Without fail, it always ended in a battle for "King of the Bed." She knew that today, more than any other, Larry would need to fight that battle.

Larry was also struggling with Neil's departure. Unlike Linda, Larry had the ability to mask his emotions. Once a decision was made, no matter how painful, he would think only of the positive aspects. He would not allow himself to second guess his decision. Larry could always find the positive of any situation. He truly was her source of strength and inspiration in times of trial and tribulation. That had been true until today. Since Neil's accident, this would be their most difficult day. Although he hid it from everyone else, Linda knew he dreaded this day. Like her, she knew he struggled with the idea of having Neil live away from home.

Sitting quietly in the living room lost in her thoughts, she suddenly heard the boys laugh, followed by a thud on the floor. Smiling, she knew the battle had begun. Soon her boys would come running into her arms, seeking asylum from the monster of the bed, their father.

The day passed quickly. They spent the morning together, having a large brunch. Larry and Linda had asked that all of their relatives say good-bye to Neil prior to Sunday.

They wanted the day to be a positive, happy time for Neil. As the time approached, they wanted to create a sense of excitement and anticipation for his new adventure. This would not be possible if the day was filled with the tears of his grandma, aunts and uncles. So Saturday had been a constant stream of relatives.

Sooner than anyone wanted, it was time to leave. While Larry packed the car, Linda took Ryan to her mother's house. They had decided it was best if Ryan did not accompany them on the trip. This was going to be difficult and emotional for Neil, not to mention them. They needed to spend this time alone with Neil.

"Doot, it's time to go," Larry called as he closed the trunk. The car was packed.

Lying on his bed, lost in his thoughts, Neil did not hear his father calling. Neil's thoughts had drifted back a few weeks; to the first time his parents told him he was going to school. He felt so special. He had often heard his brother and friends talk about school. It always sounded like so much fun. He would meet new friends. He would be like his brother, a big boy. He was so excited. Then his parents explained to him that he would be going to school at Nebraska City, eighty miles from home. They told him he would stay at the school Sunday night through Friday.

Not understanding, Neil silently protested, "Kids don't live away from home when they're only four years old!" Other than the hospital, which he didn't really remember, he had never spent a night away from home, away from his family.

Neil hadn't thought much about his new school until two days earlier. Late that night, while lying in bed, he heard his parents talking in their bedroom. His parents knew his sense of hearing was extremely acute, but they didn't realize how exceptional it really was. Many times, even though they were behind closed doors, he could hear their conversations. Most of the time he would ignore them, opting to play with some toys. However, this time he listened intently. The conversation was about his new school.

His Mom was crying, asking his Dad not to take him to his new school, to wait one year. Larry was talking in a strange voice, arguing that it was important for Neil to start school now. Then Neil realized what was different about his Dad's voice. His Dad was crying. He had never heard his Dad cry before.

This frightened him. Scared and confused, he silently cried himself to sleep. For the next two days, whenever Neil was by himself, he could think of nothing but the coming departure for school. Often those thoughts ended in tears.

Getting no response, Larry went into the house to get Neil. Entering Neil's bedroom, he saw Neil on the bed, lying in the fetal position, clutching one of his favorite "Star Wars" figures. "Doot, are you ready for your new adventure?" Larry asked in an excited tone.

"I don't feel good, Daddy." Neil replied in a halting, quiet voice.

Sitting down on the bed, Larry lifted Neil into his arms, "What's wrong, buddy?"

"My tummy hurts."

Larry didn't doubt it. His stomach had been upset all morning. Lifting Neil's shirt, he gently rubbed his stomach. "That's just because you're nervous. Anytime I start a new job, my tummy hurts just like yours. Do you know how I stop the pain?"

"What do you do, Daddy?"

"I think of all the good things about my job. Then when I get there, as soon as I start working, my tummy feels better. As soon as you get to the school, after you meet some new friends, I'm sure your tummy will feel better. So the sooner we get going, the sooner you'll feel better."

"Daddy, will you carry me to the car?" Neil asked, hugging Larry.

"Sure, Doot," Larry responded, rising to his feet.

On the trip, Neil sat in the back seat of the car, pretending to be asleep. He was afraid. More afraid then he could ever remember. He refused to allow himself the luxury of letting it show. From the front seat, he could hear his mother fighting back her tears. He was determined to be strong for her sake. Not to mention that his Dad hated it when he cried. He wouldn't let his Dad see him cry.

"Here we are," Larry announced, while he angled the Oldsmobile into a parking spot.

"Oh, Neil!" Linda said, "You should see all the neat playground equipment they have."

Neil could still hear the note of grief in her voice. He knew she was trying to sound enthusiastic for his sake.

Pretending to awake, Neil responded, "Cool, Mom." Straining to include a tone of excitement with his words.

"We'll get your bags after we have found your room," Larry explained, as they climbed from the car.

"My room," Neil thought angrily. "My room is at home, along with all my toys and my brother."

Knowing that Neil always wanted to initially get the layout of any new site, Larry immediately began a running narrative. "Off to our left there is a parking lot where you'll be able to ride bikes. Just past the edge of the parking lot is the playground your mom was talking about. It runs the length of the building on this side. She wasn't kidding, they do have a lot of pretty cool stuff."

Half listening to his dad, Neil was concentrating mainly on where they were going. Neil was able to find his way by himself. This was primarily due to his exceptional hearing capabilities, which enabled him to have an acute awareness of his surroundings, while carrying on a conversation. Also, without realizing it, Neil had developed a photographic memory. One trip to the store and he would have the route memorized. One walk through a house and he could remember the floor plan. He knew that he would undoubtedly have to travel this way many more times. More than likely, his parents would not be there for guidance the next time.

When they entered a large entryway that was filled with a number of different styles of bikes and tricycles, his Dad continued his description. "This is the dormitory entrance, and also where you store the outdoor toys. Off to your left there is a staircase which I believe leads to the upstairs dormitory for the high school age kids. To our right is the entry to the younger kids dormitory, where you'll be staying, Doot."

Larry opened the door. Neil was immediately overwhelmed by the buzz of activity that greeted them. Just inside the door, to the left, were two tables, at which a number of adults sat talking. When Neil and his parents entered the room, two of the adults hurried to their feet and came to greet them. Displaying his fear for the first time since arriving, Neil squeezed his Dad's hand and stood behind Larry, hoping that nobody would notice him.

Neil could hear a number of children playing at various activities throughout the room. Once again, Neil felt a sharp pang of apprehension in his stomach. For the first time, he realized he had never met another blind child. All of his friends were sighted.

"What if they're weird or something?" Neil thought.

His Dad took him by the shoulder, pulled him out from behind his legs and announced, "Neil, this is Mrs. Blevins. She is the house mother for your dormitory."

Mrs. Blevins took both of his hands in hers as she introduced herself.

"While your parents speak with the superintendent would you like me to show you around the dorms?" Mrs. Blevins asked in a gruff voice, which Neil would learn later, was due to smoking.

"Sure," Neil hesitantly whispered.

He allowed Mrs. Blevins to lead him away from his father's side. When they started to walk away, Neil nervously looked back toward his parents. Larry caught his nervous look and quickly slapped a large hand on Neil's back. Trying to restore Neil's usual confidence, Larry encouraged him,

"Go on, Doot. Check the place out. I think there might be a couple of things around here you'll really like."

The dormitory had a large central room with two wings, one on each end. The center room, which Mrs. Blevins referred to as the lounge, was sectioned off into three areas. There was a sitting area with couches and chairs where the children watched TV and listened to stories. There was an area, just inside the door, where his parents currently were speaking with the superintendent. It contained two tables, which were used for studying and other activities. The third area of the lounge was a pleasant surprise. This was the playroom. Three or four children were climbing on a large wooden jungle gym.

"Wow!" Neil excitedly exclaimed, "A jungle gym inside, how cool."

Continuing with the tour, she showed Neil the two dormitory wings. Each wing contained five dorm rooms and a central bathroom. One wing was for the girls and one was for the boys. Each bathroom contained a number of toilets and sinks, a large shower room with a number of showerheads, and 1 bathtub. The dorm rooms each contained 2 beds, 2 small tables, and 2 large wardrobes.

During their short tour, Neil could hear several children scattered throughout the lounge or making their way up and down the wings of the dormitory. Mrs. Blevins had introduced him to a few of them, but being so nervous, Neil had forgotten their names.

Making their way back toward the lounge, Mrs. Blevins stopped to introduce Neil to an older boy who was riding a large, four-wheeled toy. "Neil, I want you to meet Bobby. Bobby, this is Neil. This is his first day at NSVH," she explained, guiding Neil's hand toward Bobby's already outstretched hand.

"Nice to meet you Neil," Bobby said shaking Neil's hand.

"Would you like to take a ride on the wagon with me?" Bobby asked.

"Sure," Neil said, with a note of hesitation in his voice.

Apprehensively, he slipped behind Bobby onto the seat of what Bobbie had referred to as the wagon. It was nothing like any wagon Neil had used before. It was a rectangle shaped, four-wheeled wooden cart, on which two or three children could ride, front to back, with the person in front steering. Mrs. Blevins left Neil to play with Bobby and went to rejoin his parents.

Neil remembered that his parents would soon be leaving. For a moment, he began to follow Mrs. Blevins, but the prospect of riding the wagon up and down the hallways of the dormitory with Bobby was an adventure he couldn't pass up. Neil once again took his place behind Bobby.

Ten minutes later Larry nudged Linda and pointed across the lounge to where Neil was now driving the wagon and giving rides to some of the other children. Neil had already memorized the room's floor plan and was skillfully navigating around all of the furniture. Larry had just returned from carrying in Neil's bags. Watching his son interact with the other children did his heart good and erased some of his earlier misgivings.

"He'll be fine, Linda," Larry said, giving her a little squeeze.

"I know he will, but will I?" she asked, once again fighting back the tears.

"We'll be fine, too," Larry reassured her, in a halting, emotional voice. "We always find a way. Let's go say our good-byes."

Larry and Linda made their way across the lounge, where Neil and his newly found friend, Bobby were attempting to stuff four kids onto the wagon.

"We're going to take off, Doot," Larry said, laying a hand on Neil's shoulder.

"Okay," Neil said, struggling to extract himself from the mass of children who had piled on the wagon.

"I'll see you guys later," he said, as he gave each of them a hug.

"I put all of your clothes away in your room." Linda explained, giving Neil a hug. "And I. . . ."

"Don't worry about me, Mom," Neil said, interrupting her in mid-sentence." "I'll be fine. I'll see you guys on Friday."

Lost in the excitement of the moment, Neil returned to the other children. For the first few miles, on the drive home, Larry and Linda were quiet. Each was lost in their thoughts. Then, Linda broke the silence, "Larry, I hope we did the right thing."

"Linda, we had no other choice," Larry once again explained.

"We could have waited another year. We could have tried public school first," Linda replied, not accepting Larry's statement.

"We've been over this a thousand times. It won't do any good to keep questioning our decision. You know that Neil has so much to learn, so much more than the typical boy, that he had to start early. Also, the only place in Nebraska that can teach him the special skills he'll need is NSVH. Not to mention the fact that the State of Nebraska is footing the bill. You know we couldn't afford to pay for his schooling. Besides, Linda, if he started public school without the special education, he would be like a fish out of water. He would fail miserably and I'm not sure he would ever recover his self confidence."

Larry once again reviewed the basis of their decision with Linda. "I know Larry, I know. It just hurts so much. I am so afraid he will always go to school there. Did you see all of the older children?"

Acquiescing, Linda's tears once again returned. She then continued, imploring her husband, "Larry, you have to promise me, that without fail, Neil will go to public school no later than the third grade."

"That has always been our plan, Linda. I don't care what happens. I don't care what other people think. I guarantee that Neil will start the third grade at Fort Calhoun Elementary School," Larry emphatically assured her.

Sliding next to him, she laid her head on his shoulder. Relieved by Larry's strong affirmation of their plan, she quickly fell asleep. She knew that when Larry promised her something, it always happened.

Some hours later, Neil lay on his new bed. Listening to the sounds of other sleeping children, he thought about the day's events. Slowly, painfully, a new feeling engulfed his entire body. It was a feeling Neil had never experienced before, a feeling that Neil would come to know well. It was the feeling of loneliness. Powerless to overcome this desperate feeling of despair, Neil released all of the emotions of the last few days. He turned his face into his new pillow and cried. Neil's tears began to dry and his mind began to slip toward the escape of dreams. His last thought, before falling asleep was, "I'll be fine. I always have been. I'll find a way."

# The Lonely Nights

Neil gently slipped from the playground of his childhood dreams into reality. He struggled to hold onto the visions of flying on the back of Ryan's motorcycle, through the bean field behind their house. In the end, it was useless. His little arms slipped from around Ryan's waist, as the sound of the Honda 50 receded back into the land of dreams.

He languished for a moment in the warmth of his bed, tracing in his mind the path across the hardwood floor of his bedroom, through the doorway and into the bathroom he shared with his brother and parents.

In his mind's eye, he could see the treasures, which filled his room. Across from the bed was his toy box, filled to the brim with the normal assortment of toys. On top of the toy box were his favorites, the Star Wars ships. He often piloted these space ships about the room, reeking havoc on imaginary, unsuspecting foes. Next to the toy box, sat a record player and his complete collection of Disney records. He would spend endless hours listening to the stories, becoming lost in the fantasy worlds of Davy Crockett and the Rescuers.

After a long stretch, he swung his little feet onto the floor. He did not encounter the expected warmth and smoothness of the hardwood floor. Instead, the cold cement floor of his dorm room at NSVH greeted his feet.

The smile on his face, left over from the dream, instantly vanished and was replaced by brimming eyes and a quivering lower lip. The realization of his surroundings brought with it an overwhelming sense of loneliness, which he had come to know so well. He placed his tiny hands over his face and quietly let the tears fall. He wished his Mother could be there to tuck him back in bed and plant a kiss on his cheek. He wished he could slip silently down the hall and into his brother's bed. He wished his father would fly him over his head like superman and crash-land him into bed.

These were only wishes in the mind of a five-year-old boy. As he rose to make the long trek down the cold hallway to the dormitory bathroom, he heard the sound that would forever haunt his mind with the memories of those lonely nights. In the distance he heard the mournful sound of the whistle of a train, alone in the dark of night.

# The Naughty Chair

Neil bounced down the dormitory hallway with all of the characteristic vigor of an average six-year-old boy. He was pumped! Every day, after school there was recreation time. Today was his favorite activity, reading. Neil loved books. In his mind, he was always able to slip into the world of the book, to become part of the story. The problem was finding someone to read to him. Today, Mrs. Blevins had promised to read a few chapters from the "Devil's Paw." "What a name for a book," he thought.

Entering the lounge, he took his customary seat on the couch. To his left, sat Scottie, Neil's good friend. Neil hoped that someone quiet would sit to his right. Many of the children at NSVH were not only blind, but had mental disorders, as well. Neil tried to be nice to all of the children, but some of them could be very disruptive, especially during story time.

Mrs. Blevins entered the lounge and asked if everybody was ready for story time. She headed across the lounge to her usual spot next to the window. Following behind her was Mary. Neil sank a little deeper into the cushions of the couch, hoping silently that Mary would not sit next to him. "It wasn't that Mary was a mean girl," Neil thought, "She just wasn't normal."

A small Vietnamese girl, Mary constantly seemed to be in her own world. She sang to herself twenty-four hours a day. No, Neil thought, it wasn't really singing because there were never any words. For that matter, in two years of living in the same dormitory, he never heard her say more than yes or no. As far as he knew, she didn't know any other words. She also had a bad habit of chewing on her own foot.

Mary fumbled around looking for a seat. Neil cringed slightly, as Mary bumped into his legs. Her wandering hands felt over his body, looking for an open spot on the couch. "I'm sitting here Mary," Neil said, hoping to discourage her.

Finding an open cushion next to Neil, she sat down and instantly put her foot in her mouth. When the last of the children found their spots, Mrs. Blevins picked up the book and began reading. Neil quickly became engrossed in Frank and Joe Hardy. For the moment, thoughts of Mary vanished.

Then slowly, like some insane person's idea of the "Chinese Water Torture," Mary's singing began to beat at the walls of Neil's concentration. "Mary!" Neil snapped in a fierce whisper, "Be quiet!"

He shot a quick elbow into her ribs and the singing quieted, but did not stop. "Does she ever stop?" he thought. He tried to get his mind back on the story, but the sound of her singing, with a mouth full of shoe kept grating on his nerves. "Mary! Stop it!" he ordered, raising his voice.

Still, the singing continued. Unable to concentrate, Neil was getting very upset. Neil turned his attention toward Mrs. Blevins. "Nope, she'll never see me while she's reading," he calculated. Neil quickly shot his right hand up to Mary's cheek. "God, she must have that foot in there clear up to the heel," he thought. He then grasped her bulging cheek between his thumb and forefinger, pinching down hard on Mary's cheek.

"Neil!" Mrs. Blevins yelled. Neil's stomach did a large summersault. He knew he had been caught. "What were you doing?" She admonished.

"I'm sorry," Neil said in a tear-choked whisper.

"You go over there and take a seat in the naughty chair," Mrs. Blevins ordered in a gruff tone.

Mrs. Blevins, taking Neil by the arm, marched him across the lounge. She stopped at the "naughty chair." It was a large chair placed by itself, adjacent to the entrance, where anyone who entered could see the condemned student. "You sit there, until we're ready for dinner," Mrs. Blevins snapped at the downcast Neil.

She deposited Neil in the chair and rejoined the children in the sitting area. Neil was left to dwell upon his actions for the next fifteen minutes. It was Neil's one and only time in the "Naughty Chair," during the three years he spent at NSVH. For the next fifteen minutes, he struggled to hold back his tears of humiliation. With tears streaming down his cheek, he couldn't help but think, "My God! I pinched her that hard and she never did quit singing."

# A Dinner Discovery

In the large dining hall, the children stood with bowed heads and folded hands. The chimes sounded, designating the beginning of dinner. Fifty screeching chairs supplied a deafening racket as the hungry children sat and began devouring the evening meal; all except one. Neil sat glumly inspecting the food on his plate. "Salmon loaf, yuck!" He quietly complained.

He began to eat the corn. It was the only portion he found to be acceptable on this evening's menu. Neil was a picky eater, and rare was the cafeteria meal that met his high standards. He longed for a big plate full of his grandma's mashed potatoes and gravy.

Each of the students was required to eat at least half of every item on their plate. Mrs. Blevins, the housemother, was the enforcer. She was a stickler when it came to this rule. Neil cut off a smelly chunk of the processed salmon loaf and dropped it in his mouth. He chewed quickly trying to digest the entire bite before the taste could totally overwhelm him. He tried to swallow and almost lost it. It was all he could do to keep from upchucking. He managed to get it down. Then he sat for a moment trying to compose himself.

"Neil, eat your dinner," Mrs. Blevins ordered, while she helped Stephanie eat her "gourmet" meal.

Knowing what he must do next, Neil carefully listened for Mrs. Blevins. She had her hands full trying to assist the other six children at the table. Since Neil was self-sufficient, he knew she wouldn't be paying much attention to him. Neil cut a slice of the loaf and waited, hoping for an opportunity. Then Mrs. Blevins turned her attention elsewhere. When she did, Neil slid the piece of loaf into his hand. He then slid his hand beneath the table and chucked the fish across the floor. It landed under the chair of the girl sitting across the table from him.

The other children at the table could be rather messy and Neil figured a few more pieces of Salmon on the floor would go unnoticed. This tricky process continued for about 10 minutes. He tried to rid himself of enough loaf to pass inspection. Neil cut off what he felt would be the final piece of the evening. After he tossed it underneath the table, Mrs. Blevins' harsh voice interrupted him, "Neil, please remove yourself from the table and go back to your room. I'll come to see you when I am finished here."

Obediently, Neil slowly made the long walk back to his dorm room. With each step, he thought of all of the possible consequences, which might result from his deception. She would probably make him clean up his mess. He might have to help in the kitchen with the dishes. He just hoped that she wouldn't make him eat another salmon loaf.

"Who feeds salmon loaf to kids anyway?" he thought. I can see having to drink my milk, or eat my peas, but salmon loaf!"

Just then Mrs. Blevins entered his room. "Neil," she admonished, "Do you know what I just got through doing?"

"What?" Neil asked apologetically.

"I just got through picking up about a half a pound of salmon loaf off of the dirty floor."

"I'm sorry Mrs. Blevins, but I just couldn't stand it. It made me want to puke." Neil said, gaining a little confidence.

"Come here, Neil."

Rising from his bed, Neil nervously, haltingly walked across the floor to where Mrs. Blevins stood, towering in the doorway. The time for his punishment had arrived. Mrs. Blevins put her arm around his little shoulders and gave Neil a big hug.

"Next time if it's that bad just tell me, okay?" Mrs. Blevins said.

"Alright." Neil said, his fear instantly vanishing.

When Mrs. Blevins turned to leave, Neil stopped her. "Mrs. Blevins. I am sorry you had to pick up my mess, but I sure am glad I didn't have to eat that salmon loaf."

Neil could hear her chuckle while she made her way down the hall. He was also laughing to himself, silently celebrating, "Well, I got caught, but that's the first time I've been caught in a year and a half. Think of all the nasty food I got out of eating. It was worth it!"

# A Spring in His Step

The morning sun shone brightly on the well-manicured lawns and orchards, slowly stealing the nights dew from the grass and leaves. In the apple trees, the birds were singing their wake up calls to their newly born babes. Spring was the time of rebirth, renewal and always created a feeling of optimism, a signal of good things to come. At NSVH, Neil's attitude mirrored the weather. Neil loved the spring. To Neil, spring meant two things; warm weather, and that he would soon be home for the summer.

Neil skipped down the stairs, on his way to PE class. He let his mind drift toward thoughts of his family and the summer to come. He couldn't wait. His next-door neighbor, Jeannie, was going to be his babysitter all summer, while his mom was at work. Jeannie was a blast. He rode on her shoulders, as they rode around the town on her ten-speed bicycle. She would take him to the park, let him play in the creek behind the house, and take him swimming. Life was never dull, with Jeannie as his guide. Neil was suddenly brought back to reality, when he entered the gym.

"Neil! You're over here with me this morning." Coach Davis called, from the far side of the gym.

Inwardly, Neil groaned. He obediently slumped across the gym toward Coach Davis. Coach Davis was the high school coach for NSVH and was in charge of all of the schools organized athletics. He also acted as the school's mobility trainer, and it was this activity, which placed the first frown of the morning on Neil's countenance. Neil loved coach Davis, but he hated mobility training.

"Ah, come on, Coach, do we have to walk with the cane today?" Neil wined in his best, please give me pity, voice.

"Yes sir, champ, you're going to have to keep learning how to use this thing until you get it down." Coach Davis said, tapping a short white cane on the gym floor.

"I know how to walk with the cane," Neil retorted. "Anyway, I can get around everywhere without it."

"Yeah, but someday, champ, you're going to have to use this thing. You can't always rely on your memory or other people to help you get around. It's my job to make sure that when that time comes you are ready. So take this baby and lets get 'truckin'," he said handing Neil the cane.

Ten minutes later, while Neil wound his way through the residential neighborhoods of the town, he found himself contemplating his opinions on cane travel, "I don't understand why it is so important to learn to walk around

Nebraska City with a cane. I don't even live here. Why would I ever want to walk around some town by myself? I don't like using a cane and I don't need a cane! When I grow up, I will never use a cane. During the summer, when I am home, I never use a cane and I get around just fine. Between my memory and my friends, I can do everything I want, go anywhere I want, without ever using a cane. Even though the teachers complain that I don't use the cane in school, I never do. I know my way around the school just fine. I never run into anything. So, what is the point?"

Feeling a hand on his shoulder, Neil gave a little jump. He realized Coach Davis had snuck up on him, while he was thinking.

"How many blocks have you gone since you took that right back there?" Coach Davis asked in his jovial tone.

Neil knew he hadn't been paying attention to what he was doing. He had inadvertently ignored coach Davis's directions.

"Um, two?" Neil said, with a questioning tone to his voice.

"My instructions were to go two blocks and then turn left." Coach Davis reminded Neil.

"Why don't you take a little walk back the way we came, and see if you might have gone more like two and a half blocks?"

Turning around, Neil retraced his steps until he came to a street he had crossed, without even noticing.

"Do you know what you did?" Coach Davis asked, with that ever present hint of humor in his voice.

"Yeah, I walked right past the turn, without even paying attention, didn't I?"

"You sure did."

"Good thing you were back there Coach, or I could have been hit by a car," Neil replied, in the spirit of Coach Davis's joviality.

"That's what they pay me for. You would have only been about the tenth or eleventh kid I've lost during mobility training," he laughed, slapping Neil on the back.

"Now why don't you take a right here and go about a block and a half down this street. On the right hand side of the street, you'll find my house."

"We're going to your house?" Neil asked.

"I know how much you dislike cane travel, so I thought maybe we'd stop by my house. My wife baked some chocolate chip cookies last night. What do you think about that?"

"I think we'd better get 'truckin'!" Neil enthusiastically demanded.

With a belly full of cookies and milk, Neil's good humor had returned. He grabbed his cane on the way out the door and headed down the front walk.

"Hold up, champ!" Coach Davis said, hurrying to catch up with Neil.

"Grab a wing and we'll get back to the school," he ordered, sticking out his elbow for Neil.

"Yes!" Neil gratefully shouted. "Now this is the way to travel!"

Once again he felt the warmth of the sun and heard the chirping of the birds in the trees.

"What a morning," he thought. "It won't be long now and I'll be home for the summer. No cane, for at least three months."

# Diddle – Diddle – Diddle

Neil took his customary seat in the large banquet hall. It was lunchtime and he was early. Several other children also took their assigned seats. Scottie hurriedly entered the hall, taking his seat next to Neil. He was Neil's friend and, like Neil was seven-years old and blind. Scottie was gasping for breath. Neil thought that he might also be crying.

"What's wrong, Scottie?" Neil asked, laying a hand on his arm.

"I got caught in the hall by Danny. There weren't any teachers around to help me," Scottie explained, still breathing hard.

You've got to be kidding me!" Neil said with a tone of disgust in his voice. "That guy drives me nuts. Did he hurt you?"

"No, I'm alright."

As the rest of the students began straggling into the hall, Neil's thoughts were directed at Danny. He was an older boy, with several handicaps. He was blind, partially deaf, and obviously had some hyper activity problems. Danny often strolled the corridors of the school, talking to himself and making funny noises. He was eighteen years old and stood six feet tall.

Danny was constantly cornering the younger children in the hallway. Once he caught them, he would lift them high in the air. Holding them against the nearest wall, he would begin administering, what Neil and his friends referred to as, "diddling." Neil believed that Danny was only trying to tickle the children. Inevitably, unknowingly, Danny would painfully poke them all over their upper bodies, with his long fingers. While doing this, Danny would shake with laughter and repeat "diddle-diddle-diddle-diddle-diddle-diddle." Neil had experienced this humiliating act twice. He had sworn that he would never allow it to happen again. The next time Neil met him in the hallway alone, Neil would out-smart him.

After finishing his lunch, Neil turned to Scottie, "Scottie, I'm going to run to the bathroom. I'll meet you back at class."

"Alright, I'll see you there."

Leaving behind the bustle of the noisy lunchroom, Neil made his way down the hallway, toward the nearest restroom. His mind was on the story his teacher had promised to read to them after lunch. He failed to notice that another student was approaching him. Finally, when the other student was within ten feet, Neil realized that someone was there. Neil moved to the right, to avoid the other student. Suddenly, Neil froze in his tracks. He knew the other student was Danny.

"Who's there?" Danny demanded, in his usually loud voice.

Standing as still as a statue, Neil hoped Danny wouldn't hear him. When Danny began shuffling toward him, Neil held his breath.

"Who's there?" Danny continued to demand.

Barely breathing, Neil didn't move. He knew Danny was on the hunt. He had trapped his prey and was moving in for the kill. For a moment he considered turning and taking flight down the hallway. He realized this would be useless. Danny was much bigger and could easily run him down. Neil could hear Danny shuffling toward him. He had his hands stretched out in front of him, searching for his victim. Neil began edging silently to his left. The restroom was only ten feet further up the hall. "If I can just make it to the restroom," Neil thought, "I'll be able to get into a stall and lock the door."

Abruptly, Neil's planning came to a halt. Like the tentacles of an octopus, Danny's groping fingers brushed the top of Neil's head. Instantly recognizing that he had trapped his prey, Danny clutched at Neil's hair. With a quick jerk of his head, Neil pulled away, leaving Danny with a handful of empty air. Danny lunged for him. Neil dodged to the left and sprinted to the restroom.

Slamming through the restroom door, he could hear Danny close behind, wildly giggling, "Diddle-diddle-diddle!"

He tried to slam the bathroom door closed in Danny's face. It didn't work. Danny hit the door, throwing Neil backward toward the stall. Stunned, Neil staggered into the open bathroom stall. Danny slammed into the bathroom wall, rebounded and came for the stall. Neil slammed the stall door and frantically tried to engage the lock. Danny hit the door. Neil's fingers frantically struggled with the lock. Finally, with a quick turn, he secured the door.

"Diddle-diddle-diddle!" Danny kept reminding Neil, while beating on the door.

Cowering in the stall, Neil wondered how he could have allowed himself to get in this predicament. Only fifteen minutes earlier, Scottie had warned him that Danny was on a rampage. He had been stupid enough to practically walk right into him. The beating on the stall door came to a sudden halt. For a moment, Neil had trouble holding back his laughter. "I did it," he thought, "I got away from him."

Then a hand groped over his foot and closed around his ankle. Neil's stomach gave a lurch. Danny had dropped to the floor and was crawling beneath the walls of the stall. Neil kicked out with his free foot and connected with the side of Danny's head. By now, the sound of Danny's "diddle-diddle-diddle" had reached a feverish pitch. Neil kicked free from Danny's grasp and leaped on the seat of the toilet.

"Diddle-diddle-diddle!" Danny screeched.

He sat up in the stall, pulling his legs in, preparing to stand. Neil grasped the top of the bathroom stall. With one quick leap, he pulled himself up and swung over the top of the stall. Landing on the floor, Neil scrambled to his feet and headed out of the bathroom on a dead run. Howling with laughter, he heard Danny struggling to extract himself from the bathroom stall.

Neil decided that the bathroom could wait. He proudly strutted down the hall. It had been close, but, on this day, he had out smarted the "Diddler."

# A Passion is Born

Neil threw himself down on his bed, releasing a sigh of frustration. He wanted to go outside and play. His Mom said he couldn't because it was cold and raining. " I don't care if it's cold!" he thought, "I'm bored. I wish I had something to do."

Seeing Neil lying on his bed, Larry stopped in the doorway of his room, asking, "Neil, why don't you listen to one of your records, or play with your Star Wars toys?"

"I played with them yesterday, when it was also cold and raining. I've listened to all those records at least a hundred times."

It was a typical winter week in Nebraska. The weather had been cold and damp for several days. The high temperature for the day was 20 degrees. Living so close to the Missouri River, it was a damp cold that felt like it penetrated all the way to a body's bones. With each day, Neil's frustration grew. Larry was there at the order of "Miss Linda." She had ordered him to occupy Neil with something to do, "Find something to interest your son!" She had demanded.

When there was a problem, Neil suddenly became "his son." Realizing this called for drastic measures, Larry had one idea. He wasn't sure it would work, but it was worth a shot. "I have an idea, Doot. Come with me," he said, as he turned and headed down the hall.

Enthusiastically, Neil hopped from the bed and followed his Dad. Larry led the way downstairs to the family room, where he knelt in front of his new stereo system. He immediately began thumbing his way through his record collection, searching for something.

"What are you looking for, Doot?" Neil asked with a tone of excitement. Neil and his Dad both called each other by the same nickname, "Doot."

"You'll see." Larry said, in an absent-minded tone.

"Come on! Tell me what you are looking for." Neil ordered, his impatience beginning to show.

"Hold your horses. I'll find …. Ah, here it is." Larry exclaimed, pulling a record from the rack.

"What is it?" Neil asked, as Larry placed the record in his hands.

"Take it upstairs and listen to it. You'll find out."

"Okay!" Neil said scampering up the stairs.

Entering his room, he opened his little record player, which was sitting next to his toy box. Neil couldn't wait. He always loved surprises. Placing the needle on the record, he listened to the snap and pop of the record, as he waited for a new adventure to begin. Suddenly, he heard the sound of music coming from the machine. It was the sound of a marching band playing a song he had heard many times before. Every Saturday afternoon, this same music blared from his father's radio. It was the sound of the Nebraska Cornhuskers fight song.

"Oh, come on!" Neil groaned, lying on the floor. "I thought it was going to be a story."

"Be patient. It is a story," Larry explained from the doorway of Neil's room.

Startled, Neil looked up, not realizing that his father had followed him up from the basement.

"Doot, you had me all excited and you gave me some record with a marching band playing songs on it?" Neil protested.

"No I didn't," Larry said. "Keep listening."

Encouraged by his father's comments, Neil turned his attention back to the record player. Suddenly, the voice of the Nebraska Cornhuskers play-by-play announcer, Lyle Bremser, roared from the machine. "Ladies and gentlemen, welcome to Memorial Stadium and the start of the 1970 football season."

In the background Neil could hear the roar of the crowd and the sound of the marching band. For the next hour Neil sat on the floor, enthralled, as Lyle Brimser gave him the highlights of the 1970 national title season. Neil could picture each play. Jerry Tagge throws the ball to the electric Johnny Rodgers. The Black Shirt defense makes a goal line stand. Neil hung on every word, as the season was reviewed, week-by-week, and game-by-game. He jumped up and down in celebration of the team's touchdowns. He groaned in anguish, as interceptions were tossed and fumbles were lost. Finally, he relaxed in joy. Former President Richard Nixon ended the record by declaring the Nebraska Cornhuskers the national champions for the 1970 season.

The record player stopped. Gingerly lifting the record from the player, he placed it back in its protective jacket. He walked from his room and made his way down to the family room, looking for his father.

"Here's your record, Doot," he said, handing Larry the album.

"What did you think?" Larry asked.

"That was the best record I've ever heard!" Neil exclaimed, jumping into Larry's lap and giving him a hug.

"I thought you'd like it," Larry said, returning the hug.

"When is the next Nebraska game?" Neil asked, hoping it was soon.

"January first, in the Orange Bowl against LSU," Larry said.

"January first?" Neil asked in astonishment.

"Yep," Larry confirmed.

"That's a month away."

"Yep."

"I'll be home from school, for the Christmas break. Can I listen to it on the radio?" Neil asked with excitement.

"You bet you can. It's a night game. I'll even let you stay up late, until it's over."

"I can't wait! I'm never going to miss another Nebraska game for as long as I live," Neil exclaimed.

As Neil headed back to his room, he was lost in the memories and excitement of the sounds of those football games. He pictured himself throwing the ball to a wide-open Johnny Rodgers. He imagined himself dodging Oklahoma tacklers on his way to the goal line. "I can't wait for that game." He muttered under his breath, as he made his way through the kitchen, where his mother was starting dinner.

"What game?" she asked turning from the stove.

"There's only one game, Mom, the Nebraska game." he said, with a hint of disgust in his voice.

"The Nebraska game?" she asked, surprised by his response.

"Yeah, the Nebraska game."

"When did you become a football fan?" she asked.

"Today." Neil proudly proclaimed.

He did listen to the 1982 Orange Bowl on January first 1982. Nebraska beat LSU, 21 – 20, in a thrilling comeback win. It was the first game he ever listened to on the radio. Also, it was the beginning of something he would continue to do each and every game, without fail, for more than 20 years.

# The Candy Bar Tournament

"Boys, stop wrestling! Settle down, we're almost there." Linda ordered.

The trip to NSVH, though only a ninety-minute drive, was never easy. They had been making the drive twice a week for more than two years. Every Friday afternoon, they would pick-up Neil for his weekend at home. Every Sunday night, they would drop him off for the school week. She hated every Sunday trip. Though she knew it was best for Neil, emotionally, her heart broke every time she had to kiss him good-bye.

Usually on the return trips to NSVH, Neil was very quiet. He never wanted to go back, often crying and begging Linda to let him stay home for "one more day." Today, it was different. Neil was very excited. He couldn't keep quiet. The entire trip he had been chattering at a hundred miles a minute. When he wasn't talking, Neil wrestled with Ryan, practicing the moves that his brother had taught him.

"They're going to have a real wrestling mat. The bleachers will be pulled out. All the parents are going to be there and everything." Neil explained, as he stuck his head between the front seats.

"Sit back Neil. We'll be there in a few minutes," Linda once again admonished.

Linda couldn't help but laugh to herself, as she silently reflected on the past two weeks. Neil and his classmates had been learning about wrestling from Coach Davis, the school's athletic director. For the past two weekends, that's all Neil could talk about. He was constantly practicing his wrestling moves with Ryan and Larry. This didn't surprise her. For as long as she could remember, Larry and the boys had wrestled. Larry was fond of getting the children down on the living room floor and wrestling with them. He would not let them up until they cried uncle. The boys, as stubborn as their father, would not give up. Larry would continue to hold them down until Linda would inevitably come to their rescue, demanding that Larry release them. She could not understand why the boys just wouldn't say uncle.

It was good to see Neil so interested in a sport, Linda thought. He was a small boy for his age, but he had always had good balance, and seemed to be strong for his size. Linda just hoped he would do well and not be disappointed. He was so excited.

Larry pulled the family car into a parking spot at the NSVH, and Ryan and Neil jumped out of the back seat. "Take it easy," Larry ordered, grabbing Neil by the hand.

"We're supposed to go straight to the gym," Neil explained to his parents, as they made their way across the parking lot.

When they entered the gym, the noise level was high. Whispering to Ryan, he nervously asked, "Are there a lot of people here?"

"The bleachers are almost full," Ryan answered.

The size of the crowd surprised Neil. There were rarely any parents present at NSVH as most students resided at the school except for holidays and summer vacation. Today, the gym was full of parents and students. A wrestling mat had been rolled out on the gym floor and a set of bleachers lined one wall. Neil could not remember ever having the bleachers used in the gym. All of the excitement in the air was beginning to make him a little bit nervous.

"Hello there, Neil," Coach Davis yelled the greeting, as he approached Neil and his family.

"Neil's really shown a lot of interest in our wrestling program. He's quite a bit smaller then some of the other kids, but he's really done well," Coach Davis explained to Linda and Larry.

"I see that you came with your shorts on. You're ready to go. So, come with me. I'll go ahead and get us started," he said turning to Neil.

Larry knelt next to Neil and whispered, "Never say uncle." Neil laughed, raised his hand for Larry to give him a high five.

Taking Neil by the shoulder, the coach led him to the corner of the mat where his other classmates had already gathered. Tom, Tim and Scott were the other three boys in Neil's class who had entered the tournament. Neil and Scottie were best friends and they instantly began chatting about their weekends.

Coach Davis stepped to the middle of the mat and quieted the crowd with a quick blow of his whistle.

"I'd like to welcome everyone to our annual Candy Bar Tournament. For those of you who have never been a part of our little event before, here is how it will work. We have four students who will have the opportunity to wrestle against each other. Each of the children has been working on learning about the sport of wrestling for the past two weeks. This competition gives us a chance to gage how much they have learned, and gives the boys an opportunity to get a feel for the real thing. Each wrestler will receive a specific number of candy bars depending on where they place in the tournament. Now I would like to introduce the four competitors in today's event."

"First we have Tommy," he said, leading Tommy toward the middle of the mat. He continued until each wrestler had been introduced. Coach Davis then directed Scottie and Tim off to the side of the mat and announced, "The first match of the day will be Neil verses Tommy."

Coach Davis had them shake hands. Then, they placed their hands palm to palm, in the traditional start for blind wrestlers. The coach blew his whistle. Only a second before Neil had been nervous, but with the sound of the whistle, all the spectators were forgotten. Neil went after Tommy with an abandon you would never have expected from someone so small. Within seconds he had taken Tommy down to the mat and put him on his back. Coach Davis slapped the mat and blew his whistle. Neil had just recorded his first career pin.

Helping Tommy up, Neil was elated! He had won his first match and his Dad had been here to see it. Smiling, with the crowd cheering, he tried to show as little emotion as possible. His Dad taught him to be humble. He knew that for every winner there was also a loser. Walking toward the edge of the mat, he thought about how Tommy must feel, with his parents watching. All of a sudden he wasn't so excited.

Sitting on the side of the mat, he watched Scottie beat Tim in a close match, 5 – 2. Tim was a smaller boy, like Neil. "Scottie had too much size on him," Neil thought as the coach raised Scottie's hand.

Coach Davis then called Tommy back to the center of the mat, to wrestle Scottie. "Ouch," Neil thought, "Scottie has to wrestle twice in a row."

Scottie made short work of Tommy. Neil began to get worried about the prospect of wrestling Scottie.

He didn't have much time to contemplate the situation. He was called to the middle of the mat, for his match with Tim. Tim was small but wiry and strong. Neil knew that this would be a tougher match. The whistle blew. They circled one another, waiting for an opening. Finally, Neil couldn't wait any longer. He dove, grabbing Tim by the legs, unceremoniously dumping him to the mat. He received 2 points for the take down. Tim quickly came to his knees and spun around behind Neil, receiving 2 points for a reversal. The score remained tied at 2 – 2, until late in the match. Tim, who was on the bottom at the time, stood up receiving 1 point for an escape and taking a 3 – 2 lead. As the match came to a close, Neil once again dove at Tim's feet. Grabbing Tim's legs, he took Tim down in a nice double leg take down, earning 2 points and a 4 – 3 victory.

"Nice match," Neil said as he pulled Tim to his feet and shook his hand.

The coach raised Neil's hand, designating him the winner. Neil sat on the edge of the mat trying to catch his breath, while Tommy and Tim wrestled.

"Tommy needs some more practice," Neil thought, as Tim quickly took Tommy down and put him on his back.

The next thing Neil knew Coach Davis was calling him back to the middle of the mat to wrestle Scottie.

Neil had never really thought about the difference in size between himself and Scottie. Neil was the leader in their friendship. Standing next to Scottie in the center of the mat, he realized that Scottie was at least three inches taller and twenty pounds heavier. Neil calculated, "that's quite a bit when I only weigh fifty-five pounds."

The whistle blew and Neil quickly discovered that Scottie was not only bigger, but he was also stronger. The first of the three one minute periods ended with neither wrestler scoring a takedown. Neil began the second period on top and quickly gave up a two-point reversal. Scottie kept Neil on the mat for the remainder of the second period. Neil began the third on the bottom. He kept trying to get to his knees and come to his feet, but Scottie's weight was just too much for him to overcome. As the whistle sounded designating the end of the match, Neil knew he had been beaten. He got to his feet fighting back the tears and shook Scottie's hand. "Nice job, Scottie," Neil said.

Then Coach Davis raised Scottie's hand in the air and declared him champion of the candy bar tournament. All four of the wrestlers lined up in the middle of the mat and were presented with their candy bars. Neil accepted his three candy bars. "Fine job, champ," Coach Davis said, shaking Neil's hand.

Waiting by the mat for his family, Neil was disappointed and sad. It wasn't just because he was beaten. It was also the thought that his family would be leaving him and returning home.

"You did a great job, Doot," Larry said, slapping him on the back.

"Yeah, but I couldn't win that last one." Neil replied in a downcast voice.

"You did your best, right?"

"Yeah."

"You should be proud of yourself. Scottie's a big boy."

"Let's go," Larry ordered. He took Neil by the shoulder and directed him toward the exit. "We'll walk you up to the dorm before we leave."

While Neil made his way back to the dormitory with his family in tow, he thought about the day's events. It sure was tough to stomach a loss. It was something special when you got your hand raised in front of all those people. That day, he decided that he would become a wrestler.

Giving his dad a hug, he whispered, "Dad, someday I will be a wrestling champion."

# The Last Day

Neil pushed away his breakfast tray, his food practically untouched. He was too excited to eat this morning. It was the last day of school at NSVH before the summer break, but more than that, it was the last day Neil would ever attend school at NSVH. Unlike the other children, Neil would not be returning in the fall. Neil's parents had made the decision to mainstream him. He would be attending third grade at the Fort Calhoun elementary school in the fall. The prospect of living at home, with his brother and parents, had Neil on top of the world.

He rose to leave the table. Hesitantly, he waited for the sound of Mrs. Blevins' gruff voice. To his surprise, he escaped. Normally she would not allow him to leave the table without finishing his meal.

Watching Neil leave the table, Mrs. Blevins' couldn't help but smile. She loved Neil, but for three years, he had been a real challenge. A very picky eater, he would try anything to avoid eating food he didn't like. From putting food on other children's trays, to hiding the food under the table, to leaving when she was distracted, he never missed a beat.

Watching Neil sneak away, she became lost in her thoughts, oblivious to the chaos of the dining hall. She was experiencing mixed emotions this morning. The last day of school was always a sad day. On the one hand she enjoyed the three-month break from the children. Yet, helping these young children learn to cope with their unique challenges was personally rewarding.

This year she was having an especially difficult time. Neil had always been her favorite. His intelligence and his fearless approach to life made him an extraordinary child. She never really thought of him as being handicapped. She knew from past experience, that when the children went back home to be mainstreamed, she rarely ever saw them again. After today, she doubted that she would ever see Neil again.

She struggled to fight back the tears, as three years of memories of Neil passed through her mind. Gradually a smile returned to her face, when she recalled the one image that was indelibly etched in her mind. She was picturing Neil running down the halls. She never understood how, but Neil had the ability to always know where he was. Most children would walk down the halls, using the walls as a guide. Neil never walked. He would run down the middle and then amazingly know exactly when to turn. She had never seen another student with that ability and she doubted she ever would.

Returning to his dorm room, he shoved the remainder of his clothes into his open suitcase. For a moment, he stopped and reflected on how some of the kids had been treating him for the last few days. "Scottie was unusually quiet. He seemed to be sad and mad. I guess I can see where he's coming from."

Neil often felt sorry for Scottie, his best friend. Scottie's family lived in Wyoming. Neil didn't know where Wyoming was, but he knew it was far enough away that Scottie only got to go home for the holidays. He knew Scottie was always envious that Neil returned home every weekend.

Each of Neil's teachers planned special parties for the day's activities. Neil, because this was his last day, was the center of attention. He had always been a favorite with the staff. Neil was anxious for his Mom to arrive. Yet, at the same time, he was confused. He couldn't understand why so many of his teachers were sad he was leaving.

"I guess most of them are happy for me," Neil told Scottie while they were finishing their lunch.

"But I just don't understand why everyone's so sad about it?"

"They're probably sad because they don't think they'll ever see you again. Will I ever see you again?" Scottie asked, as he scooped a load of fruit cocktail into his mouth.

Suddenly, he understood why Scottie was so sad. He thought he would never see Neil again. "That's crazy." Neil said. "I only live an hour and a half away. I'll be back to visit!"

"Yeah, I guess your right," Scottie said, pushing his lunch tray away.

"Let's get back to class. Mrs. Sullivan is going to finally finish that book she's been reading us," Scottie exclaimed, rising from the table.

It was all Neil could endure to make it through the final two hours of the day. He was unable to focus on the story Mrs. Sullivan, his second-grade teacher was reading. For him, this was unusual. Story time was his favorite part of the day.

His mind began to explore the idea that in just a few short summer months he would be attending a new school. His exuberance quickly changed to apprehension. He knew he was going to have to make new friends and learn his way around a new school. His biggest concern was that he would be going to school with normal kids. He was worried about how they would treat him. He thought that they would look at him differently. Suddenly, the prospect of leaving behind NSVH didn't seem so exciting. "Well, that's three months away. I'll worry about that when the time comes," Neil silently dismissed his concern.

While these thoughts were scurrying through the corridors of his mind, there came a light tap on the classroom door. Linda entered the room. Neil hurried across the room to meet his mother. The other children also crowded around Linda saying hello and asking questions. All of the children knew Neil's family, because of their weekly trips to the school. Neil said his good-byes, making sure he gave Scottie a special hug.

"We'll come back to visit next year when school starts," Linda said, before they made their exit from the classroom.

Then they made their way across the hall to the classroom of Mrs. Winegger. She had been Neil's teacher for his first two years at NSVH. He had always been very close to her. "Oh, I'm so glad you came to say good-bye," Mrs. Winegger gleefully exclaimed.

"Yep! Were going home for the summer," Neil replied.

"You're going home for good," Mrs. Winegger explained in a quiet, somber tone.

Realizing she was crying, Neil ran to her. Wrapping his little arms around her, he tearfully exclaimed, "Don't worry Mrs. Winegger, I'll come back to see you. Remember, you'll always be my favorite teacher."

Mrs. Winegger gave him a bear hug in return. "You'd better come back. I'm going to really miss you."

"I've got to go back to my room and get my suitcase," Neil said, as they neared the exit.

"It's already in the car, baby. Your momma's on top of things."

Suddenly, Neil stopped and turned toward the dormitory where he had spent the majority of his nights over the past three years. He thought to himself, "I was hoping to see my room one last time. "Oh well, I'll see it when I come back to visit."

He turned and followed his mother out the door. At the time, Neil did not realize that it would be exactly twenty years before he would once again walk the halls of NSVH.

## Postscript — Chapter Two

*The three years I spent at NSVH, played a major role in both my intellectual and emotional development. Throughout these stories, my objective was to try and impress upon the reader the emotional impact of those years. In doing so, I feel I have committed a minor injustice to the school. I cannot emphasize enough the high level of education I received at NSVH. The student to teacher ratio was 4 to 1. Each of the students received fantastic hands on teaching. It was during those years that I learned not only the 3 R's, but also braille. Braille was totally new to me. It was the foundation of my ability to learn. Like most children, I had to learn to read and write, but I learned to do so in braille. The teachers also had the task of teaching the students to read and write in print.*

*From the time I enrolled at NSVH, my parents planned to mainstream me into the Fort Calhoun Schools. When the time came to make the final decision, they were determined that it would happen. The administrators and teachers at NSVH encouraged them to have me continue there, emphasizing that I still needed to learn the many life skills required for a blind person to function in society.*

*My parents made the decision for several reasons. They knew that the quality of my education would not be as high. I would not get the specialized attention and would be in a much larger class. However, they felt there were other reasons why I should attend the local school. Emotionally, neither they nor I could continue to have me live away from home. Also, they felt that being part of a family was an important part of growing up. Equally important was the pledge my father had made to me when I was in the hospital. My parents felt I needed to compete in the sighted world on equal terms, even though I was blind. They never allowed me to use my blindness as an excuse. They knew the key to my future success was to overcome being blind.*

*To be mainstreamed into the public school system, the state required a series of tests designed to determine my educational level. These tests were administered at Boys Town. I am proud to say that, though I was only going into the third grade, NSVH had provided me with an education level of a 6th grader. I definitely believe in the importance of mainstreaming children into the public school system, but I cannot say enough about the education I received at NSVH.*

*This was an extremely emotional time in my life. I can only say that without those years and experiences I would never have become the person I am today. Those years taught me how to think, speak, and in many ways take care of myself. I have since seen the growing pains that many college students face when away from home for the first time, and I remember those feelings not as an 18 year old, but as a 4 year old. Even now, more than twenty years later, some of those memories are more vivid then many more recent events.*

*I would like to take this time to express my most heartfelt admiration and respect to the teachers and staff at NSVH. Their love and dedication made those three years as educational and positive as possible. I would especially like to thank Mrs. Blevins, Mrs. Winegger and Coach Davis. Mrs. Blevins was my housemother for all three years. Her stern, but loving care was the source of great strength and support for me. There was many a time that a hug, or a special word from her helped me cope with my loneliness. Mrs. Winegger was my teacher for my first two years. She made learning fun and exciting and instilled in me a love for books, which I still have today. Coach Davis made the school exciting and fun, providing me with a physical outlet for my frustrations and emotions.*

    *I must also thank my parents for sending me to NSVH. Now that I have children of my own, I realize how difficult and painful that decision must have been. Their dedication to bring me home on the weekends was what allowed me to cope during each week. I did not miss one weekend or holiday, no matter how severe the weather.*

# Chapter Three

## Introduction

*As the summer days of 1982 began to creep ever closer toward the month of August, I found myself also creeping toward a number of changes in my life. The little house on Madison Street, where I spent my early years, was being sold for a larger house half a block away. My best friend and baby sitter, Jeannie Fitzgerald, had graduated high school and was going away to college. I was starting over, at a new school, Fort Calhoun Elementary School. The security of repetition and regularity were giving way to the fear of the unknown. I was about to enter, what I like to refer to as, the real world, third grade. I had always functioned well among sighted people, but up to this point this had been limited primarily to my family and friends. The prospects of the future were frightening, and for the first time I was feeling unsure about my abilities.*

*I was not concerned about learning and competing in the classroom. The tests at Boys Town had proven that I was way ahead of my class. My concerns were social. I was worried I would be considered a freak, I would be teased and ridiculed and I would not have any friends. Once again, I feared I would be alone. All I wanted to do was fit in with everyone else. I didn't want to be noticed or treated differently in any way.*

# The First Meeting

Jason Weeks lay in his bed, listening to the sound of the birds singing, outside his window. The rays of the new morning sun leaked from beneath the corner of the blinds, which covered his bedroom window, signaling another great Saturday. From the bed beneath him, he could faintly hear the snores of his younger brother, Jeff. Jason and Jeff were stuck sharing a room, while their older brother Bobby had his own room.

Lying there, contemplating his plans for the day, he remembered he had promised to meet Neil Halford today. Last night, Bobby and his best friend, Ryan Halford had been playing in the house. Before leaving, Ryan asked Jason if he would play with his brother the next day. Without thinking, he agreed to join Bobby at the Halford house in the morning.

Jason had never met Ryan's little brother, but he knew Ryan. He'd heard some stories about Neil from Bobby. Even though he was blind, he sounded like a pretty cool kid. Jason didn't care if he was blind. Anyway, he thought it might be kind of interesting to see how a blind kid did things. With this thought in mind, Jason pulled his blankets over his head and fell back to sleep.

Ten o'clock that morning found Jason and Bobby finishing bowls of Captain Crunch in front of the Saturday morning cartoons, while two blocks away, in the Halford home, Neil was playing in his room, having had his cartoon fix three hours earlier. Neil was always an early riser. This morning was no exception.

He'd climbed from his bed and made his way quietly down the hall, careful not to wake his parents and brother. He went to the kitchen and pulled his brother's chair from beneath the kitchen table. Directly above his brother's seat at the table hung a clock. Neil climbed onto the chair and felt the hands of the clock, being gentle, careful not to move them. The little hand was pointing straight down, while the big hand was pointing straight left, indicating 6:45 a.m. Hopping from the chair, he pushed it back under the table, while thinking, "Life sure is easier since I learned how to tell time at NSVH."

He made his way out to the living room and planted himself in front of the consul television, which took up the majority of one wall. He turned the volume knob all the way down and flipped on the TV. He brought the volume slowly up until he could hear the sound. He then felt the knob, which changed the channel, noting its position. Channel 3, he thought, as he flipped the knob four spots to the right, turning to channel 7, ABC. In only fifteen minutes, his favorite cartoon show, Super Friends, would begin.

It was in this same position that Larry found Neil, nearly an hour later, as he headed to the basement, to take his morning shower. "I didn't know you were up, Doot,"

"I've been up for a while sleepy head," Neil replied, turning his attention toward his father.

"Sleepy head?" Larry repeated, as he jumped on Neil and began tickling him.

Squealing with laughter, Neil struggled to break away from his father's grasp. "Shh!" Larry cautioned, "If you wake up your Mom, we'll both be in trouble. Why don't you wake up your brother, get dressed and we'll run uptown for some breakfast?"

"Sounds good to me, sleepy head," Neil said, again taunting his father. Breaking from his father's grip, he scampered off through the kitchen with Larry giving chase.

At breakfast, Ryan informed Neil, "Neil, I invited Jason, Bobby's little brother to come play with you today. He's the same age as you, and he'll be in the third grade, too."

Larry, smiled, pleased with the announcement. Larry and Linda had asked Ryan to have Jason meet Neil. They were concerned. In two months, Neil would start school in Fort Calhoun. As of yet, he didn't have any friends his age. He didn't know anyone who would be in his third grade class.

Neil sat quietly. Initially, he was upset that Ryan had asked Jason without talking to him first. He didn't know Jason. He knew Ryan's friend, Bobby, and liked him. More worried than angry, Neil wondered if Jason knew that he was blind, and worried about how he would react. Other than close friends of the family, Neil had never had a sighted friend.

Larry knew Neil was not happy. Offering words of encouragement, Larry excitedly said, "Neil, I think that's great. Won't it be fun to play with somebody your own age?"

"Yeah," Neil quietly replied.

"What's wrong, Doot? I thought you'd be excited."

"Dad, what if he thinks I'm weird? What if he doesn't like to play Star Wars?"

"You'll be fine. Just give him a chance. You never know. He may become your best friend," Larry replied, trying to get Neil to think positive.

"Jason loves Star Wars. He has about as many Star Wars toys as you." Ryan said, responding to Neil's question.

"Really! He really likes Star Wars?" Neil excitedly asked.

"He sure does," Ryan answered. Neil's mood visibly changed. Suddenly, he was excited, anxious to get home.

Playing in his room, Neil nervously waited for Bobby and his brother to arrive. He had just finished constructing a racetrack for his cars when he heard the doorbell ring. Jumping to his feet, he ran for the front door.

Bobby and Jason stood on the Halford's doorstep waiting for someone to come to the door. Ryan opened the door and ushered them inside. When they entered the living room, a small boy came skittering around the corner.

Ryan introduced Jason, "Neil, this is Jason." Neil stuck out his hand in

Jason's direction. Jason took it, giving him a nervous handshake. "Nice to meet you," they said in unison.

"Come on, I'll show you my room," Neil excitedly said, running back toward the hallway.

Following Neil down the hallway, Jason noted how Neil turned at exactly the right moment to enter his room. He doesn't seem different, Jason thought as Neil showed him his collection of Star Wars toys, which lined the shelves of his toy box. Jason was a laid back child who took most things in stride. Before long, they were both engrossed in fighting Darth Vader. While they waged war in Neil's bedroom, a friendship was born. Oblivious to Neil's blindness, unimpressed with Neil's unusual abilities, Jason was intent on rescuing Princess Leah. He thought Neil was cool and he had lots of neat toys. That's what counted to him.

Two hours later, Neil and Jason were fighting their way through the woods behind Neil's house looking for a good tree to climb. It surprised Jason when, after lunch, Neil took him out back to show him the tree he loved to climb. Grabbing a limb, Neil swung himself into the tree and effortlessly stepped from limb to limb. Jason followed, meeting Neil at the top.

Having conquered this tree, Jason suggested heading down to the creek, behind the house, in search of new trees to climb. Neil quickly agreed. After showing Jason how to lead a blind person, they were on their way. Neil showed him how he could hold on to Jason's right arm by the elbow and walk a step behind. Thus, he could feel when Jason stepped up or down.

"Leading around a blind person isn't too bad," Jason thought, as they made their way through a particularly heavy spot of undergrowth.

"Here's a good one," Jason declared, stopping at the foot of the tallest tree in a little grove.

Placing his hands on the tree trunk, Neil excitedly challenged Jason, "Race you to the top!"

Grabbing a low branch, Neil signaled the start of the race. Jason, choosing the opposite side of the tree, was determined to reach the top first. Climbing as fast as he could, Jason could not stay with Neil. "Blind or not, he's the fastest tree climber I've ever seen," Jason silently thought. Disappointed at losing, yet amazed at Neil's ability, he followed Neil to the top.

High above the ground, they sat, surveying their newly found kingdom. Neil couldn't remember being happier. All of his fears and doubts about Jason had quickly vanished. He had never had so much fun climbing a tree. Of course, he had never climbed a tree with anyone other than his brother Ryan, who was always ordering him around. This was the first time he climbed a tree with a friend. It was different. It was much more fun. He was so glad he finally had a real friend.

# The New School

It was early Friday morning. Larry stood at the living room picture window, enjoying the moment. Neil was riding his Big Wheel on the driveway below. The house was close to the street, so the driveway was short, measuring fifteen by twelve feet. That didn't matter to Neil. He would ride the trike, as fast as he could, to within inches of the street, always turning at the last minute, spinning his wheels, as he slid into a sharp turn, and headed back toward the garage. Lap after lap, Neil never once went into the street.

Watching in wonder, Larry remembered back to the first time he saw Neil racing in the driveway. It was a Saturday morning, three years ago. He was cooking breakfast in the kitchen, when he heard Linda call, "Larry, come here!"

Hearing the concern in Linda's voice, he hurried to the living room, where she was watching Neil in the driveway. "Watch the way he rides his Big Wheel. See how close he gets to the street. I don't think he should be doing that. You know how busy that street is, especially in the afternoon. What if he accidentally goes into the street?"

Dismissing Linda's concern, he jokingly replied, "Well, he'll only do it once."

"Larry!" Linda replied, disgusted by his sense of humor. He always tried to make jokes about her concerns.

Turning serious, Larry explained, "Linda, watch him. Every time, he turns just before the road. He knows when to turn. Besides, you know that he hears the cars coming, long before they reach the house. He'll be fine."

"Why don't we have him ride in the back yard? It's perfectly safe there," she pleaded.

"You know he can't spin his wheels or slide into the turns. It wouldn't be the same. This is one of those times where you have to let go of the apron strings. He needs to have the chance to play, like every other boy. If that was Ryan out there, we wouldn't even be having this conversation."

"That's not fair. It's different with Ryan. You know that."

"Linda, that's my point exactly. I won't make it different for Neil. If we want him to have a normal life, then he has to be treated like a normal child."

She knew Larry was right, but nevertheless she still worried.

His thoughts returning to the present, Larry realized it was time to go. Normally, he would be at work by now, but he had taken the day off. A week from today was going to be another big event in Neil's life. It would be Neil's first day at the local school. Larry had promised to give him a tour, which would allow him to become acquainted with the floor plan. He'd made arrangements with the principal, Mr. Schellenberger, to take the tour that morning.

Opening the front door, he called to Neil, "Doot, it's time to go."

Imagining that his trike was his father's Corvette, Neil was leading in a race with his uncle Darrell. Passing the finish line, the entrance to the garage, he slid his trike into its parking place, next to the real Corvette, and raised his hands in victory.

"Come on, Dad," he yelled, running out of the garage.

Larry, meeting Neil at the bottom of the front steps, asked, "Do you want to take the Corvette?"

He knew Neil loved to ride in the car. He thought it was a racecar. Of course, Larry knew it was the way he drove that gave Neil that idea. Neil pondered for a moment and then replied, "Dad, can we walk? I need to learn the way to school."

"That's a great idea, Doot! Let's take a walk."

The school was only five blocks from their house. On their short trek, they carried on a conversation about the third grade. Neil loved to talk. To Larry, many times it was like talking to a little adult.

While talking with Larry, Neil would carefully listen to the surrounding sounds. It would be many years before he or his parents would recognize that he had developed the ability to carry on a conversation and to simultaneously listen to his surroundings. It was as if two different parts of his brain were working independently, but equally clear.

As they approached the front doors to the school, Neil suddenly stopped. Pointing to his right, Neil asked, "What's that, Dad?'

Shaking his head, Larry answered, "That's a wall with a bench on it. It's for students to sit on, while waiting for the school to open."

Neil never stopped surprising him. This had happened so many times. Neil would somehow know there was a wall, or a desk, or a table, nearby, as if he were able to see. It happened so frequently, that Larry and Linda thought that he could at least see shadows. A year earlier, Neil's sight had been retested. After the tests, their doctor explained that there was no way he was seeing anything. He was completely blind. Doctor Crossman was considered one of the most renowned eye doctors in the country. Yet, he had no explanation for this extraordinary ability of Neil's. He had never seen it before.

Greeted by the principal, they entered the school, "Good morning, Neil. I'm Mr. John Schellenberger, the principal. I'm honored to have you come to this school."

Shaking the principal's hand, Neil replied, "Nice to meet you, sir."

"The school is open. You can go wherever you want and take as long as you need."

"Thank you. Let's get started, Doot," Larry replied.

Taking Neil's hand, they proceeded to his third grade classroom. While Larry explained the different areas, Neil walked the room, familiarizing himself with the location of the major items, desks, blackboards, etc. Then they proceeded to the other areas, which Neil would use. They visited the other third grade classroom, the cafeteria, the gymnasium and the library. In each area,

Neil would explore, while Larry would offer an explanation. The entire process took about one hour.

Mr. Schellenberger followed them, helping to explain Neil's daily routine. He knew about Neil, but this was the first time he had the opportunity to meet him. While watching Neil go from room to room, he was concerned. It was not what he had expected. Neil didn't feel the walls or the desks, he didn't walk with his hands outstretched to protect himself, and he didn't walk with a cane. He didn't believe Neil would be able to make his way without help. This was going to be more difficult than he originally envisioned.

"That's everything. Time to head home, Doot," Larry declared.

"Dad, before we go, I want to do a couple of more things."

"Sure, you name it."

"First, I would like to walk back to my classroom by myself. I want to make sure I know the way."

Letting go of Neil's hand, Larry replied, "Give it a try, Doot."

Concerned that Neil would injure himself, Mr. Schellenberger started to object. Larry raised his hand, silencing the principal.

To Mr. Schellenberger's surprise, Neil took off immediately; racing up the stairs, through two closed doors, down another hallway, turned left and stopped directly in front of the door to his classroom. He walked down the middle of the hallway, never once hitting a wall or a door.

Larry and the principal followed. Mr. Schellenberger asked, in disbelief, "How does he do that? That is unbelievable. He must have some eyesight?"

Accustomed to such questions, Larry proudly replied, "I can't answer that question. I don't know how he does it, but he's done it for years. For a while, we also thought, hoped that he could see. We've had him retested for sight several times. There is no doubt. He is totally blind. He seems to know where all the major obstacles are. It wasn't always like this. When he first came home from the hospital, he was constantly running into doors, walls, and furniture. You name it. He hit it. I can't tell you how many times we took him to the hospital for stitches. Somehow, over the years, he's developed this sixth sense.

"I do know that he has an incredible memory. It's hard to understand, but, even though he is blind, he has a photographic memory. Once he's been in a house or a building, once he's learned the floor plan, he always remembers it. I've seen him return to a house years later and maneuver through the house like he'd always lived there."

"I've never seen anything like that." Mr. Schellenberger shook Neil's hand and said, "Neil, you are going to do just fine. I'm proud to have you at our school."

Saying goodbye, Mr. Schellenberger returned to his office.

"Dad, I want to go to the cafeteria and pretend like it is lunch time."

"Lead the way, Doot."

Neil proceeded to the cafeteria, where he practiced stopping at each station, pretending to get his tray, silverware, drink and meal. Successfully completing each stop, he turned to Larry and said, "Dad, one last item. It just wouldn't be right to visit the school, without checking out the playground."

Larry laughed and then led Neil outside. Neil went from the swings, to the slide, trying out each apparatus. Then he discovered a large Jungle Gym, made from tires. He climbed to the top, crawled through the tires, swung from the tires, jumped from the tires. Patiently watching, Larry enjoyed every moment. He often called Neil "His Li'l Monkey." Neil loved to climb, and being blind hadn't slowed him down. He would climb rocks, walls, even trees.

"It's time to go," Larry called to Neil, knowing he would play for hours, if he had his way.

Walking home, they talked about his first day in school. "Neil, you did great. Monday should be easy."

"I'll be fine, Dad," Neil replied, squeezing his Dad's hand.

Though confident, Neil was very nervous. It was easy to find his way, when the halls weren't filled with students. More than the navigational challenges, he was worried about how his classmates would react to him. Being a small town, he would know most of the kids in his class. However, having been away to school for the last three years, it would still be as if he was the new kid in school.

Also, the school would be much different. At Nebraska City, he was in a class of four students; he was competing with other blind children, he was considered "the stud" of the school. Now he would be at a great disadvantage, a blind boy competing against sighted children. Though he had successfully done this for years, it was never in a structured, school setting. It had always been with relatives and friends. Though sheltered most of his life, he had experienced the prejudice of people, the cruel comments about his blindness; and most degrading, the need for people to treat him differently, to treat him as handicapped. He hoped he would be "just one of the boys" in school. He didn't want to be different; he didn't want any special attention.

In an effort to ease his concerns and to reassure his Dad, as they arrived home, he concluded, "It may take a little time, but I'll be fine."

# Third Grade

The day had arrived. Today Neil would start third grade at the Fort Calhoun Elementary School. He approached the new day, the beginning of a new chapter in his life, exhausted and with mixed emotions. Awake most of the night, his mind had been a battlefield of emotions. He was excited about going to public school, about being with sighted students. Yet, he was worried about fitting in, about being accepted by the other students.

"Would they accept him as an equal, or treat him as some handicapped freak?" This was the question that caused his sleepless night.

As the car stopped in front of the school, Ryan leaped from the car, shouting goodbye.

Neil sat still, frozen to the front seat. Linda knew he was afraid. She wanted to walk him to his classroom, but she knew she shouldn't. She and Larry had decided it would be best if Neil did it by himself. Besides, Neil had emphatically objected to the idea. His exact words were, "You can't. They'll call me a baby. Mom, I have to do this on my own."

Linda reached over, and gave Neil a hug, whispering in his ear, "Time to go. You'll be just fine."

She moved to give him a kiss and he pulled away, demanding, "Mom, not here!"

Smiling at his attempt to be older, she honored his wish, "Okay, dear. You have a great day."

Just as Neil opened the door, he was greeted by a familiar voice, "Hi, Neil. It's time to go to class."

Suddenly, his fear evaporated. It was his new best friend, Jason. Since the first day they met, they became inseparable, playing together for hours each day. The best news he'd heard about school, was that Jason would be in his class. He knew he would have at least one friend in his class. Jumping from the car, he shouted, "Goodbye Mom. I'll be fine."

Then, he grasped Jason's right arm and they proceeded into the school. Jason was a very good guide. The experience of the last two months was invaluable. They moved in unison, as one. They navigated through the crowd unnoticed, not attracting any attention to Neil.

Arriving at the door to their classroom, they were greeted by their teacher, Mrs. Goodman, "Well, hello there. You must be Neil and Jason. Each desk has a nametag on it. Please take a seat at the desk with your name."

Neil wondered how she knew their names. They had never met. He did not know that his parents had met with Mrs. Goodman, to ensure she was well informed about Neil's condition and his capabilities. One of the topics of discussion was Neil's friendship with Jason. They wanted her to help support this friendship. Jason was accustomed to being with Neil. He knew when Neil could be on his own and when Neil needed assistance. They felt he could be a great help to Mrs. Goodman. More importantly, they felt he could be an example for the other students. By watching him and Neil interact, they would not be afraid of Neil's blindness. They would see he was very independent and able to take care of himself.

Nervously, Neil followed Jason. He was afraid the teacher would make him sit in the front, apart from the other students. Being separate, being treated differently, would make it more difficult to be accepted by the students. Neil felt confident that, if he were treated like all the other students, he would be able to hold his own. He knew he would be able to overcome the prejudices of his fellow students. What he feared the most, what he knew would be an insurmountable obstacle, would be the prejudices of the adults, those in authority. Their well-intentioned, overprotective attitude could result in decisions that would set him apart.

As they maneuvered between the desks, Jason suddenly stopped. "This is your desk," he announced.

Whispering, Neil asked, "Where is my desk located?"

"It's in the second row, three desks back. My desk is in the fifth row." Jason explained and moved to his desk.

"Good morning students. My name is Mrs. Goodman. I will be your teacher for this year. I want to start by having each of you stand, state your name and tell us something about yourself."

Once the students started to introduce themselves, Neil panicked. He didn't know what to say. Should he tell them he was blind? Should he just let them find out for themselves? Decision time came faster then he expected. He knew he was next. When the girl behind him finished, he immediately stood and announced, "My name is Neil Halford. I have an older brother, Ryan. My favorite movie is Star Wars. My favorite sport is wrestling."

Mrs. Goodman was curious. She had intended to introduce him, thinking that he would not know when it was his turn. To her amazement, he arose at the proper time. She was unaware that this would be the first, of many times, that Neil would do the unexpected, would do things she felt a blind person could never do.

When the introductions were finished, Mrs. Goodman then explained the plans for the year and the daily schedule.

Mrs. Goodman then announced, "Class we have a very special student in our class. Many of you already know him. He is Neil Halford. He is blind. He will be treated like any other student. However, because he can't see, he has to do some things differently. I want you to understand how we will all work together. First, each week, I will appoint one of you to act as his guide, to walk with him to the various rooms and activities. Do I have a volunteer for the first week?"

Though necessary, Neil did not like being the center of attention. When she asked for a volunteer, he held his breath; worried that nobody would want to help. His fears were eased when she acknowledged the first volunteer, "Jason Weeks has volunteered. All of you should watch how Neil and Jason work together, so when it is your turn, you will know what to do. Also, anytime I write something on the blackboard, I will also say every word I write, so Neil will know what we are talking about."

When she finished her explanation, two people entered the room. Mrs. Goodman introduced them to the class, "Children, we have two very special guests, whom I want to introduce. They are Mr. Bender and Mrs. Ringler. Mr. Bender is the superintendent of the Nebraska School for the Visually Handicapped and Mrs. Ringler will be Neil's braille transcriber. Mr. Bender, you have the floor."

Neil was taken by surprise. He had no idea they would be coming to the class. He was worried. He didn't know what they were going to say.

"Good morning students. Hi, Neil. How are you? How was your summer?"

Neil nervously answered, "I'm fine Mr. Bender. I had a great summer. I didn't know you were coming to visit."

"I know it's a surprise. We thought it would be good to explain to your fellow classmates how school works for you. Will you help me?"

"Sure. Whatever I can do to help."

"Students for the last three years Neil attended my school in Nebraska City. He not only went to school there, he lived there. It is a very difficult school. He had to learn everything you learned in school, plus a whole lot more."

Mr. Bender then explained all of the different skills Neil learned. When it came to braille, Mr. Bender asked for Neil's help, "Neil, would you type a few sentences with your braillewriter, please?"

While Neil typed, Mr. Bender explained how braille worked, why it was necessary. When Neil was finished, he passed the paper around the class so the students could understand how Neil could read and write.

To Neil's surprise, his fellow students were very interested and asked a lot of questions. Neil answered their questions. Then each student got to type some letters using his braillewriter. They were all intrigued with how it worked. Neil was very happy, being the center of attention. It made him feel special. It made him feel accepted.

Mr. Bender finished his presentation by talking about the purpose for "mainstreaming."

"Neil is an exceptional student. He has uncommon abilities, which made him an excellent candidate for mainstreaming. Neil is the youngest student and one of the first to be integrated into public school. He will be able to do most things by himself, just like you. However, sometimes, he will require some help. I hope that each of you will be willing to help him."

When Mr. Bender was finished, Mrs. Goodman added, "I know you would not want to leave your home and have to live in a strange place. So, let's all help Neil, so he can live with his family."

Then Mrs. Ringler introduced herself and explained her role as Neil's transcriber. She would not be in class with him, but would office in the teacher's lounge. This meant that in class, he would be like every other student. Neil wanted to cheer. He had been very concerned about Sharry being in class, emphasizing his blindness, and making him stand out. Also, she didn't mention she was Neil's aunt, though he thought most students knew.

Mrs. Goodman then explained that Neil would be treated like all the other students, having to do the same work. "The only difference is that the rest of you have it easier. Neil's homework will take twice as long, because he has to use the braillewriter."

This explanation was greeted by audible "Aahs" of relief by the students. Neil was glad the kids knew how difficult it would be for him. He felt this would make life in the classroom much easier.

When their guests had departed, Mrs. Goodman made an announcement. An announcement the students had been waiting to hear all morning, "It's time for recess."

The students formed a line. Neil, holding onto Jason, was in the rear. Once they entered the playground, the line quickly disappeared. The students raced to their favorite apparatus.

"Let's hit the jungle gym," Neil suggested. Running alongside Jason, they quickly arrived at their destination. Unexpectedly, they were greeted by a challenge Neil had hoped would never come.

"What do you think you're doing, Blind Boy. You can't play here. It's too dangerous. You can't see. Go play on the grass with the girls."

The challenge had come from the class "stud," Andy. Neil didn't know him, but had heard about him. Because he was "different," Neil knew this moment was inevitable. He knew that eventually someone would challenge his right to be there. Never in his wildest dreams had he thought it would come on the first day. Neil knew this was his moment of truth. How he handled this challenge would define his role in the class. It would determine how the other students treated him.

"I'll play where I want! You're not the teacher!" Neil replied, accepting the challenge.

Andy moved closer, standing chest to chest with Neil. Neil confidently continued, "Let's race to the top and back! First one down wins!"

Since his father first brought Neil to the school and he climbed this very same jungle gym, Jason and Neil had returned many times. They spent countless hours climbing all over the jungle gym. Neil knew where every tire was. He had raced and beaten Jason many times.

Standing in the ready position, they both waited. Upon Jason's command, "GO!" they both began. Neil raced to the top, never missing a step. When he reached the top, he realized that Andy was slightly ahead. It was time for drastic measures. He had to win. Standing at the top of the gym, eight feet above the ground, he turned and jumped, landing on his feet, well ahead of Andy.

A small group of students, who heard the challenge, had gathered to watch. Once Neil landed, they cheered his victory, celebrating by giving him some "high fives."

When he reached the ground, Andy approached Neil and congratulated him, "That was awesome, Dude!"

Neil knew those words signaled his acceptance. He was no longer just a member of the class. He was part of the class.

Unbeknownst to the students, Mrs. Goodman had been carefully watching. She wanted to see how Neil would handle himself. She didn't expect him to do so well. His athletic ability and daring amazed her. When she learned that one of her students would be a blind boy, she initially had some grave reservations. She had envisioned a little boy who could not walk without help and who would need special attention in the classroom.

As the students lined up to return to class, she silently admonished herself, "How wrong could I have been? Neil is going to be an unexpected gift to my class. Just by being himself, he will unknowingly be a constant source of inspiration."

# *Friend or Foe*

Neil's third grade year had been a year of great change, in all aspects of his life. He was mainstreamed into the public school. Scholastically, he had been an excellent student, adjusting well to his new environment. Though, he knew there were signs of trouble on the horizon. The students had accepted him, for the most part. They would help him and they would play with him, but they never really became friends. There was still some distance he could not close. He only had one true friend in school, Jason.

Like all students, he had to endure some cruel jokes and petty jealousies. The difference was that they were always directed toward his blindness and the limitations it caused. They were more vitriolic, more personal than most. Someone would purposely bump into him in the hall, or trip him on the playground. Infrequent at this time, Neil chose to ignore them, but he could never forget them. He always worried; concerned that this was an ominous omen, portending more painful, cruel school years to follow.

His family life also changed. His parents worked extremely hard. Larry worked long hours, often on weekends. The family was finally experiencing the rewards of his labor. Shortly after starting the third grade, the family moved into a new house. A house they still live in today. Most moves are traumatic for the children; this was not. Though only a block away from their first house, for Neil, it was like moving to paradise.

The house the Halfords had lived in, up to this point in his life, was a small three-bedroom ranch, with 1,050 square feet of living space. It was on a small lot, closely surrounded by other small houses. The new house was a tri-level with more than 2,000 square feet. It was situated at the end of a narrow, quiet lane, on a heavily wooded, two-acre lot. Adjacent to the north was a creek and to the west was a large city park. Best of all, the thing Neil loved the most, was the swimming pool.

Larry had traded his Corvette for a 1940 Ford Convertible. Neil and Ryan always wore the latest fashions and the neatest shoes. They always had the newest toys. Times were good.

Throughout the school year, Neil's friendship with Jason had grown. They would play for hours, lost in the imaginations of the moment. Racing through the trees, splashing in the creek, swinging for the sky, they were inseparable. Jason was Neil's transportation. Together, they would explore the town. Neil would sit on Jason's "Huffy" bicycle, while Jason stood, pedaling around town. Being a small town, Neil's parents allowed him to go everywhere. Unbeknownst to Neil, wherever he went, everyone knew him. Everyone watched him carefully.

One of their favorite places was Fort Atkinson. It was located on the bluffs overlooking the Missouri River Valley, about two blocks from the Halford house. Lewis and Clark, the famous explorers of the Louisiana Purchase, had camped there, meeting with local Indians. Later, on this same site, the U.S. Army built a military post. The fort had been restored. It was the perfect place to play "cowboys and Indians." The walls of the fort and the trails surrounding the fort brought the past to life. It wasn't a game to the boys. It felt real.

Most weekends, Larry and Linda would go out, often to a restaurant and a movie. Neil, Jason, Ryan and one of his friends would usually accompany them. Neil loved to go to movies. Jason had become a great partner. Without Neil ever asking, Jason instinctively knew when to explain the movie's action and when to remain silent. Neil would also spend many nights at Jason's house. It was as if they were both members of two families.

The following summer passed quickly. The Halford's had the only swimming pool in town. Each day, the pool was the center of their lives. Used by family, friends and neighbors, it was like one constant party. Neil was a great swimmer and fearless. He would dive, he would slide, and he would play water basketball. You name the game, and he played it. In the pool, he felt like he was on equal terms. Being blind was not a factor.

With summer coming to a close, Neil began to worry about school. He learned that Jason would not be in his fourth grade class. Neil wanted his parents to transfer him to Jason's class. They refused. Having Jason in Neil's class, the first year, had been important. He really helped Neil that first year. Now they were concerned Neil was becoming too dependent on Jason. They loved Jason. They considered him to be their third son. They also felt that it was very important to wean Neil from Jason. Neil had to learn to become more self-sufficient.

The first day of school, Neil walked with Ryan to Jason's house, which was on the way to school. Jason and Neil then walked to school together. Parting ways at the door to Neil's classroom, Neil was immediately met by his new teacher, Mrs. Sweem. A young teacher, in her mid twenties, she greeted Neil, "My name is Mrs. Sweem. I am your fourth grade teacher."

Neil's nerves were immediately calmed. He didn't know why. It was her voice. The tone of her voice, something about her voice assuaged his concerns. He instantly fell in love. She was his favorite teacher.

His desk was in the front row, adjacent to Mrs. Sweem's desk. He was happy to be so close to his new love. As the day progressed, it was obvious that Mrs. Sweem had taken an instant interest in Neil. This set the tone for the entire year. In one day, Neil had become the proverbial "Teacher's Pet."

The class began without all the special attention that accompanied Neil in the third grade. After one year, all of the students knew about Neil's situation. Neil was pleased; the less fanfare, the better. He also knew that the special attention of Mrs. Sweem would cause some problems. At the moment, Neil didn't care. He was basking in the light of his favorite teacher's special attention.

As the school year progressed, it became obvious to Neil that three boys, all fellow classmates, would be his nemeses. Chad, the ringleader, Andre, his school's version of "The Giant," and Jamie, were his antagonists. They took every opportunity to call him names: "Baby," "Blind Boy," "Sissy." Name calling quickly progressed to more aggressive behavior. They would push him and trip him. They'd do anything to embarrass him on the playground. Of course, they were careful. This would only happen when the teachers weren't looking.

Though he felt embarrassed and angry, he chose to ignore them. In his mind, reporting them to the teacher would only make matters worse. Frustrated, he knew he had no choice. He would just have to live with it. Living with it was not easy. He began to hate going to school, never knowing what or when, but always knowing that they would do something. Neil began to have a problem with cold sores, the manifestation of his constant stress.

The final straw came on a Friday during a game of kickball. At recess, the students divided into two teams. When Neil's team was in the field, he would be the pitcher. A teammate would stand next to him to retrieve any balls kicked toward Neil. When it was his turn to kick the ball, they would hand it to Neil. He would then punt it and run to the base. This Friday, Chad, his most vocal adversary, was pitching for the opposing team. When Neil came to kick, Chad refused to give him the ball, demanding that Neil kick the ball like everyone else. Although Neil's teammates vociferously protested, Chad did not budge. Finally, Chad rolled the ball, demanding that Neil kick it. One of Neil's teammates caught the ball and handed it to Neil, telling him to punt it. Chad raced from the pitching mound. Standing chest to chest with Neil, he grabbed the ball and once again demanded that Neil kick the ball. Neil, realizing that Chad would not stop, quit the game. He did not want to spoil the game for everyone else. Holding back his tears, Neil returned to class.

The next Monday morning, after worrying all weekend, Neil decided he would not go to school. He was finished. Pretending to be sick, his mother let him stay with his Grandma Betty. Linda's mother lived across the street from Neil's school. With mixed feelings, he watched from her window as his fellow students played. He wanted to be there, he loved school. Yet, he couldn't continue to tolerate the abuse. At that moment, secure in the warm, loving arms of his grandma, his worries vanished.

Having been successful the day before, the next day, he once again declared his ailments, anticipating another quiet day with Grandma Betty. Moments later, his father appeared, "What's wrong, Doot?"

Neil immediately knew his father was skeptical. Hoping to belie his father's concerns, Neil answered, using the weakest, most feeble voice he could imitate, "I feel sick, Dad. My throat hurts, my cold sores hurt, I have a bad headache. I just don't feel good."

Larry, struggling to hold back a smile, continued to question Neil. "Neil, I know you're not sick. Tell me the real problem."

Tears slowly rolling down his cheeks, Neil informed Larry of the bullies and their abuse.

Instantly, Larry was furious. "How could someone do this to his boy?" he silently questioned. His immediate reaction was to take Neil to school and confront the bullies. He knew that would only make things worse. This was Neil's problem and he would have to resolve it.

When Neil had finished, Larry lifted him into his arms. Tightly hugging his son, Larry explained, "Neil, I'm sorry this is happening to you. I can help you, but I think you need to handle this yourself. I can talk to the principal or I can talk to the boy's parents."

"No, Dad!" Neil interrupted. "That won't help."

"What do you want me to do?" Larry asked.

Neil couldn't answer his Dad. He knew anything Larry did would only make matters worse. No one could help him. Larry, understanding Neil's frustration, continued, "Neil, a person can only be so patient, so understanding. At some point, and only you will know when you reach that point, you have to solve the problem."

"You mean fight them?" Neil questioned.

"That's one solution. You can also continue to ignore them. If you do ignore them, then you can't let them bother you. You can't go through the entire year worrying every day about what may come next."

"Dad, they're so big!" Neil proclaimed, voicing his fears.

"You take me down when we wrestle. They're not as big as me, right? Besides, remember what I've always told you, 'The bigger they are, the harder they fall.'"

Neil immediately hopped from his father's lap and began to get dressed. "Tell Mom to fix my lunch. I'm going to school. Today, things will change," Neil declared.

Climbing the stairs from Neil's room, Larry worried. There was no easy answer for Neil. The irony was that when Larry was in school, he was a bully. Listening to his son, he now graphically saw, through his own son, how much emotional pain he had inflicted on others. He was worried Neil would get hurt. He also knew no one but Neil could stop the pain.

Later that day, the morning recess bell rang. At the playground, Neil decided to play by himself, hoping they would not bother him. Most of his classmates, including the three bullies, were playing kickball on the tennis courts. Neil, looking towards the courts, listened, trying to determine who was winning. Unknowingly, he caught the eye of Chad.

"Hey, everyone. Look at that sissy, Neil, playing by himself. He's too afraid to play a real game." Chad loudly exclaimed, ensuring all of his classmates heard him ridiculing Neil.

The time had come, and Neil knew it. If he didn't confront Chad now, things would continue to get worse. He quickly stood up, walked to the edge of the tennis court and defiantly challenged Chad, "Come here and say that!"

Chad was surprised, but confident. He ran to Neil, stopping inches from his face. Neil could feel his breath and knew Chad was very close.

"Chad, it stops NOW!" Neil declared.

Reacting to Neil's demand, Chad pushed Neil. As he began to drop to his knees, Neil grabbed Chad by the shirt, preventing the fall. Chad's shirt still in his grasp, Neil began to swing.

"Neil! Stop that!" Mrs. Sweem yelled. She had seen the initial push and was rushing to prevent a fight.

Obeying her command, Neil stopped.

Escorted to the principal's office, they were ordered to take seats across the desk from Principal Schellenberger. "What's the problem, Chad?" He questioned in a demanding voice.

"There's no problem," Chad quietly replied.

"Neil, tell me what happened," he requested, in a stern, yet caring voice, which reflected a different attitude. Neil wanted to tell him. He wanted to tell Mr. Schellenberger about all of the jokes, all of the degrading comments, all of the physical abuse, but he didn't. Neil knew Chad expected him to tell. He also knew his Dad was right, that he was the only person who could make it stop. It certainly wasn't Principal Schellenberger. He could only make it worse.

"Nothing happened. We were just playing." Neil answered.

Seeing that neither boy was going to talk, Mr. Schellenberger gave them both a stern, but short, lecture about appropriate playground behavior. He then ordered Chad to walk Neil back to class.

Mr. Schellenberger proceeded to call each child's parents and report their behavior. He knew Chad had been picking on Neil. In time, he hoped it would subside. Never, in his wildest dreams, had he expected Neil to literally "take the matter into his own hands." While lecturing the two boys, he had to restrain himself. He really wanted to give Neil a high five and tell him how proud he was of the way he had handled the problem. Officially he couldn't condone violence, but he knew that sometimes, there was no other choice.

"Why didn't you tell him what happened?" Chad asked Neil, as they walked to class.

"I'm not a rat. I handle my own problems."

Recognizing that Neil would no longer take any of his crap, Chad stopped, and turned to Neil, took his hand and exclaimed, "You're okay."

He shook Neil's hand and then finished leading him to class.

Immediately Neil knew he had solved the problem. He could feel the respect in Chad's voice. Neil also wondered if it would ever change. In the third grade, he had to prove himself. In the fourth grade, he had to prove himself. He silently wondered if it would ever stop, if people would ever accept him as an equal.

While at work, Larry worried all day about Neil. He wondered if Neil had fought Chad. He hoped no one had been hurt. When he entered the house, his questions were immediately answered. "Larry, you and I need to talk now!" Linda greeted him with this emphatic demand. She led him upstairs to the master bedroom.

"Do you know your son almost got into a fight at school today?" she queried, already knowing the answer.

"You mean "our" son, don't you?" Larry replied, trying to calm her with his humor. It never did work.

"Seriously, Larry, Neil told me that you told him to fight Chad. Why would you ever do that?"

"I discussed the different ways he could handle Chad. Yes, one of them was to stand up to Chad, knowing it might end in a fight. To be honest, I'm glad he made that choice. Did he win? Is he okay?" Larry asked, ignoring her admonition.

"Yes, he's fine. It was only a little shoving match. Even so, now, he thinks he's the next "Hulk Hogan.""

"Linda, Neil had to solve this problem. You should be proud of him. He took a big step. This is just the first of many times in his life he will be challenged. In the future, he will have to stand up for himself. Today, he learned never to run.""

For the following two weeks, Mrs. Sweem had Chad serve as Neil's guide, hoping to kindle a friendship. It worked. Neil and Chad became friends, often playing together. During the year, Neil and Chad spent the night at each other's house. Though, at times, Neil was still confronted with ridicule, it was minimal. More importantly, he had earned the admiration of his greatest foe.

# The First Kiss

The summer of 1984 was a perpetual pool party. On the hot, humid, Nebraska summer days, the pool was an oasis. It was the source of cool relief and endless pleasure. There was always a group of cousins and friends, supervised by a teenage babysitter, who of course would invite her friends.

In early July, a new visitor began to frequent the pool. Allie, a classmate of Neil's, lived in the country. Her mother worked at the high school. She started coming to town with her mother. While her mother worked, Allie would ride her bicycle around the town, visiting her friends and classmates. One day she stopped to see Neil.

Neil was excited to see her. They had been in the same class for both the third and fourth grades. Allie was always very nice to Neil. They were both very outgoing, very mature for their age and enjoyed conversing. On her first visit, Neil and Allie spent the afternoon lounging around the pool and talking. She hadn't brought her swimsuit, so she couldn't swim. It seemed like only a short time before Allie had to return to the high school to go home with her mother. As Allie prepared to leave, Neil invited her to return and reminded her to bring her swimsuit.

When Linda came home that evening, she was excitedly greeted by Neil, "Mom, will you please call Allie's Mom and let her know that it's okay for Allie to swim in our pool?"

His animated request surprised Linda. Up until now, he had never taken an interest in girls. All of his friends were boys. He got along well with girls, but never spent any time with them. He always dismissed them as a necessary nuisance. Linda knew Allie from Neil's class and had known her mother for years. They were a very nice family.

"Why the sudden interest in Allie?" Linda asked, interested in hearing more of the story.

"She came by today. We talked all afternoon. I asked her to come back. She said she would try, but wasn't sure her mother would let her. Please call her Mom and tell her that it's okay," Neil replied, handing Linda the phone.

Linda, laughing, replied, "Okay, I'll call her, Neil. First, let me at least get comfortable."

"Okay, Mom, but please call her before you go to the pool," Neil asked, worried that Linda would ignore his request.

He was afraid she would do what she did every sunny evening, go sun bathe by the pool. His Mom loved the sun. Every summer she had a great suntan.

"Neil, I'll call her. I promise."

Just after Linda laid down on her float, planning to spend a leisure hour floating gently across the pool, Neil suddenly reappeared, "Mom, did you call Allie's mom?"

"Yes, Neil, I did. Allie's Mom said she could come anytime she wants. I think she will return tomorrow. Now leave me alone, please."

"Yeah! Thanks, Mom," Neil celebrated, as he obeyed his Mom and went to play inside.

An hour later, Larry arrived home, dinner in hand. Linda was a great cook. However, after working eight to ten hours a day at the bank, the last thing she wanted to do was cook dinner. So three to four nights a week, the family went out to eat, or Larry brought home a meal. Tonight, it was one of their favorites, fried chicken from the Long Horn, a local bar/restaurant. They had great chicken and even better salads.

Linda greeted Larry in the kitchen, announcing, "I think we have a budding new romance."

She then proceeded to explain her earlier conversation with Neil. Linda then cautioned Larry against making fun of Neil. She ordered him to remain completely silent about Allie.

The next day, much to Neil's delight, Allie returned, swimsuit in hand. She spent the entire day playing with Neil and the other boys and girls. For the next two months, Allie would spend three or four days a week playing at the Halford's. During this time, Neil and Allie became very close. They were very much alike. Both had very outgoing, laid back personalities. They enjoyed talking. Much of their time together, they spent sitting by the pool, just talking.

Then one day in early August, Neil's cousin Angie and a neighbor, Kim Miller, both twelve, decided to intervene. They spent a great deal of time at the Halford's pool and had noticed the budding romance. "Allie, come up here. I need to talk to you." Angie, standing on the deck, which overlooked the pool, called to Allie.

Allie obeyed, wondering what she wanted. Neil remained by the pool, nervously waiting for Allie's return. He knew his cousin well. She was wild. He had no idea what she wanted, but he knew she was probably up to some mischief.

After several minutes, Angie came and sat next to Neil, and announced, "Neil, Allie wants to be your girlfriend."

"No way!" Neil instinctively replied.

"Don't you like her? She sure likes you." Angie said, encouraging Neil to reconsider.

After thinking for a while, Neil agreed, "Yes, I like her a lot. Okay, I'll be her boyfriend," he agreed, even though he had no idea what it meant. It sounded grownup.

Angie led Neil inside the house, to the living room, where Kim was waiting with Allie. Then Angie began, as if orchestrating a wedding, "Allie, do you want Neil to be your boyfriend?"

"Yes," Allie, replied, her red face revealing her embarrassment.

"Neil, do you want Allie to be your girlfriend?"

"Yes," Neil replied, trying to make his voice sound deeper, more adult.

"Good. Then to make it official, you have to kiss."

Allie and Neil looked at each other, totally surprised by this requirement. Kissing had not crossed either of their minds. At first, Neil wanted to run. The more he thought about it, the more he liked the idea. One thing was for sure; he wasn't going to kiss her with an audience. Taking Allie's hand, Neil whispered, "Allie, follow me."

He knew the perfect spot. As they left, Angie and Kim's faces reflected their disappointment. They had anticipated witnessing Neil's first kiss.

Ryan and Neil lived in the basement. Their bedroom was very large, with two sets of bunk beds built into the wall. They had their own bathroom. The bedroom had a large sliding glass door, which opened directly onto the pool patio. Underneath the stairs, was a large cavity, which Neil turned into his personal fort. Neil decorated his fort with a florescent light, a radio and some of his favorite toys. He never allowed anyone, other than Jason, to enter his fort.

"I'm going to take you to my special place, my fort," Neil announced, while they descended the stairs.

Obediently, Allie followed Neil, crawling into the fort. Neil turned on the radio. "The Power of Love" by Huey Lewis and the News was playing. Listening to the song and holding hands, they sat in silence. Breaking the ice, Neil asked, "Who's going to do it first? Who's going to start?"

Allie, before Neil could finish, replied, "I'm not going to start it!"

"Well, I'm not going to start it, either."

"They said we have to do this, if we're going to be boyfriend and girlfriend," Allie explained.

Once again sitting in silence, Allie, growing impatient, said, "Okay, I'll count to three and then we'll do it." Neil nodded in agreement. Then Allie, as if afraid Neil would change his mind, rapidly counted, "One, Two, Three!"

In unison, they leaned forward and their lips met, for an instant, before they both pulled back.

Neil was so proud. He had kissed his first girl. More importantly, he didn't know why, but he liked it. Since the ice had been broken, he decided he wanted more. So moving closer, he and Allie proceeded to kiss again and again and again. Each time it lasted a little longer. Each time was more pleasant. Now, officially boyfriend and girlfriend, they departed the fort.

His first romance lasted three months. During that time, they never kissed again. One day, during school, Allie approached Neil, "I want to break up with you."

"Okay," Neil replied. He knew they would continue to be good friends.

# Scatter Ball

For most fifth graders, PE was the favorite class of the day. For Neil, it was always a time of apprehension. Each day he silently worried about what would be the game of the day. In many games, such as races, wrestling and calisthenics, he could hold his own with the best of them. However, if the game involved a ball; it didn't matter what game, just any game with a ball; it meant he could not play on his own. He would either have to sit out the game, or another student would have to help him. Either way, it made him feel "handicapped." It was a feeling he didn't like, a feeling that he fought to overcome every day of his life.

It was Wednesday, the day for "Scatter Ball." "Scatter Ball" was the favorite game of his classmates.

The game would start with all the students lined up, facing the gym wall. The teacher would throw the ball into the air, and then blow his whistle, signaling the beginning of the game. The students would run to get the ball. Whoever got the ball would then throw it at another student. If it hit the student, that student was eliminated from the game. If a student caught the ball, the student who threw the ball was eliminated. The game ended when only one student remained. The winner was considered "King of the Game," a real status symbol.

For Neil, the PE teacher would designate a student to be his partner. Neil would hold his partner's arm, following him wherever he ran. If the ball hit Neil, he was eliminated, but his partner remained. If the ball hit his partner, they were both eliminated. Most of the students silently accepted the assignment, but Neil knew they didn't like it, because they were always eliminated. Everyone considered Neil to be an easy target. He was always their first target. Neil worried this would create animosity between him and the other students.

There were two students who were exceptionally good at the game. One was Andy. Considered the "Stud" of the class, he was one of the larger, stronger students. When he threw the ball, everybody ran. His ball always came fast and hard. It hurt when you were hit. Unfortunately, Neil was one of his favorite targets.

The other player was Guy. He was very fast and could evade most of the balls, even ones thrown by Andy. Guy was Neil's favorite partner. He always talked to Neil, telling him which way they were going and when to duck or jump. With Guy as a partner, Neil always managed to stay in the game a few rounds.

This Wednesday was special. It was the last Wednesday of the school year. The winner of this "Scatter Ball" game would own the title until the next school year. Although Neil had never won, and he knew his chances were slim, he always held out hope. Today was his last chance. He was determined. Today he would be crowned "King of the Game."

Neil knew his only chance was if Guy would be his partner. He did not plan to leave that to luck. On the way to the gym, he asked Guy to be his partner. Guy, who had won the game many times, agreed. When Neil entered the gym, he immediately went to the PE teacher, Mr. Kissell, and asked if Guy could be his partner. Mr. Kissell agreed.

Grinning, Neil joined Guy and the other students, lined against the wall. Neil turned to Guy, and whispered, "Guy, we're going to win this game, no matter what."

"Okay, Neil. Let's do it. When the whistle blows, you stay here, I will run to the ball and then come back and get you."

"If you don't get the ball, I'm a dead man!"

"Neil, I will get the ball!"

Just as Guy finished reassuring Neil, the whistle blew. Suddenly the gym was filled with the sound of little footsteps running every which way. Neil stood by the wall, anxiously waiting for Guy.

Gasping for breath, Guy stretched out his arm to Neil, "I told you. We've got the ball. Take my arm and let's go kick some butt."

Following Guy's every instruction, it seemed as if they moved as one. They ducked, they jumped, and they ran. As the game progressed, Neil realized that he had never lasted this long.

"Neil, there are only six kids left. We're doing great. JUMP!" Guy yelled, as they successfully dodged another ball.

Suddenly Guy stopped.

"What is it? What's wrong, Guy?"

"Neil, the only other person left in the game is Andy! He's got the ball, so stay close and run fast!"

They slowly turned, as Guy watched Andy, waiting for his throw. Neil was elated. He was one of the last three. He had never done this well. He was determined to win.

"DUCK!" Guy yelled.

Falling to the floor, Neil waited to hear the ball fly by. Instead, the ball bounced off Guy. Neil couldn't believe it. They were so close. They had lost.

Then, to Neil's surprise, Mr. Kissel announced, "Guy you are eliminated. Neil, you have one chance to win. Andy will talk to you, so you know where he is."

Handing the ball to Neil, he continued, "Neil you throw the ball. If it hits Andy, you win. If Andy catches it or if you miss him, he wins."

Neil was excited, but also worried. He rarely threw the ball. When he did, it was usually caught. Andy began to speak, taunting Neil, "You throw like a girl. C'mon! What are you waiting for?"

Slowly moving closer, Neil followed the sound of Andy's voice. He knew he could hit Andy. Ever since he could remember, he had been able to throw accurately, hitting his target, the source of the sound. He had a lot of practice playing ball in his swimming pool. His only concern was if he could throw it hard enough. The students were silent. They didn't want to confuse Neil with additional noise. With each step Andy took, the suspense grew.

The moment had come. Neil had zeroed in on his target. He had a plan. He took the ball in his right hand, his arm outstretched behind him as far as possible, to maximize his speed. He planned to throw the ball at Andy's feet, hoping he would miss it on the short hop. Suddenly, without warning, he threw the ball. Holding his breathe, he waited, anticipating the worst.

Suddenly, the students yelled, cheering the victor. The only problem was, Neil didn't know who had won. Then placing his hand on Neil's shoulder, Mr. Kissel announced, "I hereby declare Neil, "King of the Game!"

Neil couldn't believe it. He'd won. He would be "King of the Game" for the entire summer. Neil, as "King," led his classmates back to their room.

Watching the students march from the gym, Mr. Kissel stood in disbelief. Throughout the year, Neil amazed him with his athletic ability, his fearlessness and his seemingly "sixth sense" of always knowing where he was. What he just saw was incredible. Neil, standing twenty feet from Andy, based solely on sound, had thrown a perfect strike, hitting Andy on a short hop, at his feet.

# *Jumping for Joy*

"Mom, when is Dad going to be home?" Neil impatiently asked.

It seemed like it had been hours since his father had left. That Sunday morning, at breakfast, Larry announced he had a special surprise for Ryan and Neil. He said he would be bringing it home later that afternoon.

Tersely replying, Linda shook her head in frustration, "Neil, this is the third time you've asked me that."

All day long Neil was anxious. He continually peppered her with questions, trying to guess the surprise. Unlike Neil, Ryan was much more laid back, taking it all in stride. Although she knew he was excited, he acted like it was a normal Sunday.

Linda was nervous about the surprise. She and Larry had discussed it several times. He wanted to buy it. She felt it was too dangerous, especially for Neil. He thought it would help Neil develop his coordination and balance. She feared the boys would be reckless. She knew her boys; they were fearless. Finally, after several arguments, Linda acquiesced.

"Mom, it's Dad!" Neil excitedly announced, as he ran out the front door, Ryan closely following.

She could never get accustomed to Neil's hearing abilities. Larry was nowhere in sight, yet Neil knew he was near. He knew the sound of Larry's truck and heard it long before she could. Sure enough, as Linda walked out the door, Larry turned into the driveway.

"Can you see it, Ryan? What is it?" Neil asked, eager to learn the secret.

"He's got something big in the back. It's covered. I can't see what it is," Ryan answered, stretching to get a better look.

"Come on! What is it?" Neil asked again, jumping up and down in his excitement.

"Take it easy. I can't tell," Ryan answered.

Exiting the truck, Larry was immediately met by his two boys.

"What the heck is that?" Ryan asked, now showing some excitement.

"You can't tell what it is?" Larry asked, prolonging the suspense.

"No, I can't," Ryan replied, frustrated by his father's elusive answer.

"That's because you've probably never seen one like this before," Larry proudly announced.

"Come on Dad, what the heck is it?" Neil asked, no longer able to control his excitement.

"It's a professional style trampoline," Larry said.

"Where did you get it, dad?" Ryan asked.

"I got it from a school in South Dakota. It's like brand new. The school rarely used it," Larry explained.

What he didn't say, and what he did not tell Linda, was that the school had decided to sell it, because a student had been seriously injured while using it. Larry thought it was ironic they were selling it because it was too dangerous and he was buying it for his blind son.

Thirty minutes later, Larry and Linda stood in the driveway watching the boys test their boundaries on the new trampoline. Neil took to it like a duck to water. He knew his mother was watching and seemed to be doing everything possible to frighten her.

"Neil, be careful!" Linda snapped, when Neil bounced dangerously close to the edge of the mat.

"Take it easy," Larry said. "He's doing it just to get you riled."

Larry was awe struck. He couldn't believe how quickly Neil adapted to the trampoline. Within minutes, he seemed to have measured the surface, knowing just how far he could bounce, before reaching the edge. Larry watched Neil spring three or four feet in the air and with a quick motion propel himself toward the edge of the trampoline; landing just on the edge. In the next instant, he would shoot himself back to the center, avoiding all danger.

"I wish this thing had sides on it." Linda complained to Larry.

The two boys began a wrestling match in the center of the trampoline.

"Look at them, Linda. They know exactly what they're doing. Don't worry about them," Larry said, turning to go in the house. Linda reluctantly followed, silently wondering how long it would be before they had to rush Neil to the hospital.

Later that evening, as the family watched TV, Neil jumped to his feet and announced, "I'm going to go jump on the trampoline."

"No, you are not!" Linda said, setting aside the newspaper she was reading.

"Come on, Mom," Neil whined.

"No, it's dark out there," she insisted.

"That doesn't matter to him," Larry said, turning his attention to the conversation.

"Yeah, that doesn't bother me," Neil reiterated.

"Larry, he doesn't need to be out there in the dark by himself," Linda said, throwing a warning look at her husband.

"The dark doesn't make a darn bit of difference to him, Linda. Let him go. It's right outside the door. If he falls off and breaks a leg, he won't have far to crawl," Larry said, with a laugh that Linda did not share.

They can fight it out, Neil thought, quietly exiting the room. On the way out of the house, he stopped by the garage to pick up a tetherball he used for shooting baskets. He jumped onto the trampoline and quickly lost himself in his imagination. Neil had an extremely active imagination and could usually find ways to amuse himself in any situation. He threw his tetherball in the air, holding onto the rope with his left hand and catching it in his right as it came down. Diving to the mat to catch the ball, he imagined he was catching touchdown passes from Turner Gill. After a few minutes he noticed that the ball would follow him around the trampoline, if he allowed it to roll freely on the mat. He quickly began testing his newfound ability. He would try not to allow the ball to touch him as he bounced around the trampoline. He would wait until the last possible second and then spring away leaving the ball behind.

This was how Linda found Neil nearly an hour later, when she stepped outside to call him in for bed. For a moment, she marveled at his athletic prowess. Anyone who didn't know Neil would not believe he was blind. It brought tears to her eyes. She knew that even though he was an exceptional athlete, he would never be able to participate in organized athletics. Here he was, oblivious to the world that awaited him, oblivious to his handicap, in his private world of make believe. Linda admitted to herself that buying the trampoline was a good idea.

# The Cane

In the spring of 1986, Neil was approaching the end of his sixth grade year in school. The last two years had been good. Neil was comfortable with the school and the students. He felt totally accepted and had many friends. The summer was approaching and he couldn't wait for the school year to end.

When Neil mainstreamed into public school, he was assigned an instructor by the State of Nebraska Services for the Visually Impaired. His instructor, Nancy Flurel, was responsible for preparing Neil for independent living. This involved teaching Neil how to cook, how to use public transportation and how to use a cane. Since his early years at NSVH, Neil had been working with a cane.

He hated the cane and he saw no reason to use it. In fact, Neil never planned to use the cane. It made him stand out and made him different than the other kids. Neil worked very hard to be "just one of the boys." He worked very diligently to be mobile, to get around without the cane, to not be considered unusual or weird. If he was to be unique, if he was to stand apart, it would be because he excelled, on the same terms as every other student. It would not be because he was considered different.

Anytime Neil knew Ms. Flurel was coming to visit to work with the cane, he would conveniently forget about the appointment and be away playing with Jason when she arrived. Though frustrated by Neil's refusal to accept cane travel as a necessity for his future life, Ms. Flural was very patient and understanding with Neil. Though she tried to hide it, she liked Neil. He was one of her brighter students. She knew he had a bright future ahead of him. She also believed that cane travel was a necessity for all blind people, even for someone as smart as Neil.

Ms. Flurel, whose determination matched that of Neil's, began to pressure Linda and Larry to require Neil to use his cane. She was adamant in their discussions that Neil must learn cane travel, that without it he would be greatly handicapped. Larry and Linda struggled with the mental picture of Neil slowly walking down a busy sidewalk, tapping his cane to feel the path ahead. This reinforced the reality that Neil was handicapped. For years, they did everything they could to allow Neil to be like the other children, to keep him from feeling handicapped. Reluctantly, in response to the persistent urging of Ms. Flurel, they agreed to require Neil to use his cane.

After a very emotional discussion, Neil acquiesced to his parent's demands. That Monday, he agreed to start using the cane in school. He left the house that morning, lead by his cane. When his house was out of sight, he folded up the cane, put it in his backpack and ran to meet Jason for the usual walk together to school. Thinking he had fooled his parents, upon entering the school, he learned otherwise. The moment he walked through the front doors, he was greeted by the stern voice of Mr. Ectencamp, Neil's sixth grade teacher, "Neil, front and center." Neil obediently obeyed.

Mr. Ectencamp continued, "Neil, your mother called me today and told me that you were to start using your cane. She left me with the impression that you would be using it to walk to school. I see it sticking out of your backpack, but I don't think that is what your mother had in mind."

Neil, knowing he was caught, began to plead his case, just like he did with his parents.

"Mr. Ectencamp, you know I don't need that cane. I came straight to you when you called my name, and I didn't use the cane."

Fighting to hide a smile, in response to Neil, his teacher explained, "Neil, this matter is not up for discussion. Your parents want you to use your cane and you will. I do not want to see you in the halls without it. If I do, there will be no recess for that day. Is that clear?"

Recognizing it was useless, Neil agreed. He knew he did not want to miss recess. Taking his cane in hand, he walked to his classroom. Neil moved the cane like he had been taught, but totally ignored it. It looked like he was using it when in reality he wasn't. He had walked those halls thousands of times. He didn't need a cane.

For the next few weeks, Neil would pretend to walk with his cane. The few times when he would decide not to use it, one of the teachers would inevitably catch him and make him immediately start to use it again. Reluctantly, Neil would always obey. He had no choice. Recess was always at risk.

One day, Neil was returning to his classroom from the music room, pretending to use the cane, as he always did. He was walking down the hall, not paying attention, when a younger student ran from the boy's restroom and collided with Neil's cane. Because of the way Neil was cavalierly swinging his cane, it appeared as if he purposely tripped the boy. At that very moment, Ms. Johnson came around the corner and saw the boy falling over Neil's cane. She immediately yelled,

"Neil Halford! What do you think you're doing? Come here!"

She grabbed Neil, took him around the corner and continued to scold him, "You need to watch what you're doing with that cane, young man! After lunch, I want to see you in the lunchroom, when all the other kids have gone to the playground."

Though he wanted to ask her why he needed a cane if she thought he could watch it, instead, he sheepishly replied, "Yes, Ms. Johnson."

He then proceeded to his classroom.

After lunch, with a heavy heart, Neil patiently waited for Ms. Johnson. He knew he was in for a real tongue-lashing. When she finally arrived, she pulled two chairs out and placed them facing each other, a foot apart. She sat in one and Neil sat in the other.

To Neil's surprise, she began very quietly and calmly,

"Neil, do you know how important it is for you to learn to use this cane?"

"Yes, Ms. Johnson," Neil responded.

"When you grow up, go to college, and eventually get a job, you will need the cane. For the rest of your life this is going to be your transportation. The cane will enable you to succeed. This is how you are going to get around," Ms. Johnson adamantly explained to Neil.

He always liked talking with Ms. Johnson. Unlike most teachers, she never talked down to the students. She had an uncanny ability to communicate with them at their own level. Ms. Johnson was the one teacher who strongly believed Neil needed to use the cane. Everything she had just said to Neil, she believed was very true. In an effort to bring her point home to Neil, she turned to an emotional argument, "Neil, do you ever want to make out with a girl, in the back seat of a car? Do you ever want to have a girlfriend? Do you want to date girls, go out with girls and have a good time?"

Ms. Johnson knew that most sixth grade boys, including Neil, had begun to be interested in girls. She hoped that this argument would finally convince Neil of the value of the cane. Continuing, she admonished Neil,

"If you ever want to do these things, then it all starts by using this cane. The cane will give you your independence. The cane is what will make those things happen."

Stoically, Neil sat listening, occasionally giving her a polite nod. Little did she know that her argument was having the reverse effect from what she intended. The more she pleaded with Neil, the more determined he became. The more she explained to Neil, the more resolute became his purpose.

What he wanted to say, what he was thinking, but what he never said that day was, "I'll show you! I'll show you! One day, you'll see, when I don't use this cane, when I do things my way, when I live my life my way. I'll do all those things you are describing and much more, but I will do them the way I want to do them, because I can! I'll not only kiss a girl in the back seat of a car, I'll drive the @&?%$ car. I know I can. I'll show you that I don't need this dumb cane. Someday I will be accepted because of who I am, because of what I do, not because of a cane."

When Ms. Johnson finished, Neil thanked her and returned to class. For the rest of the afternoon, Neil ignored his teacher. His mind was focused on his conversation with Ms. Johnson. As each minute ticked by, Neil became more determined. He had decided that the cane was history.

That night he announced to his parents he would never again use the cane, and he didn't. From that point on, Neil never again walked with a cane.

### Postscript — Chapter Three

*In the spring of 1986, my graduation from sixth grade marked the end of a difficult, yet significant phase of my life. When I started third grade, I was a frightened, insecure little boy who felt all alone. When I walked out of the Fort Calhoun Elementary School for the last time, I was confident in my ability to function at school and in every day life. I was no longer fearful of the "sighted world," but felt like I was part of it, like I belonged. Socially, I had gained the acceptance of most of my fellow classmates. I had developed some lasting friendships. I was no longer the "blind boy," I was just Neil.*

*Though, at the time, I was too young to realize it. Now, as I reflect back, I was closing a very important period of my life. Physically, emotionally and socially, I'd greatly matured. The teachers, the staff and my Aunt Sharry all played vital roles in my development, during those years. I owe them a debt of gratitude.*

# Chapter Four

## INTRODUCTION

*The next six years would mark the greatest changes in my life. It would also be the most exciting time of my life. That first summer I gave up the Star Wars and the "He-man" toys. They were boxed up and put in storage. Also, I cast aside the storybook records and my little record player. They were replaced by a stereo system my Dad purchased for me. Music became and would remain a large part of my life. Cable TV had finally come to Fort Calhoun. My passion was All Star Wrestling. Saturday nights on WTBS, I would cheer my newfound heroes, Rick Flair, the Road Warriors, Hulk Hogan, and Andre the Giant. I also discovered the Library of Congress. They provided an endless supply of books on tape. My appetite for reading became insatiable. My early favorites were the Hardy boys, but eventually I graduated to some of the popular modern authors. My favorite authors were Stephen King and John D. MacDonald.*

*Sports became a large part of my life. I was and to this day still am an avid Nebraska Cornhusker football fan. My interests soon expanded to all college football and boxing. My greatest sporting interest became wrestling. Ryan, my older brother, was on the high school team. Eventually, I would join the high school football and wrestling teams. Through the exercise and physical fitness demanded by these sports, I became a strong, agile athlete. This added to my confidence and my self-image.*

*Socially, my interest in girls soon took center stage. Though I didn't know it at the time, I would meet my future wife, while in high school. Also, I developed five close friendships with Jay Weeks, Chris Nelson, Seth Tamisiea, Jason Husk, and Kirt Ringler. To this day, they remain my best friends.*

# Waterlogged

It was a hot and humid August day. Ryan and Neil had been anxiously waiting for this day to come. For the last week, it seemed to Linda like the boys were constantly asking her if it was time to go to the lake. Finally, the time had arrived. Today, they would learn how to water-ski.

Their destination was Lake Manawa, a small lake located five miles south of Council Bluffs, Iowa, which was adjacent to Omaha, but separated by the Missouri River. A family friend, Frank Starr, kept his boat docked at the Lakeshore Country Club, which was located on the lake.

Frank greeted the family after Larry parked their car. Leaping from the car, the boys raced toward the lake.

"Stop!" Larry demanded. The boys, knowing the consequences, stopped in their tracks. "We will all walk together to the boat. Wait for Frank to show you the way," Larry ordered the boys.

The route to the boat docks took them past the country club's swimming pool.

"Neil, they have a separate diving pool with a high dive!!!" Ryan excitedly announced.

"Frank, can we go jump off the diving board?" Neil pleaded.

Thinking that Neil meant the low board, Frank replied, "No one else is in the diving pool, so sure, go ahead.

To Frank's surprise they started climbing the ladder to the high board. He knew they were both excellent swimmers, but he was concerned about the twenty-five foot drop to the pool.

Ryan went first. Running to the edge, he jumped and safely landed with a large splash.

While Neil climbed the ladder, all eyes from the swimming pool watched his every step. Once on the board, he slowly inched his way, carefully feeling for the edges of the board. Once at the end, he hesitated.

"Jump, Neil, it's a blast!!" Ryan shouted his encouragement.

Neil didn't hesitate. Shouting "Geronimo!" Neil leapt off the board. Carefully watching Neil's descent, Frank heard some gasps coming from the pool area. Entering the pool with a splash, he quickly bobbed to the surface.

Ryan had remained in the pool, safely away from Neil's landing zone. In case Neil had a problem, he would be ready. Through their young years Ryan was always near, always ready to come to Neil's aid when required. Larry and Linda had never said anything to Ryan. From the day Neil returned home from the hospital, Ryan immediately assumed the role of protector. He went unnoticed to many, even Neil, but Larry and Linda always knew that Ryan was watching over Neil.

"That was awesome!" Neil exclaimed immediately upon breaking the surface. "Can we do it again?"

"No, boys. It's time to go skiing," Larry pointed to the boat.

It was a Thursday afternoon, so the lake was not crowded. Frank was pleased. He knew that teaching these boys to ski was going to be a real challenge. Few boats meant few wakes, which meant a smoother lake. The smoother the lake, the easier it is to ski. The water temperature of the lake was 77 degrees and the air temperature was 84 degrees. It was a great day to ski.

Once they reached the middle of the lake, Frank stopped the boat. "Who wants to go first?" he asked.

"I will!" Ryan excitedly volunteered. Neil was glad Ryan was going first. Until he actually climbed onto the boat, Neil was confident. With each wave that rocked the boat, Neil's resolve slowly evaporated.

After Ryan put on his vest, he and Frank jumped into the lake. Larry would drive the boat, while Frank would help Ryan. Next, Larry threw the skis and the ski rope into the water.

"First we will put on your skis. The plan is for you to ski between my legs. Once we are up and you are balanced, I will let go and fall back in the water, leaving you to ski alone," Frank explained.

"Let's do it!" Ryan urged, with an excited grin.

"Whoa, there are some things you need to know first. You lay in the water, on your back with the skis about half out of the water and your knees bent. Hold the ski rope between your legs. Stretch out your arms with just a slight bend at the elbow. The boat will slowly move forward until the rope is tight. When you are ready, you shout, 'GO!' The boat will accelerate, pulling you out of the water. It is very important that you don't use your arms to pull yourself out of the water. Your arms remain stretched. To get out of the water you push down on the skis, like you were standing up. Once up, keep your knees slightly bent to help absorb the bumps. To go left, push out with your right ski and vice versa. Never pull your arms in. If you do, you will fall. When you fall, don't forget to let go of the rope. If you don't, the boat will pull you deep into the water. Did you get all that?"

Nervously nodding "yes," Ryan tried to remember everything Frank had just told him. Frank put on his skis, then swam around Ryan, straddling him and gripping the rope handle. "Are you ready, Ryan?" Frank checked one last time. Again Ryan nodded.

"Then give your Dad the signal."

"GO!" Ryan shouted.

Frank knew this was going to be difficult. Ryan only weighed 125lbs. It would not take much speed to pull him out of the water. However, to pull Frank out required maximum acceleration; more than Ryan could handle. He would almost immediately fall. So instead, Larry was going to slowly accelerate. This would put tremendous strain on Frank's legs. Frank would have to use his legs to fight the force of the water, until the boat had reached a speed that would lift him out of the water. Without Ryan, it would take seconds. With Ryan, it would be an exhausting 30-40 seconds.

Larry slowly started to accelerate the boat. Ryan did an excellent job of holding his skis straight, not allowing them to get tangled with Frank's skis. After what seemed like an eternity to Frank, with his legs burning, they finally popped out of the water.

To Frank's amazement, Ryan was a natural. After a couple of early near falls, Ryan was doing great. He remained balanced and never tried to pull in the rope. Frank then had Ryan practice moving to the right and left.

"Ryan, you're doing great. Ready to try it on your own?"

"Yeah, let's do it!"

Spreading his skis wide, to avoid hitting Ryan, Frank let go of the rope and fell into the water. He then watched Ryan ski around the lake several times without falling. Finally, Larry brought the boat to a stop, next to Frank. As the boat came to a stop, Ryan slowly sunk into the water.

Climbing into the boat, Ryan exclaimed, "Neil, that is awesome!! It's really easy and you go so fast!" Ryan then gave a blow-by-blow account to Neil, repeating Frank's instructions and how it actually felt to ski.

"Doot, are you ready to go?" Larry asked.

With Ryan's success, Neil's confidence returned. The combination of Neil's athletic ability and his strong desire to always do whatever his brother could do, had often proved a winning combination in the past. He was sure that today would be no different.

"I'm ready!" Neil shouted, and jumped off the boat into the water. Frank followed. He was pleased at how easily Ryan had mastered skiing. He hoped that Neil would be the same. Unfortunately, because Neil only weighed 70 pounds, Frank could not ski with him. Unlike Ryan, Neil would be on his own.

After Frank once again gave his instructional speech, Neil acknowledged he was ready. The plan was for Frank to help Neil get into position and then hold him until the boat accelerated. Frank would then let go and Neil would ski. Being so light, the boat would only have to reach a speed of about 10mph and Neil would pop out of the water.

Almost immediately there were problems. Neil was unable to keep his skis steady. Even though the skis were children's skis, Neil did not have the strength to hold his skis against the waves. Frank waited for a calm in the lake, set Neil's skis and gave Larry the "GO" signal. Larry slowly accelerated the boat. Neil's legs did the splits and he planted his face in the water. Forgetting Frank's admonitions, Neil kept hold of the rope. The boat dragged him about forty feet before stopping. The entire time, Neil's head was under water. Finally, out of breath, Neil let go. His head immediately popped to the surface.

While Larry repositioned the boat, Frank swam to Neil. He was anxious to go again. There were several more attempts, each one unsuccessful. Neil would lean to the left, then the next time lean to the right. Larry would accelerate too fast or accelerate too slow. The only positive thing was that Neil had learned his lesson. Anytime he started to fall, he would immediately release the rope. Frank was happy. Instead of swimming forty feet each time to reach Neil, he would only have to swim about 20 feet. Even so, after Neil's sixth attempt, Frank was exhausted.

Neil was getting frustrated. Ryan had skied on his first attempt. After six tries, Neil was still floating in the water. In an effort to bolster Neil's flagging spirit, Frank, explained how it had personally taken him two days and probably forty attempts before he finally learned to ski.

His spirit and determination renewed, Neil ordered his Dad to try again. Before, the next try, Larry and Frank traded places, due to Frank's exhaustion. This made a world of difference.

The combination of Frank's ability to move smoothly and consistently when accelerating the boat and Larry's strength in the water, proved successful on the third attempt. Neil bounced out of the water, assumed a balanced, steady position and skied around the lake.

Watching, Frank shook his head in disbelief. Once again Neil had done the impossible. Frank knew he was at such a disadvantage. Neil could not see any of the approaching waves. He could not anticipate. He could only react.

Frank finally stopped the boat by Larry. Neil was so excited. He kept slapping the water in delight. Larry swam over to him and gave him a big hug.

"You did it, Neil!! You were great!" Larry exclaimed.

"Dad, it was awesome!! I almost fell a few times, but I managed to keep my balance."

"Let's get back in the boat, Neil," Larry said, as he started to remove Neil's skis.

"Dad, don't. Please let me ski again. I want to start without any help." Neil pleaded.

After checking with Frank, they decided to let Neil try. Frank's experience with teaching other people to ski taught him that once the person had skied, his balance and ability to handle the waves would be almost instinctive.

Larry hopped in the boat. On Neil's shout of "GO!", the boat accelerated. To the delight of everyone, Neil was once again skiing.

They spent the rest of the afternoon at the lake. With the sun beginning to set, Neil was skiing for the last time. Driving the boat, Frank looked back to check on Neil. He saw Neil, skiing across the water, framed in the setting sun. The picture was almost surrealistic. It was a fitting end to an incredible day.

# Those Lazy, Hazy,
# Crazy Days of Summer

Neil slowly opened his eyes. Like every other weekday morning, he awakened to the muffled hum of the vacuum cleaner. Without looking at the clock, he knew it was 6:30 in the morning. His mother was like an alarm clock. Every morning, before going to work, at exactly 6:30, she would vacuum the carpets. Finally, an hour later, when his parents and brother had all left for work, he fell back to sleep.

After his early morning nap, Neil arose and headed for the kitchen. He loved the summer. For eight hours every weekday, he had the house to himself. This morning, he decided to have bacon and eggs for breakfast. As he was finishing the last piece of bacon, he heard familiar footsteps walk through the door. It was his best friend, Jason Weeks. During the summer, they were inseparable. They spent almost every waking hour together.

"Hey, Jason. What's up, dude?"

"Not much. What's on the agenda for today?" Jason asked, plopping down on the sofa and turning on the television.

"Same old @%?&$!. Nothin' special."

"Want to hit the bottoms this morning, before it gets too hot?"

This meant Jason wanted to take the ATV on the trails of the flats, the Missouri River bottomland. Just east of their house, below the bluff, was a large wooded area with many challenging trails. The two of them had spent hundreds of hours exploring the trails and racing through the woods.

"Sounds good. I want to take a quick shower, first," Neil yelled, heading downstairs.

Standing in the shower, the hot water massaging his body, he reflected on all the fun Jason and he had on the ATV over the years. It all started two years earlier on Christmas Day, 1984. They had just finished opening all of the gifts from under the tree. He remembered thinking how disappointed he was. Usually he was deluged with presents. That year, his take had been slim. Then, his father announced,

"There is one more gift. It's for you, Ryan. It's a new stereo system. I had to keep it at Grandma's, so you wouldn't find it. Get your coats on. Let's go."

Ryan jumped to his feet, grabbed his coat and raced to the door. Larry grabbed him, "Whoa, there, Ryan. Wait for us. You can't go anywhere until I get the car."

Neil slowly put on his coat. The frown that covered his face reflected his jealousy.

Ryan was getting a big gift, and he wasn't.

Larry, standing by the door, fought to hide his smile. Ryan was so excited and Neil was so sad. Neither one of them knew what awaited them outside. Larry knew it was cruel. He also knew the boys would be ecstatic, once he opened the door. Led by Ryan, they walked out the front door.

Sitting in the driveway was a new Honda 125 ATV. "Awesome, Dad! It's awesome!" Ryan exclaimed, jumping on the seat.

"What is it?" Neil asked.

"Neil, you won't believe it! We've got our own ATV!"

Even though it was Ryan's gift, he unselfishly declared it was for both of them. He didn't think twice about allowing Neil to use the ATV. Also, he knew that Neil would not be satisfied with being a passenger. Someway, somehow, he knew Neil would eventually drive the ATV.

Neil hopped on behind Ryan, and asked, "Dad, can we take it for a ride? Please, Dad?"

For the next few minutes, Larry explained how to operate it. Because of their excitement, he knew they weren't hearing much of what he was saying. He wasn't concerned. Ryan had driven his friends' ATVs many times. Tossing Ryan the keys, Larry cautioned, "Be careful, Ryan. The streets are very slippery. Once around the block and come right back."

Before Larry completed his order, Ryan was flying down the alley with Neil behind him, clinging tightly to his brother.

Larry and Linda stood in the driveway, holding each other.

"They were excited. I knew they'd like it. I'm not sure it is fair to Neil. Even though it was great that Ryan told Neil he would share it with him. He's so good with Neil, always sharing with him. Ryan will be able to use it all the time. I don't think Neil will be able to use it much. We probably should have gotten him something else."

Linda, hugging Larry, offered her encouragement, "You know Neil. Where there's a will, there's a way. If I know Neil, he'll be driving it before long."

They laughed and walked inside. A short time later, the boys excitedly ran into the house. They pleaded with their Dad to continue riding. After some hesitation, Larry acceded to their request.

That afternoon, Neil called Jay and eagerly told him about the exciting new gift. Later that day, Jay came to visit. After a crash course in the operation of the ATV by Larry, Jay and Neil took off, with Jay driving. Once out of site, Neil ordered,

"Okay, Jay. It's my turn to drive."

Neil jumped in front and took off. He controlled the throttle, the gearshift and the brakes. Jay sat behind Neil and held onto the ends of the handlebars. This allowed him to steer. Before long, they were racing through the streets.

"Larry, come here!" Linda ordered. She was staring out their large front window.

"What is it?' Larry asked, joining her at the window.

"You're not going to believe this. I told you it wouldn't take long."

"What are you talking about?"

Just as Larry finished his question, the ATV went speeding by the house. "Nothing stops that kid," Larry exclaimed.

He and Linda watched for several minutes, laughing at the ingenuity of their youngest son.

It wasn't long before Neil and Jay tired of driving the streets. With Jay driving, they decided to explore the trails in the nearby woods. After several trips up familiar trails, Neil once again became the driver. When it was time to return home, Neil decided to take a new trail. He thought it would be a short cut back to his house. Racing along the unknown path, Jay suddenly shouted, "Stoooop!"

Neil slammed on the brakes. The ATV slid to a stop.

"What's the problem?" Neil asked.

"It's a dead end," Jay explained.

"What do you mean, it's a dead end. It can't be," Neil objected.

"The trail goes straight up the bluff. It's really steep. There's no way we can make it."

"There is a trail, right?"

"Yes, but . . ."

"We can make it. Come on you wuss. Let's go for it," Neil interrupted Jay.

"Okay, but we need to go back a ways and get a good run at it," Jay hesitantly instructed.

Once in position, Neil revved up the engine. When he was ready, he released the brake. The ATV bolted forward with the front tires lifting off the ground. Racing forward, they reached a speed of 30 mph. They quickly reached the hill and started the climb. Neil had the ATV at full throttle. About half way up the hill, Neil down shifted to get more power. The front wheels once again left the ground. This time, due to the sharp incline, slowly but surely it started to fall backwards. Helpless, Neil shouted, "We're going over!"

Jay slid off the back of the ATV and Neil quickly followed. Landing on his back, Neil held his legs in the air, anticipating that the ATV would come falling back on him. He was right. His right foot made contact with the throttle on the handlebar, causing the engine to rev. Lying there, Neil heard the ATV fly over him and then tumble down the hill.

"Jay, are you okay." Neil asked, laughing.

"Yeah, I'm okay. You're crazy, dude." Jay replied, joining Neil in his laughter.

They then slid down the hill to the ATV. After rolling it back onto its tires, Neil tried to start it. To their surprise, it started immediately. Neil hopped back into the driver's seat and asked, "Where to now, dude?"

"I've had enough excitement for today. Let's head home," Jason suggested.

Upon arriving back at the house, Jay carefully inspected the ATV, assessing the damage. Neil, nervously asked, "Well, what's the bad news? If we damaged it, Ryan's going to kick my @%?&$!."

Jay, trying to sound concerned, replied, "I think he's going to do more than kick your @%?&$!. It's pretty bad."

"What do you mean? There can't be that much damage," Neil anxiously pressed Jay for more information.

"The right front fender is cracked, the gear shift is bent, the rear lights are broken, the front . . ."

Neil interrupted, knowing he was kidding, "That's so much BS. I know the gear shift isn't bent." Jay began to laugh, quickly joined by Neil, who was silently relieved.

Neil was jolted back to the present by Chris, who shouted down the stairs, "Get your lazy @%?&$! out of the shower. Daylight is burnin'."

Unbeknownst to Neil, while he was daydreaming in the shower, Chris and Seth had arrived on their bikes. There was always someone coming over. Chris was usually leading the pack. The attraction of Neil's toys, the ATV, the trampoline and most of all, the pool, resulted in a daily neighborhood party.

The four friends spent the morning racing and doing tricks on the ATV. Finally, their hunger forced them to stop for lunch. After a quick sandwich, they decided to spend some time on the trampoline. Of course, just jumping and doing flips was not enough. Their trips to the trampoline always ended up in a tag-team wrestling match. After several matches, with each of them posing as their favorite professional wrestling star, even this got boring.

"Hey, dudes, I've got an idea. Help me move the tramp next to the shed," Chris ordered, with a sense of excitement in his voice.

Always up for a new adventure, the boys obeyed. There was a shed in the back yard, which was fourteen feet by ten feet and stood ten feet high. Once the tramp was adjacent to the shed, Chris exclaimed, "Watch this!"

He then proceeded to bounce on the tramp, until he reached the required height. With one last jump, he bounced off the tramp and landed at the peak of the shed's roof. Chris proudly stood on the roof, while the other boys cheered. Then, without any warning, he jumped from the roof, did a flip and landed back on the trampoline. In unison, the other boys shouted, as they all climbed onto the trampoline, "I'm next. It's my turn."

Of course, it being Neil's trampoline, he prevailed. Chris stayed on the trampoline with him. Neil checked out the location of the shed and examined the roof, to get a feel for its height and slant. Once Neil was comfortable with the roof, he began to bounce on the trampoline. After several bounces, he took one final jump and bounced to the roof. He landed at the peak. Upon making contact, he fell to his knees, grabbing the roof.

"Hey, dude, that was a real rush!"

Rising to his feet, Neil faced the trampoline and leaped off the roof. He safely landed on the trampoline. "What's that, dude? No flip! You're a @%?&$!" Chris admiringly chided Neil.

Before long, everyone was taking turns roof jumping. As with most boys their age, after a while, it too became boring. So, they decided to make it more interesting. They returned to their first love, wrestling on the tramp. Only this time, the roof of the shed was used as the top rope of the ring. In professional wrestling, some of the most daring, most effective moves are initiated with the wrestler jumping from the top rope, which encloses the wrestling mat.

A tag-team wrestling match ensued for hours. Late in the afternoon, with the boys bruised and sore, they decided it was time to relax by the pool. It had been their most exciting and roughest match. They would jump from the roof, land on their opponent and try to pin him. Though at times it was painful, none of the boys wanted to appear weak, so they all just grinned and continued to wrestle. Neil had taken the brunt of the attacks. He did not know for sure from whom or when an attack would come. Neil always retaliated, giving as good as he got. In the end, they all limped to the pool.

After a brief rest, they were all in the pool, ready for another game. The game was Marco Polo, Neil's favorite. Of all the games they played, this was the one game where he was not at a disadvantage. In fact, he had a decided advantage. Marco Polo is a form of tag played in a swimming pool. The person who is 'it' must keep his eyes closed. However, to find the other players, he can call out, "Marco." The other players are required to stop swimming and respond by yelling, "Polo." The person, who is 'it' then tries to swim to one of the other players and tag him. Once a player has called out, "Polo," he can swim away. Because of Neil's acute hearing ability and sense of feel, he would know where people were without ever calling, "Marco."

Every day, about 5:00 p.m., each of the boys, except Jay, would usually go home. Each morning, Linda would leave a list of chores for Neil to do while she was at work. Linda usually would arrive home about 5:30 p.m. Of course, Neil would procrastinate. Every day at five, Jay and Neil would rush around, completing the list of chores.

That night, while Linda was cooking dinner, she happened to look out the kitchen window, which overlooked the backyard and pool. Curious by what she saw, she sternly called out, "Neil, come here!"

"What do you need, Mom?" Neil asked, upon entering the kitchen.

"Why is the trampoline sitting next to the shed?"

"Mom, it's so cool. You should have seen it. We use the shed as the top rope for our wrestling matches. Just like Hulk Hogan, I jump off the rope, hitting my opponent and pinning him to the tramp," Neil excitedly exclaimed.

Linda had assumed it was something like that. She knew that if it involved the trampoline, it also involved wrestling. Neil was a daring, fearless boy, who wanted to do what the other kids did. Most of the time, he did. Long ago, she had given up trying to protect him. She couldn't stop him. Yet, this seemed a bit extreme. So, she admonished him, "Neil, this is too much. Jumping off a roof is not acceptable!"

Neil had been anxiously awaiting her reply. He knew she was going to object. Responding with his prepared answer, Neil explained, "Mom, the roof is only ten feet high. I jump higher than that on the trampoline. It isn't a big deal. I'll be okay."

Knowing that she would never win this argument, she offered a compromise, "Neil, it is dangerous. I'll allow it as long as you promise never to do it unless there is someone else present. Never do it by yourself. Is that understood?"

"No problem, Mom. Watch me from the window. I want to show you how high I can jump," Neil announced, as he rushed out the door.

Nervously, she watched Neil effortlessly and precisely jump back and forth from the shed to the trampoline.

# *Gone Fishin'*

It was early June, 1989. Ryan had graduated from high school and Neil had completed his freshman year. Neil was looking forward to another fun summer.

One evening, Linda called to Neil, "Neil, come here. I have a surprise for you."

Neil, unaware of what it could be, raced upstairs in response to his mother's order. "What is it, Mom?"

"Your uncle Darrell and cousin Ross are going to Canada for a week of fishing and they have invited you," she explained.

Neil didn't have anything special planned. He liked Darrel, who everyone considered the wild and crazy uncle of the family, and he and Ross were good friends. Two years earlier, Neil went on a fishing trip with them to South Dakota. He had a great time. They'd caught more fish than they could ever eat. Excitedly, Neil agreed to go.

On Monday, June 26, at 8:30 a.m., Darrell and Ross pulled up in front of Neil's house in Darrell's brand new 1989 Ford F150 pickup. It was shiny black with a matching camper shell. The bed of the truck was carpeted and carpeted benches lined both sides. They loaded Neil's gear into the back of the truck and Darrell, Ross, Neil and Darrell's English Springer Spaniel, Cilica, began their journey to the north. Darrell explained they were taking Cilica for the bears. He said bears were afraid of dogs but not humans. Neil didn't know if it was true or if his uncle was just trying to frighten them.

Two days later, they arrived at their destination, the Green Bay Resort on Caddy Lake. It was about ninety miles East of Winnipeg, Canada, on the border of Manitoba Providence and Ontario Providence.

They unloaded their gear into their cabin and immediately hit the lake. Darrell had rented a sixteen-foot Lund boat with a small ten-horse power, Mercury fishing motor. The boat had three swivel seats, designed for fishing.

For the next two days, the conditions were idyllic. Warm sunshine, calm waters, and hungry fish, made for exceptional fishing. Though the weather was beautiful the water was cold, with a temperature of fifty degrees. Each night they would dine like kings, enjoying the rewards of the day's catch.

There were a series of lakes, each separated by tree covered, mountainous terrain. By blasting through the mountains, several long, narrow tunnels, connecting the lakes, had been created. The chain of lakes totaled one hundred and five miles. Only seven feet wide, with minimal clearance, each tunnel was about two hundred feet long, with rocks jutting out of the curved overhang.

For Neil and Ross, their favorite part of the trip was navigating the tunnels. They loved the sense of adventure and discovery they felt, as they slowly meandered through these narrow waterways. To traverse the tunnels, they had to crouch down in the boat. The clearance was so tight that the seats barely cleared the top of the tunnel.

Then the weather changed and the rains came. For the next day, they were relegated to their cabin, as the temperature dropped, accompanied by pouring rain. Listening to baseball on the radio and playing cards was their entertainment. The following day, the rain diminished to a steady drizzle. Bored, tired and undaunted, they decided to brave the weather and resume their fishing.

It was still very cold. Each of them dressed in warm clothes. Long johns, jeans and sweatshirts were the order of the day. In addition, they each wore rain pants and poncho. To ensure he would not go hungry, Neil loaded his pockets with food and drinks. In all, Neil probably weighed an extra fifty pounds.

After several unsuccessful hours of fishing on the lake, they decided to try the adjacent lake. Darrell was in the rear of the boat, steering, Neil was amidships and Ross was in the bow. To reach the tunnel, they had to navigate through a narrow inlet, which was marked by floating boxes. Each box signaled a large underwater rock, which had to be avoided. Darrel slowly piloted the boat toward the entrance of the tunnel. Inching closer to the tunnel he felt the boat suddenly being pulled by an unexpected current.

His previous trips through the tunnel had been uneventful. Then, as the boat rounded the last curve, Darrell saw the problem. The rain had raised the water lever to a point where the tunnel was almost full. The water from the higher lake, Caddy Lake, rushing through the tunnel to the lower lake, South Cross Lake, had created a strong current.

Trying to maneuver the boat, Darrell turned away, to escape the strong current. It was too late. It caught the bow of the boat, forcing it into the tunnel. Darrell knew the water was too high for the boat to clear the tunnel. He knew they would capsize. Throwing the engine into reverse, he gunned it, hoping to back away from the entrance. Unfortunately, the current was much stronger than their little ten-horse power motor. When the boat lunged backwards, the current began to drag the back of the boat under water. The boat slowly, but inevitably, rolled on its side and capsized, throwing its passengers into the water.

All three were excellent swimmers, but this was a very dangerous situation. Neil quickly swam to the surface, as he followed the boat into the tunnel. With less than a foot of clearance, he was fighting for every breath, while fending off the rocks with his arms. Ross and Darrell had managed to grab the boat. "Neil, over here! Grab the boat!" Darrell ordered.

He was very concerned. No one was wearing a life jacket. To make matters worse, they were all wearing extra clothes packed with food. He knew their only chance was to stay with the boat.

Continuing to scream for Neil, they knew he would follow the sound of their voices. Neil began to swim to the boat, but it was more difficult than he had thought. His wet clothes and all of the food he had stuffed in his pockets were weighing him down. He struggled with each stroke until he finally reached the boat, grasping it as a lifesaver. Then he heard Cilica bark. It was the most frightening bark he had ever heard. For a moment he didn't know from where it was coming. Then he realized that the barks were coming from under the boat. He concluded that Cilica must be trapped in an air bubble.

Neil was not concerned about himself. He was safely floating through the tunnel with the boat, but he was very worried about the dog. "Get the dog Darrell! We have to save the dog!" He screamed.

The rush of the water through the tunnel created a loud, echoing roar, which made it difficult for the three to hear each other. Darrell screamed his reply, "Forget the dog. She'll be fine. Stay with the boat. Just, stay with the boat. We'll ride it out! We'll ride it out!"

Neil obeyed. He had no choice. The boat was careening through the tunnel, bouncing off the walls. They were constantly fighting to avoid the onrushing rocks. As the light at the end of the tunnel quickly approached, Ross saw that something was blocking their only exit. At first he couldn't make out what it was. Then he realized that someone had placed strips of tape across the opening.

"Dad, there's some tape blocking the tunnel." Ross yelled his warning. Darrell turned, looked and pronounced, "What the @&?*$! is that! Don't worry guys. The boat will break right through it. Just hold tight to the boat."

Within seconds, they broke through the tape. Exiting the tunnel, the current pushed them into the lake. Fortunately, two park rangers were there, waiting for them in a boat. They had just finished taping the exit to the tunnel, warning people of the current.

All three released their death grips on the boat and swam to the rangers. One by one they were lifted into the boat. Just as they were about to leave Ross spotted Cilica, who was dog paddling towards them. Once the dog had been rescued the rangers started toward the dock, which was across the lake. On the way they passed the boat, which had proven to be their lifesaver. The engine was gone and the boat was destroyed, with dents and holes throughout the hull.

An hour later they were back at their cabin, huddling in front of the fire. With their adrenalin still pumping, they relived the events of that day. Each time the story became more exciting and more dangerous, if that was possible.

Undaunted, they spent the next two days fishing and then returned to Nebraska with the biggest fish story of their lives.

# A Change of Heart

Neil finally reached his breaking point. Chad, Jamie and Andre, had been his nemeses since third grade. For the last eight years, Neil and the "Three Amigos," as he referred to them, had an erratic relationship. Sometimes they were friends, sometimes they barely tolerated each other and sometimes they harassed Neil. Neil never knew what to expect. Inevitably, at some point during the school year, there would be a practical joke, a snide remark, or a push in the hall. In some manner, they ridiculed him for being blind. Except for the initial confrontation in the fourth grade, Neil chose to ignore them. There were many times his friends wanted to confront the three and "teach them a lesson." He always stopped them.

This week had been the last straw. Monday, in his history class, the "Three Amigos" were the source of laughter by a small group of students seated in the rear of the room. Neil didn't pay any attention. Throughout the years, they had been the class clowns, providing a constant source of entertainment during school. Neil just assumed that they were up to their old tricks.

Each day the laughter continued. Eventually, Neil learned that the joke was about him. They would tap on their desks, emulating the sound of a galloping horse. The tapping would begin slowly, and then accelerate, creating the sound of a horse running at full speed. Suddenly, they would stop with a loud slap on the desk, as though the horse had struck something. This would bring raucous laughter from their little group.

When he first realized what they were doing, Neil became nauseous. The feelings of loneliness and insecurity, which had haunted his days as a child, suddenly overwhelmed him. Vivid memories of his childhood came rushing back. These feelings were quickly replaced by an anger, which he hadn't felt in years. An anger fueled by the pain of ridicule.

Neil controlled his temper. He didn't react. His demeanor was stoic, not displaying any emotion. He did not want to give them the satisfaction of knowing he knew about their sick little demonstration. Each day he returned to class, hoping their derision would stop. It didn't!

The day was Friday. The day it would all stop. Today would be the showdown. He hadn't told anyone about his plans to finally end their years of ridicule. No one knew, not his friends nor his parents. He did not want any help. Three against one, the odds were not in his favor. He had surprise, speed, strength, anger and righteousness. They had size and numbers.

He was strong for his size. For the last two years he had been diligently working out, improving his strength and agility for wrestling. The wrestling season had just ended. It had been a great season. He was confident of his abilities. Even so, he knew he would likely incur some injuries. It didn't matter. It all had to stop.

Approaching them, he developed his strategy. Chad, though the smallest, was the ringleader. He would be Neil's first target. Then would come Andre, who sat to Chad's right. He was the largest and strongest of the three, and Neil's greatest threat. If Neil was still standing, then he would deal with Jamie.

"So you think being kicked in the face by a horse is funny!" Neil challenged, standing in front of Chad's desk.

Chad began to rise, knowing from Neil's voice that the fight was on. Neil grabbed Chad by the collar, to ensure he knew where he was, and exclaimed, "Let me show you how it feels!" Before he completed his words, Neil's right fist slammed into Chad's face. The crunch of breaking bones and Chad's scream of pain, as he fell backwards, told Neil he had hit his target, Chad's nose.

Andre was the first to come to his friend's defense. He grabbed Neil on the left shoulder, planning to spin him around to meet his right fist. When Neil felt Andre's hand on his shoulder, he reacted instinctively. After hundreds of hours of practicing wrestling moves, Neil moved without hesitation. He grabbed Andre's arm and did a leg sweep. Bouncing off the desk, Andre fell to the floor. Instantly, Neil was on him, repeatedly punching him.

Someone clumsily climbed over a desk behind him. Knowing it was probably Jamie, he waited until he could feel him near. He released his hold on Andre, turned, and blindly swung at Jamie. With a combination of luck and his incredible hearing, Neil's punch landed hard, in the middle of what Neil thought was Jamie's stomach. He heard Jamie gasp for breath as he fell against a desk.

Neil arose and stood alert, not knowing from where the next attack would come. Suddenly, the class was cheering, calling his name, "Neil! . . . Neil!"

Finally, all the years of frustration, humiliation and anger were over. His adversaries were vanquished. He was the victor. Closing his eyes, a sense of total and complete relief washed over his body.

"Neil! . . . Neil!" Abruptly, Neil sat up. He couldn't believe it. The voice he had heard was his mother's, calling him to get up. He wasn't in the classroom; he was at home, asleep in bed. Standing over him, Linda said, "It's about time you woke up. I've been calling you for several minutes."

Realizing that it had all been a dream, Neil responded, "I'm awake, Mom."

"Your bed is a mess. It looks like you were wrestling in your dreams."

"Something like that," Neil answered, a broad smile slowly covering his face.

Slowly eating breakfast, Neil knew his revenge could never be more than a dream. In reality, in the real world, everyone faces some form of ridicule. In his case, it just so happened that it was more personal than most. Neil reasoned, "What did it matter if they had a few laughs at my expense. It wasn't hurting me. I have some great friends. As long as I have friends, I don't care what anyone else thinks."

His recent successful wrestling season gave him a newfound confidence, both physically and socially. From that point forward, he decided he would never again confront them about their juvenile derisions. Anytime he met them, at school or at a party, he would always treat them with respect.

The years of adversity had truly made him a stronger person. He no longer held any contempt for their laughter. If anything, he felt sorry for anyone who could harbor such animosity in his heart. He knew that many people viewed him as a source of inspiration. At that moment, he understood he had grown up.

Even though he'd had a change of heart, he thought, silently smiling, "I know I could beat those dudes."

# I Made It Through the Rain

The bell rang, signaling the end of Neil's fourth period English class. Jumping to his feet, he gathered his books and made his way to the door. The halls were quickly filling with students, but Neil was unaffected. Before his first day as a freshman, Neil had walked the school many times, memorizing the entire floor plan. Now, in his junior year, automatically, without thinking he navigated the halls. It just came naturally. Though Neil discarded his cane in elementary school, he rarely collided with another student. If there was a collision, it was almost always one of his good friends, joking with him.

"Where're you going in such a hurry?" asked Chris, his best friend and locker mate.

"I've got to get to the gym. It's my last practice before the talent show tonight." Neil replied, unceremoniously dumping his books on the floor of his locker.

"That's right, you're singing tonight, aren't you?"

"Don't even act like you forgot," Neil answered, giving Chris an elbow to the ribs.

"Are you still insisting on singing that Barry Manilow song?"

"You bet. Barry kicks butt," Neil retorted, turning to make his way to the gym.

"You remind me of my Mom!" Chris chided.

Neil chuckled to himself. His friends were always giving him crap about some of the music he liked. He considered himself a music connoisseur. The popular music of his time, Metallica, Ozzy and Aerosmith, were his favorites. However, he also enjoyed the music of the sixties, the seventies and "easy listening" music. Because of his broad musical interests, he was often the brunt of his friends' jokes, but he didn't care. Neil had never based his opinions on what his friends thought were cool.

In the gym, there was a large stage and preparations for the evening's festivities were in full swing. It was Friday, March 29, 1991. That evening, the Fort Calhoun High School was holding its annual talent show. It was always a big event. The town usually turned out in full force to watch the most talented students perform.

He had been a member of the choir and the swing choir for the last three years. Tonight, he would perform with the swing choir. That was not what brought him to the gym. Tonight, he would also be singing his first solo. He was going to sing "I Made It Through the Rain" by Barry Manilow.

"Neil, come over here!" Called Mrs. Boeka, his choir teacher.

"Are you ready?" She asked, taking his arm to lead him to the stage.

"As ready as I'll ever be," Neil replied, trying not to let his apprehension show in his voice.

"I thought we would have Holly accompany you to the stage. She can lead you to the microphone. Then she'll exit the stage. When you are finished, place the mike back in its stand and take your bow. Holly will then return to guide you off stage. How does that sound?" Neil liked Holly. They were both members of the school choirs. She was pretty cool and cute as well.

"That's great. Oh, here is the accompaniment tape I'll be using," Neil acknowledged, while handing Mrs. Boeka the instrumental music tape for his performance that night.

The remainder of the day passed quickly. Before he knew it, Neil was next to the gym doors, nervously listening to people crowd through the public entrance on the opposite side of the gym.

Larry and Linda made their way into the gym, stopping to pick up a program. Linda perused the program, searching for Neil's name. Her stomach gave a nervous leap when she discovered that he was the last act.

"Larry, Neil's going to be the last act of the night," she announced in a whisper.

"Great! The grand finale!" Larry exclaimed, giving her arm a reassuring squeeze.

"I sure hope he knows what he's doing. Neil was very nervous when he came home this afternoon. His final practice didn't go well," Linda cautioned, reflecting Neil's concerns.

"Linda, you and I both know that kid thrives on being in the spotlight. He has ice water in his veins. When he hears the applause of the crowd, he will be just fine," Larry answered, knowing Linda was much more nervous than Neil.

"I hope you're right."

Holly Hassel, his partner for this evening, joined Neil. He was tense. It was partly caused by nerves, but more from anticipation. He was excited to finally perform in front of his friends and family. The song was chosen because he felt the words embodied much of what he had endured over the years.

"Are you ready?" Holly asked, taking Neil's arm.

"Actually, I think I've forgotten the words," he replied, turning to Holly with a worried look on his face.

"Oh my God! I don't know the song. I can't help you!" Holly exclaimed, thinking Neil was serious.

Breaking into a smile, Neil explained, "I'm just kidding. I'm going to nail this song."

Ms. Daley, the show's Master of Ceremonies, announced Neil's name. Holly lead him to the stage. The crowd politely applauded, welcoming Neil. A hush of anticipation fell over the audience. Neil took a deep breath, trying to control his shaking legs.

The music began to play. Immediately, all thoughts of his surroundings disappeared. Neil put sixteen years of feeling into the performance, as he began to sing,

"We dreamers have our ways
of facing rainy days
and somehow we survive . . .

. . . I made it through the rain
and found myself respected
by the others who
got rained on too
and made it through."

Neil was gifted with a strong tenor voice. He hit the final note of the song, giving it his full vocal force. The final notes of the music slowly died away. Once again, his apprehension returned, when he was greeted by complete silence. He didn't understand that the crowd was stunned by the power and emotion of the moment. They were emotionally overwhelmed.

Mrs. Daley rushed to Neil. Tears streaming down her face, she gave Neil a hug and whispered, "You were terrific!"

As if on signal, the audience erupted into a thundering applause. With that one song, Neil had touched the emotions of every person there. They had spent fifteen years watching him grow from a victim of an unfortunate accident into an inspiration for many people. From his parents and friends, to his teachers and neighbors, they all felt a sense of pride, a sense of participation in Neil's accomplishments. In their hearts, they knew that Neil had in deed, "Made It Through the Rain."

# H-O-R-S-E

*H-O-R-S-E is a game of basketball where two or more players compete, on a shot by shot basis. When one player makes a shot, all succeeding players must make the same shot. When a player misses, he gets a letter, starting with H. When a player has missed five shots and gets the letter E, he is eliminated from the game. Once a player misses a shot, the next player is free to shoot any shot he desires, until a shot is made. Then the shot elimination process begins again until someone misses. The last person remaining wins.*

Jason Husk dribbled the basketball a few times, eyed the basket and took his shot. The minute the ball left his hands he knew he'd made it. "That one felt good," he bragged, when the ball split the net.

Rebounding the ball, he delivered the ball to Neil with a quick bounce pass. Neil caught the ball and assumed the spot Jason had just vacated.

It was a warm evening in mid-June. After a lazy afternoon of lounging by the pool, Neil and Jason were stepping up the pace with a friendly game of H-O-R-S-E. Neil recently completed his junior year of high school and Jason his freshman year. They were both members of the wrestling team. Jason wrestled in the 103 pound weight class and Neil in the 112 pound class. Their close proximity in weight made them daily practice partners in the Fort Calhoun wrestling room. They spent many afternoons trying to beat each other on the wrestling mat.

Their competitions forged a mutual respect and fast growing friendship. Jason was an outstanding wrestler and an even better basketball player. He usually got the better of Neil and his friends in the game of H-O-R-S-E.

A few years earlier, Larry erected a large garage next to, but separate from their house. It had a wide driveway, which with the addition of a basketball hoop, became a basketball court for the boys and their friends.

"I've got this one," Neil boasted, as he dribbled the ball.

Jason watched while Neil prepared to try and equal the shot he had just made. He marveled at some of the shots Neil was able to make. It seemed that every time they played, and they had played hundreds of games, Neil would make some incredible shot. A shot that would be considered great, if made by a sighted person, let alone by someone who was blind. Neil released his shot. Jason watched as the ball bounced off the back of the rim and fell through the hoop.

"Pure luck," Jason admonished. Rebounding the ball, he prepared to take his turn.

"Oh, come on, dude. It's all skill," Neil sarcastically replied, stepping to the side of the court.

"That's rad," Jason thought, then watched as his next shot bounced off the front of the rim.

Ten minutes later Jason found himself in the closest game they had ever played. They both had H-O-R. Each had missed three shots. It was Neil's shot. He picked a spot about twenty-five feet out and eight feet to the left of the basket.

"Ooh, you're going to try and finish me off," Jason exclaimed.

"You could hit this one with your eyes closed," Neil joked, with a broad smile on his face.

"Give me a little net," Neil ordered, squaring up to the basket.

Jason knew this meant Neil wanted some sound to help him gauge the distance of the shot. The net on the basket was made of chain. If you shook the pole the net made a jingling noise. This allowed Neil to hone in on the basket. Jason shook the pole. When the net had come to rest, Neil released his shot. It was a beautiful shot, catching nothing but the net as it fell through the hoop.

"Yes!" Neil yelled, celebrating by dancing around the court.

"That was a hell of a shot," Jason said, measuring the distance to the basket. Jason moved to the spot of Neil's shot.

"This is for an S?" Jason nervously asked.

"It's a sure S. As soon as you get the nerve to take the shot, I'll be in the lead." Neil mockingly challenged.

Jason launched his shot. Instantly, he knew he'd missed. Even before the ball had bounced off the rim, Jason declared, "Give me an S."

"My pleasure," Neil laughed, returning to the exact spot of his previous shot.

"Oh, we're feeling lucky today, are we?"

"I told you, man, it's all skill," Neil repeated.

"Nothing but net!" Neil predicted, as he shot the ball. The ball proved him correct. The shot swished through the basket.

"The pressures on now," Neil proclaimed, hoping to make Jason nervous.

"I was just giving you a little lead," Jason laughed.

Taking more time than usual, Jason finally let the ball fly. The ball bounced twice on the rim and fell harmlessly to the ground.

"Give me an E," Jason said, slapping Neil on the shoulder. "That's the first time you've ever beaten me."

"Well, you know what they say about the sun shining on a dog."

"How the hell do you do it, man? You make shots that most people who can see couldn't make."

"You want me to give away my secrets? That'll cost you." Neil laughed.

"C'mon man, I'm serious. I know when I give you net, you use the sound to somehow judge the direction and distance, but I don't know how. When

I close my eyes and you shake the net, I always miss the shot by a mile. What's even more amazing is when you take shots without asking for any net. How do you know where the basket even is, let alone how far?"

"The answer is simple, but hard to explain. There are three things. Have you ever noticed that I always play in my bare feet?"

"Yeah, I always thought that was weird."

"I do it because I know every crack and crevice in this driveway. I can feel them with my feet. By the feel, I can tell where I am at and thus, where to shoot."

"No way! That's flat impossible, dude."

Jason couldn't believe Neil could have such a great memory. He could barely memorize the multiplication tables and Neil could memorize hundreds of little cracks in a driveway. Incredulous, Jason wanted to learn more,

"Go on, tell me more."

"I picture everything in my mind. You know how many of the sports psychologists teach the pro athletes to close their eyes and imagine, visualize what they want to accomplish. Well, I do the same thing, except I don't have to close my eyes. I picture the basket, it's height and distance."

"Are you trying to tell me you're a blind Isaiah Thomas?"

"No. Michael Jordan."

They both laughed, caught up in the fantasy of the moment.

"The last factor is the most difficult to explain. It is my hearing. You know how people say when you lose one sense, the other senses become more sensitive, more acute?"

"Yeah. I know you can hear better than me. You're always hearing cars long before I can see or hear them, but I don't understand how that helps you shoot a basketball."

"My hearing has developed to an unusually high degree. It is much more acute than even that of most blind people. I don't know how or why, but it's like . . ."

Neil paused, struggling for a way to describe it to Jason. He had never discussed this with anyone before. All of his friends just took his abilities for granted. They just considered him one of the "guys." He was concerned Jason would think this was all BS, that he wouldn't believe him, or, even worse, that he might look at him as some kind of freak. Hesitantly, he decided to continue.

"I guess the best way to describe my hearing is to say that it is like a bat. I hear the sound come back from objects. By the echoes, I can tell distance and size."

"You can actually hear sound waves bouncing off the basket?" Jason asked in disbelief.

"Yes, that's exactly what happens."

"You're telling me that you have some super human hearing? I guess I should start calling you Batman!" Jason and Neil laughed.

"No, I'm not super human. I think everyone has the same capability, but because they can see, they don't use it."

"I understand, but how do you explain the fact that very few blind people have your hearing capabilities?"

"I'm not sure. I think it's because I live and compete in the sighted world. If I had not developed my hearing, I would have failed. It was not a conscious decision on my part, but rather my body responding to the demands of my environment."

"That's pretty awesome!" Jason responded with a tone of real respect and admiration.

"Enough of this sentimental crap! Let's go play a game of football on the Nintendo. Maybe I can get lucky twice in one day," Neil challenged.

Then, they raced to the house, ready to do battle again.

# *Hangin' Out*

"What are you going to do tonight, dude?" Neil asked into the phone.

"Ah, I think Jay and I are going to go see "Childs Play II." Why don't you come with us?" Chris suggested, from the other end of the line.

"You guys aren't going to that party up on the high road tonight?" Neil continued, with a tone of surprise in his voice.

"No, I feel like @&?%$! today. I hurt my shoulder in the game last night. Partying doesn't really appeal to me tonight."

Chris was referring to last night's pounding the football team received by Arlington High School. Calhoun was in the midst of setting a state record-losing streak, which had now reached twenty-seven straight losses. The streak dated all the way back to Neil's freshman year, three years ago.

Neil was accustomed to Chris' weekly Saturday morning moans and groans. He was the starting running back. Their friend and quarterback, Jesse, couldn't seem to make any completions, except to the opposing team. Chris usually took the brunt of the punishment, as Calhoun tried to pound out a victory on the ground.

"If you went to the party, after a while, you'd be feeling no pain," Neil suggested, knowing that would not happen.

"Yeah, I know. You know how that goes. I always go with good intentions. By the time the night's over, I always end up getting buckled."

"Alright dude. I'll give Jesse a call. Maybe he'll run me out there, for a little while tonight. I'm betting there will be quite a few chicks there," Neil wishfully speculated.

"Yeah, I know. It'll do me some good to stay away from them as well," Chris joked, accentuating it with a short laugh.

"You can take one home for me."

"Okay dude, I'll catch you later," Neil concluded.

"Stay out of trouble," Chris admonished and then hung up the phone.

Later that evening, Neil lay on the couch watching college football. His parents were preparing to go out for the evening.

"What are you doing tonight?" Linda asked, taking a moment to slip on her shoes.

"I'm going to go out with Jesse."

"Oh, what are you two planning to do?" she asked, trying to pry a little more information out of her son.

"I don't know. We may stop by a party this guy's having up on the high road."

Larry entered the room and gave his usual fatherly warning, "Be careful."

"I know, Dad," Neil said, letting out a sigh of frustration.

"Yeah, I know you think you know, but remember, you hang around crap you start smelling like it."

Neil silently shook his head. He had heard all his Dad's one-line warnings a million times before. Neil knew he wouldn't get out of the house without listening to at least one more. He was not to be disappointed. "You do what you want. Remember, I'll give you just enough rope to hang yourself."

"Where are you two going?" Neil asked, changing the subject.

"We're going to see a movie."

"Well, have a good time," Neil said, ushering his parents toward the door.

"Remember what I said," Larry added, on his way out the door. "Watch yourself."

Larry and Linda trusted both boys. All of their friends were basically good kids. They were lenient with the boys. If they made a mistake, they were punished, but that seldom happened, or at least they rarely knew about it. They were proud of their boys. Even so, they were not naïve. The boys were both teenagers and they knew that meant anything could happen.

As his parents backed out of the driveway, Neil headed for the shower. After a leisurely, fifteen-minute shower set to an obnoxiously loud dose of ACDC, Neil jumped into his regular weekend attire; a nice pair of jeans and a polo shirt. He hurried back upstairs to catch the end of the football game on ESPN, while he waited for Jesse.

Two hours later, Neil and Jesse arrived at a large, A-frame house. It was a large acreage located on what the locals referred to as the high road. The high road was a commonly traveled, back way through the hills, from Fort Calhoun to Omaha. This particular house was newly constructed and located two miles west of Fort Calhoun. Making their way toward the house, with the sound of loud music reverberating through the walls, Jesse described the house to Neil.

"You should see the size of this place. It's huge. Its got four decks on the back. Whoever built it put some money into this sucker." he ended, as they reached the front door.

Upon entering the house, they were greeted by Chris, whose parents owned the house. It just so happened they were away, on vacation. Chris, a contemporary of Ryan's, was twenty-one. After making the rounds of the house, they parted ways. Jesse stopped to talk to some girls. Neil began chatting with his former grade school nemeses, Chad and Andre. Neil had memorized the floor plan during his initial tour of the house.

"This house is awesome," Neil commented to Andre.

"Yeah, you should see this thing. It's got three floors, each one slightly smaller than the one below. You look out from each floor onto the floors below." Andre explained, finishing off his glass of beer.

"Each level has a deck too, don't they?" Neil asked.

"Yeah, it's a pretty cool place."

Andre then turned to talk to some new arrivals. Mingling again, Neil ran into Tracy. She was a really cute girl from school. After a few minutes of unsuccessful flirting, Neil once again entered the throng, searching for Jesse.

It was about an hour later when Neil heard someone come stumbling through the front door, hollering, "Cops!" Neil immediately heeded the often-expressed advice of his older brother, who had always told him, "If you're ever at a party and you hear someone yell cops, there are two things you do. The first thing you do is drop your beer. The second thing is run like hell."

Ryan was somewhere at the party as well. He had come home from college for the weekend. Ryan was the furthest thing from Neil's mind. He knew that Ryan would not come to his rescue. It was every man for himself. In less then ten seconds, Neil found himself standing alone.

Heeding his brother's advice, he turned and ran up the stairs to the second floor. Turning to his right, he rushed into an open bedroom and opened the closet door. A girl screamed. Neil slammed the door and headed up the stairs to the third floor. As Neil reached the top of the stairs, he heard Chris talking to the cops at the door.

"Oh @%?&$!" he thought. "My Dad was right. He gave me enough rope and I'm about thirty seconds away from hanging myself."

Just then he remembered hearing someone say there was a fourth level. It was an attic that could only be reached through the ceiling. Neil ran over to the bed, in the middle of the room. Two girls from Omaha, whom he had been talking to earlier, were huddled together, not knowing what to do.

"Come on!" Neil whispered. "Hop on the bed and climb into the attic."

"There's a board over the hole," one of the girls shot back.

"Who cares?" Neil exclaimed, jumping onto the bed.

"I'll knock it out of the way. Where is it?" he asked, moving toward the middle of the bed.

"Right above you," another girl responded.

Neil leaped toward the ceiling with his hands raised above his head. His hands hit the board covering the hole and knocked it aside. Neil took another leap. Grabbing the ceiling above him, he pulled himself through the hole. He stuck his head through the hole and whispered to the girls below.

"Come on. I'll help you up," he said, lowering his hand to the girls. His hand was grasped by one of the girls and he quickly pulled her up.

"Where are the others?" He asked.

"There's a ladder on the deck that leads up to the attic level," she explained.

"You mean to tell me there's a ladder down there and I just set the world high jump record getting up here?" Neil admonished.

"Yep. Let's get this hole covered up and go out on the deck.

"There's a deck off of the attic?" Neil asked.

"Yeah. Now come on," she said, pulling Neil toward the door.

He found himself on a small deck, which was still under construction. It was missing some boards on one corner. Neil took inventory of his surroundings. He noticed Andre was making his way up the ladder.

"Somebody come over here and help me pull this ladder up," Andre ordered. Neil stepped forward to help, but was beat to the punch by Jesse.

"Jesse, I didn't know you made it up here, too," Neil said.

"Yah. Now let's make sure we don't get caught," Jesse said. Andre and Jesse then pulled the ladder up from the deck below.

"There are too many of us up here. The cops are sure to see us," Jesse explained.

"Why don't some of us climb up on the roof?" Neil suggested, turning toward the house.

The roof was a mere two feet above his head. Neil placed a foot on the deck railing and hoisted himself onto the roof. Lying on the roof, he held the edge with one hand frozen in fear. He hadn't realized that the roof was so steep. The roof sloped downward at a sixty-degree angle. It was all Neil could do to keep from plunging down the slope.

He groped around the roof with his right hand, until he felt a wire running down the curve of the roof. He grasped it with his right hand and secured himself. Feeling safer, he finally began to relax his straining muscles. Unexpectedly, Jesse joined Neil on the roof. Jesse and Neil lay side-by-side, holding on to one another and the wire running down the roof.

Annie, one of the girls from Omaha, and Kelly, a girl from Fort Calhoun, joined them. Neil and Annie tightly clutched each other, hoping they would not slide off the roof. Little did Neil know at that time, but nine years later, the girl he was hanging on a roof with, would become his brother's wife. The cops came out onto each deck, slowly working their way to the top. Searching the deck with the beam from his flashlight, one of the officers asked Chris,

"What's up on that upper deck?" The beam of a flashlight began to play over the darkened deck.

"Oh, that deck's not finished yet," Chris explained, pointing out the missing boards.

"Okay, well let's head back in," the officer ordered.

Giving a silent sigh of relief, Neil tried to relax, even though his muscles were screaming in protest. The four of them lay on the roof of the house for nearly an hour before the all clear was given.

"Holy @%?&$!" Jesse exclaimed, lowering himself to the deck.

"Now that was the epitome of a night of hanging out!" Neil joked, helping the girls down from the roof. His comment was met by nervous laughter from each of the participants.

"That's just like you, dude," Jesse said. "I'm up there scared @%?&$! and you're up there laughing about it."

"You think I wasn't afraid," Neil replied. "There's nothing to do about it now but laugh and learn."

They made their way down the stairs and out the front door. "Well, I guess I got lucky and dodged the noose again," Neil thought as he jumped into Jesse's jeep. "Jesse, let's get the hell out of here."

# Wrestling With the Past

Neil awoke and slowly, painfully stretched his body, feeling the protest from his strained muscles. He mentally took a quick inventory of his tortured body and catalogued the damages.

"My legs are so tight. My left cheek stings from a large mat burn, a wrestler's badge of honor. When my right arm moves, it is greeted by a sharp pang of pain, the price of being subjected to several contorted wrestling holds."

He knew only a long, hot shower and an hour of stretching would allow him to walk normally. Gradually, stiffly, he rose from the bed. With each agonizing step, he haltingly moved toward the shower. Standing five feet nine inches, he weighed 125 pounds. It felt like every inch of his body was begging for a hot shower. After a long, steamy shower, he returned to bed. He'd followed this same routine for the last four years. This time would be his last.

It was Sunday, February 17, 1992. The day after Neil completed his four-year wrestling career for Fort Calhoun High School. Lying in bed, his mind drifted back to the beginning of it all.

His freshman year, he had been one of only three freshmen to join the high school wrestling team. Images of his first team practice vividly returned. Listening to Ryan at the dinner table, Neil became acquainted with the practice routine. For three years, Ryan spent many nights with Neil, teaching him the different wrestling positions and moves. Neil was unsure if Ryan did it to help him, or if he just enjoyed inflicting pain. It was the only time Ryan could beat him up, without incurring the wrath of their father.

Through Ryan, Neil knew most of the school's wrestling team. Some of them were Ryan's best friends. They always treated him as one of the team. During the summer, many of them had spent endless hours at the Halford's pool. Yet, he was still nervous. They accepted him as Ryan's brother. They always treated him as their equal.

Playing with them was one thing. Being part of a competitive wrestling team, where he could affect the success of the team, was another matter. Neil was afraid he could not live up to Ryan's success. He was concerned the team would consider him a liability, someone unable to carry his load.

To make matters worse, one of his best friends and summer wrestling partner, Seth Tamisiea, unexpectedly transferred to an Omaha Catholic high school. All summer they had practiced wrestling, anticipating joining the team together. Now, he would be forced to face the team, to face the season without his sidekick.

In addition, Ryan was a great wrestler. He qualified for the state tournament as a sophomore and just missed going his junior year. As a senior, Ryan expected to once again qualify for the state tournament. Neil feared he could not match his brother's success.

He had faced these fears before and had always overcome them. This was different. His success or failure would be played out on a wrestling mat, for all to see. After dressing, he slowly, hesitantly entered the gym. The team had already commenced the practice.

"Over here, Neil" Coach Jim Meyer ordered.

"Welcome to the team. I think you know everyone on the team. Chris Nelson will be your practice partner," Coach Meyer explained, placing Neil's hand on Chris' shoulder.

Neil was relieved. He knew Chris. Chris was a good friend of Seth's. Much bigger than Neil, Chris was six feet tall and weighed one hundred sixty pounds. Neil, skinny but wiry, only stood five feet seven inches and weighed ninety-seven pounds. With his first takedown, Neil's apprehensions vanished. Instantly, Chris and Neil became best friends. For the next four years they were inseparable, on and off the wrestling mat.

After one month of practice, it was time for the "wrestle off." The "wrestle off" was how the varsity team was selected. Each week the top wrestlers in each weight class would wrestle each other, with the winner wrestling on varsity for that week. Every week there was a new "wrestle off." Ryan easily won his match and would wrestle at 119 pounds. Chris won his match and would wrestle at 152 pounds. Though weighing less than one hundred pounds, Neil had to wrestle a sophomore, Jeff Shaner, for the 103 pound position.

Smiling, Neil recalled his first weekly "wrestle off." Though Jeff had a losing record as a freshman, he was expected to be the starter at this weight. The match had been close, with Neil leading throughout. Then, with ten seconds remaining, Jeff escaped Neil's hold, earning one point. The match was tied at 9 – 9. In overtime, Jeff won with a quick take down off the whistle.

That evening, at the dinner table, Neil sheepishly announced to his parents he had lost the wrestle off. He would not be wrestling varsity for the first meet. Even now, four years later, he could still feel the sting of that defeat. While his parents and brother tried to console him, Neil made a silent vow he would never allow it to happen again. For the remainder of the season, each week, Neil and Jeff would wrestle off for the varsity position. Jeff never again defeated Neil. By the end of the season, Neil was consistently pinning Jeff.

Though Neil was relegated to being a cheerleader for the first tournament of the year, he was anxious for his brother to start the year with a first place victory. Ryan easily won his first two matches. Then disaster hit in the finals. He was wrestling Marty Smith from David City Aquinas. He was the older brother of a wrestler who would prove to be Neil's archrival for most of his wrestling career. In the third period, ahead by three points, Ryan was thrown to the ground, landing on his right shoulder. Hearing Ryan shouting in pain, Neil rose from the bench. "Neil, Ryan has dislocated his shoulder!" Chris excitedly explained.

Chris described the scene, while Neil continued to stand. Paramedics were called and Ryan was taken to the hospital. Neil remained with the team, though his thoughts were with Ryan. Anxious to get home, to find out about Ryan, it seemed as if the school bus ride back to Fort Calhoun took forever. When Neil finally arrived home, he was greeted by Ryan with his shoulder wrapped and his arm in a sling. He explained he would be out for several weeks, but that the prognosis was good. He would be able to return in time to qualify for the state tournament.

Neil's first match was a dual meet at home, against Lyons-Decatur. His opponent was a senior, Mitch Climer. That night, the gym was full. This was unusual for a wrestling match. Neil knew that much of the town had come out to see how he would perform in his first varsity start. It was like a family reunion. His parents, his aunts and uncles, cousins, grandmother and many family friends, were all in attendance. He was determined to win. Neil did not want to disappoint all those who had helped him through the years. His hopes were quickly shattered. Neil was pinned in the first thirty-five seconds of the match.

The shame of his first varsity loss returned. It was a feeling he grew to know very well that first season. He ended the season with a record of 6-16. The one highlight of his freshman season came in front of the home crowd. At a dual meet with Weeping Water, Neil was matched up against a returning state qualifier Gary Sorenson. Neil gave up an early takedown and was down 2–0 going in to the second period.

Sorenson chose to assume the down position. On the referee's command, Neil took his place atop his opponent. Upon the command of the referee's whistle, Neil rapped his left leg around the inside of his opponent's left leg and assumed the cross body ride. Neil was experienced with this hold. He was often tortured in this position by Ryan during their nightly living room wrestling matches. Sorenson struggled to come to his feet. Neil reached across Sorenson's body snatching his right arm and placing it behind his head. He then leaned back, placing Sorenson in what was to become Neil's signature pinning combination, the guillotine. Neil pinned Sorenson and the crowd went crazy. Neil had provided them with the first upset of the night and of his young career.

His first wrestling season, although disappointing, was inconsequential when compared to his brother Ryan's season. This was his senior season, his last opportunity to be a state champion. Ryan was ready. During the off-season, he had worked hard to improve his strength and endurance. Neil knew Ryan was expecting to have a great season. Then he was injured. Neil would have sacrificed all of his victories, if it could have helped Ryan make it to the state tournament. Neil knew Ryan was good enough not only to qualify for state, but also to win.

Ryan recovered quickly and was cleared by the doctor to wrestle in the first tournament after the Christmas break. It was important that he do well so he could earn a high seeding for the district tournament. He returned with a vengeance.

In his first tournament, he made it to the finals where he met Joe Morris.

Ryan was tentative, not his usual aggressive self. He was not yet confident that his shoulder had totally recovered. In the third period, he was trailing 10-6. Ryan was determined to win. He needed five points, a take down and a near pin, all in one move. With thirty seconds remaining, he charged, taking Morris to the mat. As they landed, he rolled, forcing Morris on his back. Ryan had done it. He earned the five points. He won the tournament. Neil, followed by the entire team ran to Ryan. The entire Fort Calhoun audience cheered. They knew their potential state champion was back.

He won the next two tournaments and finished second in the third, losing a close match to a wrestler rated first in the state. Ryan continued to win. He was ranked third in the state when disaster struck again.

It was the last meet before the district qualification tournament. Neil was ill with the flu and remained at home. Ryan was scheduled to wrestle an opponent he had already defeated three times that season. In the third period, Ryan had a comfortable lead. Both wrestlers were upright, jockeying for position. In one last effort to pin his opponent, Ryan charged. He managed to get a good hold and then took his foe to the mat. As they fell, Ryan landed on top, his right shoulder taking the full weight of the fall.

Larry and Linda were anxiously watching when they once again heard Ryan cry out in agonizing pain. Larry and Linda rushed to the mat. When they arrived, their worst fears were realized. Once again, Ryan's right shoulder was dislocated.

Chris Nelson called Neil and told him what happened. Neil greeted Ryan at the door. He was anxious to hear the news. Unlike the first time, the news was not good. Ryan would need surgery on his shoulder and he would never wrestle again.

Ryan and Neil stayed up late that night, reminiscing about all of their years of wrestling. Several hours later, they both succumbed to their bodies' demands for rest. Rising to retire to bed, Neil turned to Ryan and declared, "Bro, I'll win a medal for both of us."

Upon the conclusion of that disappointing season Neil vowed he would do whatever it took to become a better wrestler. He swore he would not allow himself to endure another season with so many defeats. Neil knew his technique was good. It was his size and strength that held him back. He needed to hit the weight room with a vengeance. However, lifting weights required a partner.

His newly found friend and practice partner, Chris suggested he work out with the track team. Chris ran hurdles for the track team. The prospect excited Neil. Neil asked the track coach, Mr. Skrdla. Knowing of Neil's commitment to wrestling, the coach encouraged his participation. "I'll be holding you accountable just like the other members of the team," the coach warned. Mr. Skrdla followed through on his promise. He required Neil attend each practice and pushed him to the max.

When his sophomore season began, Neil weighed 110 pounds. He chose to wrestle in the 112-pound class, rather than cut weight back down to 103 pounds. At the time, he felt cutting weight would be detrimental to what he had been trying to accomplish physically. He had lifted weights all summer. Neil was just beginning to gain some weight and strength. He felt that losing weight would be counterproductive.

Once again, Neil was disappointed. He finished the season with a record of 8-18; only two more wins than the previous year. The success of his practice partner, Chris, exacerbated his disappointment. Chris reached the goal of every high school wrestler. He qualified for the state tournament. Even though Chris went 0–2 at the state tournament, Neil was envious. He longed to match the success of his friend.

Many times Neil debated whether or not he'd made the right choice. He had dedicated so much of his time and effort to wrestling. He had not wavered in his commitment. Yet, he had shown negligible improvement. Neil wondered if his lofty goals were achievable, "Could a wrestler who had only won fourteen matches in two years compete in the state tournament?"

In the spring of 1990, Neil once again dedicated himself to working out with the track team and improving his strength. Chris had turned 16 and could drive. He was Neil's daily transportation to weight lifting during the spring and summer. They worked out together, pushing each other in the weight room. Outside of the weight room, their friendship continued to grow.

Finally, after two years, Neil's relentless weight training and conditioning were showing tangible results. At the beginning of his junior season, he stood five feet nine inches tall, weighed 123 pounds and could bench press 180 pounds. With the encouragement of his brother, Neil made the decision to make a drop in weight and return to the 112 pound weight class. Ryan felt Neil would not lose any of his strength and power with the weight loss. For his size, Neil's strength was exceptional. Ryan was confident Neil would dominate this weight class.

When Neil made the decision to drop the weight, he discussed it with his parents. Though they were concerned, they knew Neil had dedicated many long hours to ensure he would have a successful wrestling season and qualify for the state tournament. Linda required Neil to adhere to a strict vitamin and protein plan, to ensure he would have the minimum required to maintain his health.

Neil had long since left the picky eating days of Nebraska City behind. Eating was now a source of great enjoyment. The 11-pound weight loss was difficult. Each week he struggled to reach his weight. Starting every Wednesday, he would eat only a minimal breakfast, no lunch and a frozen Weight Watcher's dinner. He would run each night. Each day closer to the wrestling meet, his workout became more intense. No matter how hard he worked, no matter how little he ate, it always seemed that he would just barely make the weight. Every Friday morning he would weigh himself. Sometimes, if he weighed 115 pounds or more, he would not drink or eat until after the weigh-in on Saturday morning. Many times he would strip naked at the weigh-in, shedding every possible source of weight, to qualify at 112 pounds.

On Saturday he would weigh 112 pounds. By Saturday evening, after eating all day, his weight would return to 120 pounds. Neil reflected on the many Sunday evenings he spent at the high school, working to shed the pounds he put on the day before. His cousin Kirt would join him. They would run two miles through the halls of the school, while the other kids played basketball in the gym. He would then weigh himself to gauge his progress. If he wasn't satisfied, he would jump rope for 3,000 consecutive jumps. Food was always on his mind. It was the first thing he thought about when he awoke in the morning, and it was the last thing he thought about before falling to sleep each night.

On the wrestling mat, Neil began to reap the rewards of his two years of dedication. The first tournament of the season at Bennington High School was one of the toughest tournaments the team would attend all year. Neil started his season off with a quick victory, easily pinning his opponent in the first period. His next opponent was the returning state champion, Vincent Smith of David City Aquinas, the younger brother of the wrestler who first dislocated Ryan's shoulder. He wrestled Smith extremely close through the first period, trailing 2–0. Late in the second period, Smith caught Neil in a Half Nelson. A few seconds later, Neil was counting the ceiling lights, as Smith recorded a pin.

Neil didn't allow the loss to slow him down. He wrestled his way back through the losers bracket, winning a chance to wrestle for 3rd or 4th place. Neil lost a close match, 4–2 to a wrestler from Boys Town, settling for fourth place. Having earned his first varsity medal, Neil was happy, yet he felt he could have done better. He vowed to perform better the following week, to wrestle smarter and with more heart.

The next tournament was at West Point, Nebraska. In his first match of the day, Neil locked up with a wrestler from Wayne. After a hard fought 6 minutes, the match was tied. Giving up a takedown at the beginning of the overtime period, Neil was quickly defeated. He was extremely upset. Neil knew he was a better wrestler than his opponent. If they wrestled again, he believed he could win. Neil dispatched his next two opponents in quick succession. For the second straight week, Neil found himself wrestling for 3rd or 4th place.

His opponent was the wrestler from Wayne, who had beaten him earlier in the day. When he took the mat, Neil vowed not to make the same mistake twice. He quickly shot in, scoring a two-point takedown. With the first period coming to a close, he locked his opponent in a cradle and scored three back points. Starting the second period, Neil took the top position. He felt he could work his opponent into a pinning combination. Shortly after the whistle blew, Neil slipped in his leg and assumed the cross body ride. Fifteen seconds later he had pulled his opponent's arm behind his head and tilted him back into the Guillotine. The referee slapped the mat. Neil extracted himself from his opponent and helped him to his feet. Though pleased with the improvement over the previous tournament, Neil still had his sights set on a first place medal.

The team was at Loganview for the next tournament. Neil was seeded third. The 112-pound weight class had only five wrestlers. Neil received a bye in the first round. His first match of the day was to be against a returning state qualifier from Columbus-Lakeview. Neil gave up a takedown in the first period and fell behind 2–0. He began the second period on top. After working his opponent for the first minute, he was able to turn him on his back, receiving

3 back points. Neil rode his opponent out in the third period, not giving up any points. He won, 3–2. Neil was elated. He'd made the finals for the first time in his high school career.

Once again, he was matched against Vincent Smith. After a close, tough two periods Neil was put on his back, yielding his second pin of the season to Smith. When he received his second place medal from the Loganview cheer-leader, the crowd cheering in the background, Neil promised himself that a first place medal would be in his near future.

It would be two meets and three weeks later before Neil fulfilled his promise. Neil was able to pin his way through the Weeping Water tournament. He would always remember this tournament. Not because he was the tourna-ment champion, but for another reason, a much more malicious reason.

Neil wrestled under the same rules as everyone else, with one exception. At the beginning of a match, or anytime during the match, if the wrestlers parted, had no contact, then the match was halted. The referee would bring the wrestlers together and they would touch hands. Each would have one hand on top and one hand on the bottom. This was done to ensure that Neil would know the general proximity of his opponent. Even with this consideration, Neil was still at a great disadvantage. He could not see what his opponent was doing. He could never anticipate, he could only react and his reaction could only come after his opponent had made contact.

After his quarterfinal pin, Neil was standing at the edge of the mat, talking to a freshman teammate, Monte Christensen. Suddenly, without any warning, he felt a hand on his shoulder. Yanked around, he found himself face to face with the irate father of the wrestler he had just pinned. "You make me sick! You don't belong here! You get an advantage. If you can't wrestle like everyone else, don't wrestle at all!" The father yelled, his voice rising with each word.

He did not respond to this tirade. Neil was embarrassed. Also, concerned that this parent might get physical, he braced himself to repel an attack. After another two minutes of ranting and raving, the parent returned to the stands. Neil never responded. Even after the man left, he remained stoic, unable to move. In all of his years, he had endured the jokes, the sarcastic comments, and the insults. But always, they had come from other students. This was the first time he had been the subject of a verbal attack by a parent. Even worse, never had he been subjected to such a personal, vindictive verbal attack.

While the father delivered his tirade, Monte ran to get Larry, who imme-diately rushed to Neil's aid. "Neil, are you okay?" The concerned voice of his father jarred Neil from his almost shock-like trance. "What happened?"

Neil didn't want to tell his father. He knew Larry would react, that he would confront the parent. Neil wanted to win this tournament. He wanted to wres-tle. He didn't want to be the cause of two fathers arguing, or worse, fighting. When it came to protecting his sons, Neil knew his father had a temper. He knew his Dad would not allow this to go unchallenged.

"Oh, it's nothing, Dad. Just some angry parent," Neil answered, hoping to assuage the situation.

Not satisfied with Neil's response, Larry turned to Monte. "Monte, what happened?" After relaying the facts to Larry, Monte pointed out the parent in the bleachers.

Larry was irate. He did not interfere with Neil's problems with other students. He felt it was important that Neil deal with those challenges. That was the real world and Neil had to learn to make his own way. This was different. This was a parent putting his hands on Neil. More importantly, this was a parent contesting Neil's right to live and compete in the sighted world. He could not and would not let this challenge go unanswered.

Immediately, Larry proceeded up the bleachers, until he stood directly in front of Neil's adult adversary. "Did you put your hands on my son?" Larry loudly challenged. The father sat stoic, giving no reply.

"Stand up you @&?&%! I'm here, if you want to push someone around." Still, no movement, no response came from the bleachers.

"What? You only yell at boys! You can't make your complaints to a man, you spineless @%?&$!"

His face red with anger, Larry issued his final warning, "If you ever put your hands on my boy again, if you ever say another word to Neil, I'll be back and it won't be to talk."

Giving the man one last, stern stare, Larry returned to Neil, who was now standing with his coach. "I can have the man ejected, if you want Larry?" Coach Meyer asked.

"No. I don't think he will cause any more problems."

Then, his anger instantly turning to concern for Neil, Larry quietly encouraged Neil, "Neil, don't let that @%?&$! bother you. Stay focused. You have a great chance to win this tournament. The best way to respond to people like him is to win."

Neil listened to his Dad. His shock turned to determination. In the final match, Neil pinned his opponent in the second period.

Still lying in bed, Neil reflected that never before and never after, would he ever be the subject of such a vicious verbal attack. Not wanting to dwell on the negative, his thoughts once again returned to his wrestling exploits.

The following week Fort Calhoun had a home dual with it's local wrestling rival, Bennington. Larry's brother and his wife lived in Bennington. Their son, Ross was a freshman and wrestled for Bennington High School. Ross had been wrestling much of the season at 119 pounds, but was now wrestling in the 112-pound weight class. Fans from both schools were hoping to see the two cousins tangle on the wrestling mat. Neil had no intention of satisfying them. He would not wrestle Ross.

Though confident he could beat Ross, he also knew it could create unnecessary tension within the family. Also, Ross was having a good year. Neil did not want to dash his dreams of a state qualification. Neil didn't need the victory. It was better for everyone if they didn't wrestle.

He asked Coach Meyer if it was possible to move him to 119 for this night's event. Coach Meyer allowed the move. Neil felt that a possible family conflict had been avoided. Then, shortly after taking their places at the side of the mat for the start of the dual meet, the opposing team's coach told Coach Meyer he was moving Ross up to the 119-pound class to wrestle Neil. Coach Meyer pulled Neil aside and addressed him, with concern in his voice,

"I know you don't want to wrestle your cousin if it can be helped. I respect that decision, but their coach has decided to move Ross up to wrestle you at 119 pounds." Neil's stomach took a sudden plunge.

"If you don't feel it will have a difference on the overall outcome of the meet, coach, I would rather not wrestle him. If you feel that my forfeiting the match will cost us the meet, then I will go out there and beat him."

"Honestly Neil, we both know that Bennington has a very good team. It's going to be tough for us to win this dual. I'm going to have you sit this one out."

As Coach Meyer removed his arm from around Neil and turned toward the scorer's table, Neil grabbed his arm and gave it a squeeze. "Thanks coach," Neil said, acknowledging his coach's sacrifice.

He knew Coach Meyer wanted him to wrestle. Neil liked and admired Coach Meyer. The coach's decision to allow Neil to forfeit the match, without once questioning Neil's reason, only served to reinforce Neil's respect for his coach. He was very calm and never seemed to get excited or upset, no matter how well or how poorly the team did. Coach Meyer did not motivate the team by yelling and screaming or giving some "rah-rah" speech. He inspired his students by treating each one as an individual, with respect. Each wrestler liked him so much that they always tried to do their best for him, to win for him.

The next week was the conference tournament. After handily winning his first two matches, Neil faced a small wrestler named Tyson McCoy. He was an excellent wrestler. Neil lost, getting pinned in the first period. He received the second place medal.

After a week off, a week during which Neil practiced with renewed intensity, the team wrestled at a small tournament in Fremont. Neil was seeded first. Easily reaching the finals, he fifteen pointed his opponent in the second period, winning the tournament. Because of his excellent performance, he placed second in the voting for the outstanding wrestler of the tournament award.

The following week, the district tournament was held in David City, Nebraska. Neil entered the tournament with a record of 23-6. He was seeded second. The first seed was Neil's nemesis, Vincent Smith. When Chris read the seeding chart to Neil, he stopped at one name. Ross Halford, Neil's cousin, was wrestling in the 112 pound class and was seeded third. This meant that to qualify for the state tournament, Neil would most likely have to beat his cousin.

He won his first match 5-0. In the second match, the quarterfinal match, Neil wrestled a boy who only weighed 97 pounds. Unlike Neil, who was constantly fighting to lose weight, this boy struggled to make the minimum required weight to qualify. It was no match. Neil pinned him 33 seconds into the first period. After the referee slammed the mat announcing the pin, Neil's family went wild. Neil was now in the semifinals. One more victory and he would qualify for the state tournament. Their elation turned to concern when they learned that Neil's semifinal opponent would be his cousin, Ross.

Even though he had avoided wrestling his cousin earlier, Neil was determined. The only person standing between Neil and his dream of reaching the state tournament was Ross. Cousin or not, he was going down.

Nervously, Neil walked onto the mat. A victory over his cousin was necessary to reach his dream. One more victory and he would be going to Lincoln. Standing, hand in hand with Ross, he anxiously awaited the referee's whistle, the signal to begin.

On the whistle, both wrestlers jockeyed for position. They would each shoot for the legs, each always being forced to reassume the upright position. Then with the two-minute period about to end, Ross shot for Neil's legs. Neil answered by placing Ross in a front headlock. Shucking him to the side, Neil took Ross to the mat, earning 2 points for the take down. Neil then immediately assumed his favorite position, the Cross Body Ride. While Ross struggled to free himself, Neil, while in the Cross Body Ride, laying diagonally on Ross' back, lunged across his body, forcing his left side up and his right side down. He then reached back with his left arm, put Ross' head in a lock, and rolled, forcing Ross on his back. This was the Turk position and resulted in a near pin. When the period ended, Neil was awarded three points and led 5-0.

Neil won the toss for the second period and chose the top position. In response to the referee's whistle, Neil immediately threw his left leg around Ross's left leg and went into the Cross Body Ride. Grabbing Ross's right leg, Neil caught Ross in the "Banana Splits." Ross' legs were spread wide as Neil rolled, forcing Ross' butt into the air and his shoulders to the mat. Within seconds the referee slapped the mat. Neil had pinned his cousin in the second period.

Releasing Ross from the hold, he grabbed Ross' hand and helped him to his feet. After the referee had raised Neil's hand, signifying his victory, Ross immediately put his arm around Neil, congratulated him and guided him off the mat. Neil knew Ross was disappointed. He was within one victory of going to state, as a freshman. Even so, as young as he was, Ross displayed great sportsmanship.

Warmly rapped in his covers, Neil reflected on the stark contrast between Ross, who had been so gracious in the face of defeat, and the irate father of a losing son.

Once again, trying to forget the stupid ranting of an ignorant and immature man, Neil's thoughts returned to his victory celebration. When Neil walked off the mat, his coach and teammates immediately greeted him. Following their hugs and high fives, his father grabbed him, lifting him into the air. Behind his father was a throng of family, teachers and friends. The fans were going crazy, cheering wildly.

He had never before felt such exhilaration, such pride, and such a sense of accomplishment. Ever since his first wrestling tournament at the NSVH, he had one goal, to qualify for the state tournament. Now, eleven years later, his dream had finally come true.

The time for Neil's final match arrived much sooner than he anticipated. Shaking hands with Vincent Smith, Neil sensed the crowd's anticipation. The crowd was alive, cheering before the match even began. For most of the first period, they both jockeyed for position, neither one successful. Then, with ten seconds remaining, Vincent managed to grab Neil's leg, resulting in a takedown. At the end of the first period, Neil trailed 2-0.

Starting the second period on the bottom, Neil made several failed attempts to escape. Eventually, Vincent maneuvered Neil into a deep Half Nelson hold, which resulted in a pin. Neil left the district championships with mixed feelings. He was excited that he had qualified for the state tournament, but very discouraged by his poor performance in the final match.

The following Monday, Neil immediately began to prepare for the state tournament, with Chris Nelson, who also finished second in the district tournament. Chris would be going to Lincoln with Neil.

The next day at school Coach Meyer informed Neil that an Omaha sportscaster for WOWT, the Omaha NBC affiliate, was going to be at practice that afternoon to interview Neil. Upon arriving, they started by filming Neil while he practiced with the team. After five minutes, Coach Meyer noticed the film crew was packing up their equipment, preparing to leave. He approached the reporter and asked, "That was quick. Did you get everything you needed?"

To his surprise, the reporter replied, "There isn't much of a story here."

"What do you mean?" Coach Meyer questioned.

"It's obvious Neil can see. He has some sight," the reporter explained.

Coach Meyer was not surprised by their conclusion. It was not the first time someone had mistakenly thought Neil could see. He responded by asking, "Why do you think he can see?"

"He just ran the halls of the school with the team and didn't hit anything. He didn't use his arms to protect himself. There, look at him right now. He walked straight to the bathroom door and opened it like anyone else. He has to be able to see."

In an effort to explain Neil's abilities, Coach Meyer told the crew, "If you are expecting to film Neil running into something, it just isn't going to happen. He instinctively knows where things are. Neil is the only wrestler I can't sneak up on. He senses when I am near."

Then the coach asked, "Which eye do you think has sight?"

The reporter responded, "It's obvious that it is his right eye. You can see that his left eye has been seriously damaged."

Coach Meyer saw Neil returning from the restroom and called for him to join the discussion. The coach ordered, "Neil, show this reporter which eye is your glass eye."

Neil responded by tapping his glass eye and answering, "It is my right eye."

The reporter and camera crew immediately began to unpack their equipment and spent the next two hours filming and interviewing Neil. That night Neil was on television. Later that week, a reporter for the Omaha World Herald also interviewed Neil. At the moment, Neil didn't realize how his life would change. For the next year and a half, he was about to have his "fifteen minutes of fame."

That Thursday morning the team left for Lincoln. Upon arriving at the Bob Devaney Arena, Neil was overwhelmed. It was huge. The arena seated twelve thousand. On the floor were eight mats, meaning eight matches would run simultaneously. This tournament always filled the seats. The wrestling community was a very close-knit group of parents and fans, who avidly followed their home teams.

Neil's first match was against Chuck Gomez from Cozad. Neil dominated, winning 13-0. When the referee raised Neil's hand in victory, the crowd exploded. Neil had never before been the subject of such a thunderous ovation. When the excitement of his victory subsided, he came face to face with his new reality. People would stop him, pat him on the back, and praise him for his performance. Parents, fans, even other wrestlers couldn't wait for the chance to congratulate Neil. Wherever he went that day, someone was always accosting him. He couldn't even find privacy in the restroom.

Shortly after the match, he and Chris walked to the concession stand. When they opened the doors to the hallway, a barrage of reporters mobbed Neil. Sticking microphones in his face, they all were simultaneously asking questions. After responding to the questions and posing for the cameras, he proceeded to the concession stand. Chris was more excited than Neil, who seemed to take all of the attention in stride.

"Wow, you're going to be on television. You're a celebrity! Man, the girls are going to dig this!" Chris excitedly exclaimed.

"Chris, it's no big deal. Tomorrow, someone else will be the center of their attention."

Neil explained.

This wasn't the first time his victories were publicized. Neil didn't like the attention. He knew the only reason the reporters were interested in him was because he was blind. Neil struggled most of his life to not be considered different, but to be "just one of the boys." He wanted to be considered a great wrestler, not a great blind wrestler.

Leaving Chris with his dreams of celebrity, Neil went to the locker room to be by himself. The next match was the quarterfinals. It was crucial and he wanted no distractions. He knew he had to keep his head in the moment, concentrating on his next opponent. If he won this match, he would win a medal.

His opponent was Troy Glover from Centennial, Nebraska. Troy was a senior and two-time runner up at the state tournament. The first period ended tied 2-2. In the second period, Neil was on top. Late in the period he nearly pinned Troy, resulting in an award of 3 points. Neil led 5-2. In the third period, Neil began on top. With less than a minute to go, Troy did a sit out. When Neil tried to re-establish his position, he dropped his head over Troy's right shoulder. Troy grabbed Neil's head, rolled him and pinned him.

Neil was crushed. He was a minute away from placing in the state tournament. One careless move and he lost. Neil still had a chance. If he went undefeated in the wrestle back round, he could still win a medal. He won his first match 8-0. However, in the next match, he lost. His record at the state tournament was 2-2. He returned home without a medal.

Though sad about not earning a medal, about not fulfilling his promise to Ryan, Neil had reached his goal. He had qualified for the state tournament. In his sophomore year, Ryan qualified and then went 2-2, just like Neil. Neil had at least equaled his brother's success.

For several weeks, Neil took a break. Then, once again, he turned his attention to wrestling. His new goal was not just to earn a medal at the state tournament, but also to be in the "Parade of Champions." Neil had attended the parade, sitting in the stands for the last four years. To him, it was the most exciting and inspirational ceremony in high school sports.

During the state tournament, just before the final matches, all of the finalists are lined up, each opponent on opposite sides of the arena. Then as they play the song, "We are the Champions," the opponents walk to the center of the mat on which they will wrestle, shake hands and begin warming up.

That spring, Neil again worked out with the track team. During his junior year, Neil had established a good rapport with his young history teacher, Steve Owens. Mr. Owens was very inspirational to Neil. He would quote famous people in class trying to motivate his students. His class was always fun. He made history come alive. Also, probably because of his age, Mr. Owens seemed more like a fellow student than a teacher.

Unbeknownst to Neil, he also inspired Mr. Owens. He had been astonished by Neil's wrestling success and had decided to try and help him. Mr. Owens believed that with some help, Neil could even do better. He met with Neil and offered to help him work out each day. Neil excitedly accepted his offer.

Initially, Mr. Owens obtained the workout plan used by the University of Nebraska at Kearney's wrestling team. Using that program, he developed a plan for Neil. For that entire summer and the next fall, up to the start of wrestling practice. Mr. Owens would pick Neil up every Monday, Tuesday, Thursday and Friday at 5:15 a.m. at home, drive him to school and then work out with Neil for two hours. Neil was determined; he pushed himself to the maximum.

The day before wrestling practice started, Mr. Owens called Neil into his classroom. Handing Neil a piece of paper, he said, "Neil, I want you to braille this quote and hang it above your locker. Then, any time you get discouraged, any time you have doubts, I want you to read it."

"Would you read it to me now?" Neil asked, curious to learn whom Mr. Owens was quoting.

"Sure. It's a quote from John Wooden. 'Success is peace of mind, which is a direct result of self-satisfaction in knowing you did your best to become the best you are capable of becoming.'"

During the following season, Neil read this quote countless times, in search of his lost inspiration.

At the start of November, wrestling practice began. Neil dropped weight, going from 133 pounds to 120 pounds. During this period, Neil set the school record for the bench press as a percent of weight. Weighing 120 pounds, he bench-pressed 205 pounds. Neil was prepared and eager for his senior season. Like Neil, the entire team was ready. The team was projected to win the district tournament and was ranked eighth in the state. Neil and Chris were elected captains of the team.

Neil planned to wrestle in the 112-pound class, but couldn't make the weight. So, he wrestled in the 119-pound class.

The first tournament of the year was at Bennington. As a returning state qualifier, Neil was seeded first. In the first match, Neil lived up to his reputation, pinning his opponent in 50 seconds. The second match was against James

Rock from Boys Town. For the first two and a half periods, Neil dominated him. He took him down, put him on his back, put him in Cradles, put him in Chicken Wings. With less than a minute to go, Neil was leading 11-0. Neil was on top, riding him. Then, James did a sit out. In an effort to prevent his escape, Neil accidentally hung his head over his right shoulder, the same mistake he made eight months earlier in the state quarterfinal match. The result was the same. James grabbed Neil's head, rolled him over and pinned him.

Devastated by the loss, Neil's confidence was crushed. Twice he made the same mistake, twice the same result. Neil wrestled back and took third place.

For the next five weeks, Neil was on a roller coaster. The next tournament, Neil didn't place. Then he won a dual meet.

After the Christmas break, Neil asked Coach Meyer if he could wrestle at the 125 pound class. He felt that the weight loss was sapping his strength. Wrestling at the higher weight, Neil lost his first match. He was totally dejected. Neil was getting pushed all over the mat. His record was 6-9. He knew he was better than that. Physically, he had never been stronger. After this loss, Neil was seriously considering quitting the team.

Upon returning home, he went straight to bed. He didn't want to talk to anyone. Lying in bed, unable to sleep, he heard his dad walk down the stairs and open his door. Taking a seat on the bottom step, Larry quietly said, "Neil, I want to talk to you."

"Can't this wait, Dad? I'm really not in a talking mood," Neil replied, not in the mood for another of his father's lectures.

"No Neil, this can't wait. I am very concerned about you," Larry replied and then continued, "Though your record doesn't show it and I know you don't feel like it, you are an outstanding wrestler. You are underestimating your physical and mental abilities. Neil, you are so much better than what you are showing on the wrestling mat. You have never been in better physical condition. Everything that is occurring to you on that mat is due to your mental attitude. The only way you can change the outcome of this season is to do it up here," Larry emphasized by tapping his temple with his finger. "It all begins and ends right here," Larry explained, once again tapping the side of his head. "You can do it. It's all in your mind. You're a winner. The problem is that you have convinced yourself that you are a loser."

Not expecting, nor wanting any response, Larry then rose and returned to his bedroom. Neil laid awake all night thinking about what his Dad said. He knew his Dad was right. For four years he worked to build his strength. He knew, just by wrestling his teammates, that he was one of the strongest wrestlers on the mat. None of his losses had been the result of losing to someone stronger.

Lying there analyzing his season, he determined the loss at Bennington had been his downfall. It had destroyed his confidence. Neil knew he must start over and forget about the first half of the season. He decided he would wrestle at 119 pounds. Motivated and determined, he pledged that a new season would begin that night.

The next tournament was at David City, where he wrestled well, taking second. He then took second at the Weeping Water tournament. His success continued through the conference tournament, where he found himself in the finals, wrestling Bob Kuchura, whom he had lost to earlier in the year.

He wrestled hard; he wrestled smart, but still found himself trailing after two periods, 4-2. In the third period, Kuchura, who was on the bottom, kept crawling out of bounds, to keep Neil from scoring any points. Neil lost, but felt good. He took second and had wrestled well. He was beating the wrestlers he was supposed to beat and wrestling the others close.

Neil entered the district tournament with a record of 21-13, nowhere near as good as the previous year. Even so, he was seeded second behind a wrestler from Tri-County, Byron Beerenstrauch. Neil won his first match by pin, won his second 11-0, and won the semifinal match 15-0.

The final match was one of the most unbelievable of Neil's career. The lead bounced back and forth. Neil would score a takedown, and then Byron would escape. With fifteen seconds remaining, Neil reversed Byron, taking a 10-9 lead. Then, with eight seconds left, Byron reversed Neil, taking an 11-10 lead, which was the final score. After shaking hands, they walked off the mat together to a standing ovation. The entire crowd rose, applauding and screaming. Everyone knew they had just watched an incredible match. They also knew these two gladiators would meet again at the state tournament.

Once again, Neil was the darling of the press. The following week there were more interviews at school. The Wednesday night before the state tournament, Neil and Chris went to the Prairie Life Center. It was a fitness center frequented by the Fort Calhoun wrestling team. Neil was trying to lose some weight. He went into the sauna, where a man was reading the newspaper. The man finished his reading and put down his newspaper. He looked up at Neil. Then he grabbed his newspaper and looked at it again. Then looked at Neil again, and exclaimed, "You're the guy in the newspaper!"

"I guess so," Neil replied.

"Yeah you're the guy right here on the front page of the sports page! You're the guy in the newspaper!"

"Yes, I am."

He then began to pepper Neil with questions about his wrestling. Neil politely tried to answer his questions, privately wishing he could escape.

The next day, Valentines Day, February 14, 1992, the state tournament began. In the first match, Neil won 12-0. In the quarterfinal match, Neil's opponent was the returning state runner up. In the first period, Neil took a lead, 2-0. As the match continued, Neil's opponent was constantly fleeing to the out of bounds. Each time the referee would call them back to the center, Neil sensed that the referee was becoming frustrated with this stalling tactic. The referee was Phil Pasali. Neil knew him well. He had refereed many of Neil's matches. Finally, with fifteen seconds remaining in the period, the referee once again brought them to the center of the mat. When the referee blew his whistle, the kid immediately stood up and ran toward the out of bounds, dragging Neil behind him.

The referee helped Neil back to the center of the mat. Neil's opponent was walking off the mat.

"Hey, you! Get over here!" The referee shouted to the other wrestler. The referee grabbed him and asked, "Are you okay?"

"Yes."

"Well then get the heck in here and get down!"

At that point there was thirteen seconds left in the first period. Neil was on top. When the whistle blew, Neil immediately caught him in a cross face cradle. His shoulders hit the mat and the referee immediately slapped the mat, signaling a pin. Neil jumped to his feet. This victory had guaranteed him a medal. This was the first time Neil had celebrated a victory while on the mat. He always tried to be a good competitor. Neil never liked to show emotion, win or lose. He felt strongly that how a person acted after the match often showed more about that person than the match itself.

Regaining his composure, Neil pulled his opponent to his feet. After being announced the winner, Neil received a standing ovation, from the crowd of eight thousand people. Neil felt overwhelmed. His teammates, family and friends mobbed him, celebrating his victory. Shortly thereafter, came the press.

The semifinals were on Friday night. Warming up on the mat, Neil was apprehensive. His stomach was tight and he was shaking. Neil wrestled a close match, losing 4-0. With this loss, he lost his last chance to be in the "Parade of Champions." Though disappointed, Neil could not dwell on this defeat. The next day he had to wrestle again. If he won, he would then wrestle for third or fourth. Neil won, dominating 10-0.

In the final match of his high school wrestling career, he was once again pitted against Byron Beerenstrauch. This match was completely different than the previous one. They both knew each other so well, that it was a low scoring, defensive battle. Neil lost 2-1, placing fourth in the state tournament.

Later that afternoon, when they called the winners to the medallist stand, Byron approached Neil,

"Neil, I would be honored if I could walk you to the medallist stand."

Two young men, who had waged war in the trenches of the wrestling mat, proudly marched together, to be honored for their dedication and success. When Neil was presented his medal, the crowd erupted, standing, applauding and shouting his praises. To his surprise, the other wrestlers all turned to him and applauded. This was the honor that meant the most to Neil.

After receiving his medal, his parents and brother all congratulated him. As Ryan hugged Neil, Neil whispered,

"I did it. I finally won our medal. It took three years, but I did it. This is our medal."

Lying in bed, Neil was amazed how he could still recall all of his wrestling matches in such detail. He was proud of his success, but he was sad that it was over. It was time to move on. Today, that meant a big, big breakfast. He had four years of starvation to make up for and he wasn't going to waste any time. His father had promised to take him to the restaurant at the top of the Red Lion Hotel, for their breakfast buffet. Hearing his father call, Neil was ready to go in fifteen minutes. They spent two hours eating and talking. Neil couldn't remember the last time he ate so much. Neil started with the breakfast selections. He had a ham and cheese omelet, eggs benedict, and several servings of sausage and bacon. It had been months since he had eaten any meat. Then came the pancakes and syrup. Once Neil was full, he and his Dad talked, reliving his wrestling career. After an hour, Neil was ready for more food. This time he attacked the dessert table, eating some cheesecake, several pieces of pie and some carrot cake. Larry, who was known as a big eater couldn't keep up with his son. He watched in awe while Neil ate entrée after entrée. Finally, Neil announced he was full.

On the way home, Larry suddenly turned very serious and said, "Son, I am so proud of you. What you have accomplished is beyond my greatest expectations."

Tears streaming down his cheeks, Larry struggled to continue, "When I first stood over your crib at the hospital and saw you lying there so helpless, in such pain, I whispered a promise in your ear. I swore to you I would do everything I could to allow you to be like all the other children, to be normal. Neil, never in my wildest dreams, did I imagine this. You are a walking miracle. I am honored to be your father."

# Graduation Day

Sunday, May 24, 1992, a day that once seemed a hopeless dream was now a reality. It was a day of personal victory and celebration. It was Neil's high school graduation. Linda rose early that morning. She and Larry had spent most of the night reminiscing. Remembering the accident and the many challenges Neil faced; reveling in Neil's many accomplishments; the night was a mixture of tears and laughter.

The graduation ceremony was not until 3:00 that afternoon, but there was much to be done. They were having Neil's graduation party at the house, right after the ceremony. Linda anticipated a large crowd. This was more than just a family celebrating their son's triumphs. It was a community celebration. From the day of Neil's accident to this very day, many people helped the family. Rightfully so, they all felt a personal pride in Neil's graduation.

While Linda was preparing the food for the party, Larry entered the kitchen. "What's for breakfast?" he asked, hugging her from behind and giving her a little peck on the cheek. It was a rhetorical question. He knew she had no intention of cooking breakfast.

Ignoring the question, Linda immediately began to list Larry's tasks for the day. She was the cook. Larry was to prepare the picnic area. They had a beautiful setting. Their house was situated on a two-acre lot, surrounded by large trees. The kitchen exited to a large redwood deck with two levels. From the lower deck, several steps lead to the patio, which surrounded the swimming pool.

Over the years, the house had been the scene of many parties. So Larry knew exactly what Linda wanted. Linda was very nervous and wanted everything to be just right. Larry was a big practical joker. He loved to get "Miss Linda," as he called her, to react. Today there were no jokes. He worked quietly and diligently, obeying her every command.

Yesterday, Larry spent most of the day mowing and manicuring the lawn. Even with a riding mower, the size of the lot made it an all day project. It had been an unusually warm spring, so the pool was already cleaned and in use.

Neil and Ryan slept late, making an appearance just before noon. Linda knew this was the result of a late party last night and their desire to avoid any work.

Lunch consisted of cold cuts. It was every man for himself.

Even though the ceremony did not begin until 3:00 p.m., Linda wanted to get there no later than 2:00 p.m. to ensure the family could sit together, close to the stage. The ceremony, like all the years before, was held in the high school gym. The combination of bleachers and chairs positioned on the floor accommodated about five hundred people. Each year it was standing room only. The high school graduation was Fort Calhoun's social event of the year. People came, regardless of whether they had a relative graduating. At times like this, the town was just one big family. This year, it would be especially crowded. The town's favorite son, her son, Neil was graduating.

With strong encouragement, which Larry called nagging; Linda managed to get her family to the school by 2:00 p.m. To her surprise, the gym was already beginning to fill. She spotted the seats she wanted. Like an Army sergeant, she marched to the seats, her family following in step. There was Linda, Larry, Ryan, their friend Frank, Linda's sister Marla, her husband Dave and their two children, Linda's mother, Linda's brother David, his wife Sharry and their two children, Larry's brother Darrell, his wife Betsy and their two children: seventeen in all.

The program detailed the ceremony. It listed all forty-one graduating seniors. Neil was one of the main participants in the ceremony. He sang in the choir, he had a solo, he was the recipient of two scholarships, and of course, he would get his diploma. This was one of the proudest moments of Linda and Larry's lives.

While his family was finding their seats, Neil gathered in the school's common area with his fellow graduates. He had mixed feelings as he found his assigned position in the procession. This school had been the site of some of his greatest accomplishments. His wrestling conquests, his scholastic achievements, his musical talents, and most importantly, his ability to compete in the sighted world, were the product of his years at this school. He felt confident. He was prepared to take the next step in his life's journey, college. Neil was graduating with a 3.4 GPA and achieved a score of 25 on his ACT college entrance tests. He was anxious to go to college, but he was also sad. He would miss the friendships he had forged over the years and the comradeship of his fellow students and teachers.

By the time the ceremony began, the gymnasium was filled. As expected, it was standing room only. Unexpectedly, the ceremony began on time. The National anthem was followed by the procession of the graduating seniors. The local pastor offered a prayer followed by a welcome from the school superintendent. The valedictorian and salutatorian then gave their speeches.

During their speeches, Linda looked around the crowd. Suddenly her eyes met Sharry Ringler's, her sister-in-law. They both instantly started to cry. Sharry had played a major role in Neil's success. In fact, just the other night, Neil, Larry and her, while reminiscing, had talked about how big an impact Sharry had on Neil's life. They all agreed, that without Sharry, Neil could not have attended the Fort Calhoun schools.

It all started during Neil's second year at NSVH. Sharry often accompanied Linda on Fridays, when she would drive to Nebraska City to bring Neil home for the weekend. At the time, she was not working. Many times, when Linda had a conflict, Sharry would drive down to pick up Neil. For some time,

Neil's school counselor had been encouraging Linda to have someone in the family learn braille. Unlike most students, Neil returned home every weekend. She was concerned that if Neil could not return to the school for several days, either because of illness or poor weather, he would quickly fall behind the rest of his class. If a family member learned braille, he could keep up with his schoolwork when he was home.

One day, while at the school with Linda, Sharry unexpectedly volunteered for the job. Linda was not surprised. Sharry had an insatiable appetite for learning. The counselor, not allowing her any time to reconsider, immediately provided her with a braillewriter, a "Cheat Sheet," some paper, and the address and telephone number to the Library of Congress, which supervises the national certification program for braille transcribers.

Larry and Linda were ecstatic about Sharry's interest. For some time they had been discussing the possibility of transferring Neil to the Fort Calhoun schools. They knew they would have to have a braille transcriber to assist Neil. This was problematic because they knew there were few certified transcribers in the state of Nebraska. Sharry was perfect. She loved children and they loved her. Also, she could be a very stubborn person. This proved to be a valuable asset, especially in dealing with the teachers.

Sharry immediately contacted the Library of Congress and registered for the certification course. It was a two-year program. Mrs. Bender, the wife of the superintendent and a teacher at the NSVH, volunteered to help Sharry by reviewing her work. Every Friday, when Sharry came for Neil, Mrs. Bender would check Sharry's work. Sharry enjoyed the education.

She operated a day-care center out of her house. The kids would arrive at 6:30 a.m. She would put them in bed and study, until 8:00 a.m. Then, while they were taking their afternoon naps, she would study braille. After the parents picked up the kids, until dinnertime, she would study. At night, she would enlist the help of her husband, Linda's older brother, David. After their two children were in bed, Sharry would relax in the tub, while Dave sat on the bathroom toilet, quizzing her on the meanings of the different symbols. This was her daily routine. Her motivation and determination paid off. She became certified in a record six months.

When Neil transferred to the Fort Calhoun schools, Sharry quickly became much more than just Neil's transcriber. She became his advocate, ensuring Neil received the same education as the other students. The teachers were often not prepared for Neil. The summer before each school year, Sharry would meet with Neil's teacher and obtain a list of books and textbooks Neil would be using. She would then have them transcribed by the time school started. The school provided an office for Sharry, to ensure Neil and the teachers had access to her during the school day.

Often the teachers would make decisions they thought would help Neil, when they actually hurt him. Sharry was a constant advocate and educational guardian for Neil. Linda remembered one glaring example. In the third grade, Neil's first year at Fort Calhoun Elementary School, his teacher would give the students twenty spelling words each week.

Early in the year, Neil showed Sharry his spelling words. There were only ten. Sharry went to the teacher and inquired why Neil was given only ten words and the other students were given twenty. The teacher indicated that she realized how difficult and time consuming it was for Neil to braille all the words, so she didn't want to overload him with work. Sharry's reply was to ask the teacher when she thought Neil would learn the other ten words. From that point on, the teachers at the school treated Neil the same as the sighted students.

Sharry worked long hours, for low pay, going the extra mile to help Neil obtain an education. Larry and Linda owed her a debt they could never repay.

Abruptly, Linda's thoughts returned to the present, when Mrs. Boeka, the choir director and music teacher, stood and moved to the music stand in front of the choir. The highlight of each graduation ceremony was the school choir. For years, the choir was rated as one of the best in the entire state. Neil sang with the choir all four years of high school. During that time, each year the choir received the highest rating in the state, and Neil, as the choir's featured soloist, also received the top rating. Neil had a beautiful tenor voice. On her signal, the choir arose in unison. Neil, taking a microphone in hand, immediately walked to Mrs. Boeka. He whispered to her. Looking surprised, she motioned with her hands for the choir to wait. Neil stepped to the edge of the stage and faced the audience.

Linda and Larry looked at each other, their eyes questioning, "Do you know what's going on?" They didn't.

Neil began to address the crowd, "Before I sing this song, I want to take a moment to thank you. 'Corner of the Sky' is one of my favorite songs. As you know, since a very young age I have struggled to find my 'Corner of the Sky.' Graduating from Fort Calhoun High School has been one of my dreams. Each and every one of you have helped me. Some have played a large role in my life and some have helped me in small ways. I know if I had lived any place else, I would not be here today. You have all helped me find my 'Corner of the Sky.' I dedicate this song to you as a token of my appreciation."

With tears streaming down her face, Linda turned to Larry. To her surprise, even Larry, who considered himself to be a "man's man," was wiping his eyes. She was so proud of Neil. Times like this reminded her of what an extraordinary young man Neil had become.

Motioning to Mrs. Boeka, Neil signaled he was ready. Fighting back her tears, she tapped her baton and the song began. Neil never sounded better. As he sang, each word carried a special meaning that day.

"Everything has its season
Everything has its time
Show me a reason and I'll show you a rhyme . . .

. . . Rivers belong where they can ramble
Eagles belong where they can fly
I've got to be where my spirit can run free
Got to find my corner of the sky."

Finishing the last word, Neil returned the microphone to its stand and took his seat with the choir. The crowd immediately erupted into a standing ovation. When the applause subsided, the choir sang another song. Then, several short speeches followed.

Frank Starr, who had been raised in large cities, primarily Detroit, was impressed by the ceremony. He was one of seven hundred students in his graduating class. His ceremony had been long, tedious and absent the emotion and sense of real love that filled this gymnasium. The role that religion played in this ceremony pleased and surprised him. In cities all over the country, people were suing and winning; taking the separation of church and state to the extreme. Here, the local minister gave an invocation, presented a short sermon and ended the ceremony with a benediction. A reflection of their lives, God played a large role in this ceremony.

"Neil Halford," the president of the School Board called his name. Neil rose and was escorted by Holly Hassel, the student who was named next. When Neil received his diploma, the crowd once again rose, offering another standing ovation. It was a sign of their respect, but also their way of saying good-bye.

## POSTSCRIPT — CHAPTER FOUR

*My graduation from high school marked the close of the most significant time in my life. During these years, I developed into the person I am today. My personality, my sense of humor, my love for sports, my self-confidence and my physique, were all developed during high school. They challenged me mentally and academically, teaching me logic and expanding my horizons. I was happy with the person I became and loved the life I was living. My greatest strengths were the product of my four years of wrestling. Aside from my physical strength, my greatest asset was my determination. Through the highs and lows of my wrestling career, I learned that to reach a goal, I had to be determined, dedicated, and willing to make whatever sacrifices were necessary. Because of my special challenges, every success in my life has required extraordinary effort. To this day, I have an unwavering resolve, a sense of purpose, which guides me through my life. It is the key to my every success, large or small.*

*After graduation, I was overcome with a strong feeling of sadness. I knew my life was about to change. I would be leaving behind four of my best friends. Jay and I had been inseparable since the third grade. He planned to stay in Fort Calhoun, I was going away to college. Seth had joined the Navy, and Jason and Kirt were still in high school. I was concerned that our friendships would not survive.*

*I was also closing the door on my wrestling career. For the last four years, I dedicated much of my life to wrestling. My parents also devoted much of their time in support of my wrestling. My mother was my greatest fan. Without her support, I would not have had the success I experienced. Every night, she would have to prepare a special meal for me to conform to my wrestling diet. Mom also provided me with special treats at every meet. In addition to me, she was like a second mother to my best friend, Chris, feeding and cheering him.*

*It was after my graduation that I learned about her greatest contribution to my wrestling success. Mom was and still is very superstitious. My senior year, after the Christmas break, I won my first match against a strong opponent. From that moment on, for each meet, my Mom made sure I wore the same underwear, socks and hat.*

*Although it required great dedication and sacrifice, it was fun and exciting. The lessons I learned on the wrestling mat have served me well in life. Knowing it was over, I felt empty, like a part of me had died. There was a void in my life I didn't know how I would fill.*

*As you can tell from the stories, my house was a popular gathering place. Through the years, the ATV, the trampoline and the pool were the center of entertainment for my friends and me. My summers were so much fun. It was as close to living in Disneyland as I can imagine. I realized I led a spoiled and charmed life. I knew it would soon come to a close.*

*With my life in such a state of flux, there was only one thing to do. I concentrated on women, parties, and spending as much time as possible with my friends. It was a summer to remember.*

# Chapter Five

## Introduction

*With the summer quickly coming to an end, my thoughts turned to the future, my college years. To my surprise, the powerful memories of the last time I left home for school, returned. Even though I was much older, many of the same emotions, fears and apprehensions resurfaced.*

*At the same time, I was excited. I was anxious to finally leave the security of my family and the small town, and enter the "real world." I was ready to be a man, with no strings attached, no parental supervision. Quickly and abruptly, I was greeted by the harsh realities of life. The most significant shock was money. I never worried about money. My parents always gave me what I needed. My parents still helped me, but, now, I was on a tight budget. This was an unexpected curve ball, which considerably affected my social plans. I couldn't believe it! I had to get a job! Suddenly, the "real world" did not seem as enticing as I first thought.*

*In spite of the early reality check, college was challenging and fun. My college of choice, the University of Nebraska at Kearney, proved to be fortuitous. It was large enough to offer an excellent curriculum, but small enough that I did not feel like I was just a number. It was more like a community than a school. In many ways, it was much like living in Fort Calhoun. The publicity I received during my high school wrestling career proved helpful. It seemed like everywhere I went, people recognized me from the numerous newspaper and television reports. Having my best friend, Chris, as my roommate, also helped. He was well acquainted with the challenges I faced each day and instinctively knew when and how to help. More importantly, Chris was a "chick magnet."*

# The College Years

In preparation for college during his senior year, Neil took the ACT test. This is a nationally certified series of tests, which is required for admittance to college. Because of Neil's special circumstances, special arrangements were taken to administer the test. Normally a testing site, usually a large auditorium, is designated. All the applicants take the test, which has certain time requirements, in the presence of several monitors.

His test was administered at the Fort Calhoun High School. His Aunt Sharry, who had been his braille transcriber throughout his public school years, read him the test. Neil would tell her the answer and she would mark his answer on the form provided. With the more difficult math problems, Neil would use his braillewriter to assist with the calculations. The way Neil was required to take the test, especially when he had to use his braillewriter, was time consuming. Even with this disadvantage, Neil did very well, scoring a 25. Thus, he was eligible to attend any of the private or public colleges in Nebraska.

Neil and his parents spent many hours during his senior year of high school discussing his selection of a college. Financially, Neil's choice of colleges was limited to Nebraska. Because he was blind, the State of Nebraska paid for all of his college expenses; tuition, room and board, books and readers. A reader is a student hired by the state to read textbooks required by the various classes. He was allowed forty hours per month. Neil's only requirement was to maintain a grade point average of 2.5 or better.

Finally, to the delight of his parents, Neil chose to attend the University of Nebraska at Kearney. There were several reasons for his choice. It was an outstanding college, which was large enough to offer Neil a wide selection of potential majors, yet small enough to allow Neil to flourish socially. Ryan attended the same college and would be a senior. As he had done many times before, once again Ryan would be Neil's mentor and protector. This especially made Larry and Linda feel more comfortable. Neil had visited Ryan at college several times. Thus, he already knew some students and was familiar with the campus.

Chris Nelson, who Neil first met at Fort Calhoun elementary school, was now one of his best friends. He was more like a brother than a friend. During their senior year in high school, due to problems between his divorced parents, Chris lived at the Halford's. Linda and Larry considered him to be part of their family.

They decided to attend the same college. Out of a sense of security, of having a good friend in a strange, new place, Chris wanted to follow Neil. Neil didn't mind because Chris was always surrounded by beautiful women. This had proved advantageous to Neil during high school and he hoped it would continue in college.

The week before school began, Larry, Neil and Max went to the school. Max was Neil's guide dog. Earlier that summer, Neil spent a month in Rochester, Michigan, becoming acquainted with Max and learning how to work with a guide dog. He could no longer rely on friends and family to assist him and Neil still refused to use a cane. So, Max was the answer. In two short months, Neil and Max had become great friends. Kearney was about two hundred miles west of Fort Calhoun. For two days, Larry, walked the campus with Neil and Max, familiarizing them with the location of all of his classes, his dormitory and the other major buildings.

Finally, the day arrived. The Saturday before the classes were scheduled to start, they packed Larry's pickup truck with all of Neil's and Chris' belongings. Then, Linda, Larry, Chris, Neil and Max crammed into the truck and drove to Kearney. Chris and Neil were to be roommates. Their room was on the third floor of the dormitory called Manor Hall. After hauling everything up three flights of stairs, the men went to Ryan's apartment to watch a football game and relax. Linda spent several hours organizing their room. Linda was a perfectionist, a neat freak. She preferred to work alone. Larry learned long ago to never bother Linda when she was cleaning. Several hours later, when the men returned, the room was immaculate and the refrigerator was fully stocked.

After his parents left, Neil and Chris decided to check out the nightlife. There was a dance at the student union. Neither Neil nor Chris enjoyed dancing, so they hung outside the union. Chris would give Neil a "blow by blow" description of the women, but they never really met anyone. Finally, bored, Chris exclaimed, "I feel like a dork, let's get out of here."

They returned to the dorm and spent the rest of the night in their room, falling asleep early. It was not what they had planned, what they had dreamed would be their first night on campus.

Lying in bed, Neil was overwhelmed with emotions from the past. Since his three years at the Nebraska School for the Visually Handicapped, this was the first time he had left home. The fears, the loneliness, and the frustrations returned in a rush. Once again, he silently cried himself to sleep.

Monday morning came and Neil was up early. Being an early riser, he scheduled morning classes, with his first class starting at 8:00 a.m. On the other hand, Chris loved to sleep late, so he scheduled afternoon classes. Neil and Max left early for his class, to ensure he had plenty of time, in case something went wrong. He inherited this from his mother. Linda was always early for everything. She hated being late.

It was a cold, rainy morning. En route to his first class, the sidewalk split into a Y. His class was in Founders Hall, which was to the right. Confused by the lack of a distinct intersection, Max continued to the left. After a while, Neil realized they hadn't turned right. From his exploration with his Dad, he knew he needed to go to the right. He was sure they had missed the turn. He and

Max retraced their steps. On the second try, Max again stayed to the left. Again, they returned to the dorm and started over. For the third time, Max went left. Neil was now getting frustrated. He was worried he would be late for his first class. He was getting soaked and was sure that he looked like a "dork." If anybody had been watching him, he was sure they would think he was crazy.

"Can I help you?" a strange voice asked. "Where are you trying to go?"

"I've got a class in Founders Hall." Neil replied; relieved help had arrived.

"You missed the turn. It's not very far. I would be happy to take you."

"Thanks. It's my first day and I don't want to be late for my first class." Leading Neil by the arm, they quickly arrived at the intersection. "I can find my way from here. Thanks, again." Neil said, as Max began to lead him down the right path.

"Good luck. Don't worry. You've got plenty of time before the class starts.

Following Max's lead, Neil was relieved. One Good Samaritan wiped away his fears about his ability to negotiate college life. He was kind, he was helpful, and he wasn't condescending. He accepted Neil without any question. This one encounter had renewed Neil's self-confidence.

Neil arrived at the classroom early. He sat in the front row. Max silently laid next to his desk for the entire class. Neil preferred the front row. He felt like he was more a part of the class. It also quietly brought him to the attention of the professor, to ensure the professor was aware of Neil and wouldn't forget to speak when he wrote on the board.

After the class was over, Neil approached the dais and announced, "Professor Briner, my name is Neil Halford."

"Welcome to my class, Neil," the professor replied enthusiastically.

"I wanted you to be aware I am in your class and to assure you that nothing special will be required. The only thing I ask is that when you write on the board you also say what you are writing," Neil explained.

"I was aware you would be attending this class and am very glad to meet you. As you can see from this first class, I constantly talk, so your request won't be a problem. Also, arrangements have been made for you to take tests for all of your classes at the counseling center, with the assistance of a reader. If you have any problems or questions, feel free to discuss them with me. I'll be glad to help anyway I can."

Neil thanked Professor Briner and headed to his next class. After his last class, he returned to his dorm, to find Chris just rising from a long sleep. "How were the classes?" Chris inquired.

"They were great. The professors were super. I really feel good about our decision to come here. Everyone is very friendly and supportive," Neil enthusiastically explained.

The first week was a time of adjustment, as Neil and Chris once again started studying. Though they were outgoing and readily introduced themselves to the other students in their dorm, they had not made any real friends. It seemed like everyone was just an acquaintance. Thursday night, Neil and Chris were playing poker with a deck of Neil's braille cards, gambling with their laundry money. Neil was fleecing Chris.

"Damn, dude, are these cards marked? Do you have some special braille code?" Chris asked sarcastically.

"No, I'm just a better player."

"It's just your usual stupid luck," Chris shouted, throwing in another losing hand.

Attracted by Chris' yelling, a student, unknown to either of them, suddenly appeared in their doorway, "What's happnin', dudes?" he asked, curious about the reason for all the noise.

After introductions and Neil's boasting of his poker expertise, they learned he was their neighbor, living two doors down. His name was Arthur. Everyone called him Art. Art decided to join the game. Even though Neil's luck continued, with him winning about ten dollars from each of his fellow card players, Art and Neil became friends. Art became one of Neil's few, lasting, college friends. During the four years Neil was at college, he got to know almost everyone, but only made a few close friends.

Later that first week, Ryan took Neil and Chris to his fraternity house. He was a member of the Sigma Tau Gamma fraternity. Both of them had been to several of the Sig Tau's parties, when they visited Ryan the previous year. So, they knew most of Ryan's fraternity brothers. Those students who are interested in belonging to a fraternity attend "rush" week. During this week the fraternities hold open houses for the students to visit and decide which fraternity they want to join. In Neil's and Chris' case, they had already decided on Sigma Tau Gamma.

Sigma Tau Gamma was the only fraternity, which was not housed in one of the new dormitories on campus. They had opted to remain off campus, in the old, colonial house which had been their home for years. Located off campus, it was the only fraternity, which did not have to adhere to the college's dry, non-drinking rules. Of course, Neil always insisted that this had no bearing on his decision.

From that point on they never spent another weekend night at their dorm. Every Friday and Saturday night, they would party at the Frat house or attend a party sponsored by another fraternity. The fraternity house had converted the basement into a large party room. It seemed like every weekend was a continuous party. Neil was surprised so many people knew about him. He hadn't realized how widespread the notoriety he received during his last two wrestling seasons had been. It seemed like at every party and most of his classes, someone would always come up to him and tell him they had read about him.

Jodie Halford, Neil's cousin, also attended this college. She was a sophomore. Ryan and Neil were close to her and her younger brother, Ross. Jodie was a beautiful young lady, who was popular. Many of the school's football players were friends with Jodie. She lived in a house near the campus. Neil quickly fell into a routine of visiting Jodie every Thursday night and accompanying her to a party. The students had a tradition of distributing a list of all upcoming parties, every Thursday afternoon. Jodie knew the best parties and was always welcome. Accompanying Jodie got Neil into these parties and access to many beautiful women.

Neil did not see Ryan as much as he and his parents had anticipated. Ryan lived in an apartment. He was a senior and seriously involved with a young lady named Julie. Ryan, though a member of the fraternity, was not very active. Occasionally, Neil would see him at a frat party. Once a month, Ryan would invite Neil and Chris to his apartment for steak and beer. Neil liked being independent from Ryan. He knew if he ever needed help, Ryan would always be there.

Blessed with an extraordinary memory, Neil was able to take "short cuts" when studying. He based all of his studying on the notes he would take in class. He had been provided with a Braille and Speak. This was a small braille-writer, about the size of a walkman. While in class, he would type his notes on the braillewriter. When he studied for a test, the machine would verbally read his notes. This would save him the hours it would take to read the notes in Braille with his fingers. The Braille and Speak could be directly connected to a printer, enabling him to then print out his notes for other students. Neil quickly became renowned for his extensive notes. He was in great demand by many study groups.

The State of Nebraska provided Neil with the funds to purchase his required textbooks. In the four years Neil was at college, he never opened one textbook. He relied totally on his notes and discussions within his various study groups. Neil would score average, B's and C's, on his tests, but would always get an A on his essays, which generally accounted for a large part of each class' final grade. Neil was an outstanding writer. Whenever a paper was due, he would always wait until the night before the due date. With the help of a six-pack, he would spend the night writing the essay.

All of his tests were administered in the counseling office. A reader would read each question and Neil would choose the appropriate answer. The reader would record the answer. Once complete, the reader would deliver the test to the appropriate professor for grading. The first semester, Neil was struggling in his Psychology class. Going into the final exam. He had a low C average. When he walked into the counseling center to take the Psychology final exam, he discovered his reader was Michelle. Neil had met her through his cousin, Jodie. They had been to many of the same parties.

When they were alone in the conference room, Michelle asked, "Are you ready, Neil?"

"I guess. I'm really nervous. I have a C average in this class. If I don't do well, my grade point average will be a disaster. If I don't get at least a 2.5 average, I will lose all of my funding."

Michelle, trying to encourage Neil, replied, "Neil, I am sure you will do well. Just listen carefully, as I read each question."

"I'll try. Let's get started."

Michelle then proceeded to read the first question. It was a multiple-choice test. After reading the question, she read the four possible answers. Neil hesitated, then answered, "I think it is B."

"You need to listen very carefully," Michelle cautioned. She then proceeded to reread the answers, strongly emphasizing the A answer. Neil immediately understood what she was doing and changed his answer to A. They proceeded to do the entire test. Anytime Michelle would repeat the answers, Neil knew he had selected the wrong answer and would carefully listen for the answer she emphasized, changing his answer accordingly. Neil was not surprised when he learned he had received an A on the final exam, giving him a GPA of 3.1 for the semester. This was the only time this ever happened, but Neil knew it couldn't have come at a better time.

The second semester was a continuation of the first, with an emphasis on the parties. He again achieved a 3.1 GPA.

His sophomore year proved to be very eventful. Neil and Chris moved into an apartment where they lived for the next three years. In an effort to maximize their party time, Chris and Neil made a major mistake the first semester. They decided to take classes that were only scheduled for Tuesdays and Thursdays. This meant they would be in school for almost eight hours each of these two days, but would have no classes on Monday, Wednesday and Friday. It did not work as planned. They would often skip their late afternoon classes. Many of these courses would penalize students who skipped classes, thus lowering the student's final grade.

In addition, Bill Davis, the head of campus security, offered Neil a job answering the telephones. Neil's predecessor had also been blind, so their system was voice activated. Neil accepted the job and worked ten to fifteen hours per week until he graduated. Neil's social life continued to prosper. He became even more active in the fraternity. This combination almost proved fatal for Neil's college career. He only achieved a GPA of 2.1 for that semester. The second semester he changed his schedule and did much better, bringing his GPA for the sophomore year up to 2.9. Thus, he was allowed to keep his funding.

He had learned his lesson. The last two years of college, he continued to work, but he returned to a more reasonable class schedule and cut down on the drinking and partying. He became serious about a girl in Fort Calhoun, Carrie Conradson. They went steady for his last two years of college. This greatly curtailed his social life, as he was falling in love.

Neil graduated on May 3, 1996, with a combined GPA of 3.36 and a Bachelor's Degree in Sports Administration. He had completed his degree in four years. Neil made the Dean's List, in his last semester. Unfortunately, Chris dropped out of college after his sophomore year. He continued to live with Neil and worked as a security guard at the school.

All of Neil's relatives came to Kearney for the graduation. The graduation ceremony was held in the sports arena. Neil did not use Max, but rather a fellow graduate, to lead him to the stage to receive his certificate.

After the ceremony, the Halford's hosted a big party at the local Holiday Inn, where they were all staying. The ceremony ended at noon, so the party began with a large buffet lunch at the pool. The party continued at the pool throughout the afternoon. That night, the party adjourned to the bar, where a band was performing. The celebration ended in the early morning hours.

After a large family breakfast, Larry, Linda, Chris and Neil went to the apartment and loaded Larry's truck with all of Neil's belongings. Chris planned to remain in Kearney and to continue to work. When they started the long drive home, Neil sadly realized that another chapter in his life had closed.

# Making Friends

"Thanks, guys. See you tomorrow," Neil waved when they drove away.

He'd spent the night partying at the frat house. Slightly inebriated and tired, he talked some of his brothers into driving him back to the dorm. Walking toward the entrance, he heard people yelling. He couldn't make out what they were saying, but he could tell something was wrong.

Entering Manor Hall, the words became clear. There were several voices, pleading, "Think about what you're doing! Don't jump! Things can't be that bad, Tim!"

Stumbling up the stairs, Neil wondered what was going on and who was Tim. When he reached the third floor, he saw a crowd gathered by his room. Reaching the crowd, he asked the nearest student, "What the @%?&$! is going on?"

"It's Tim! He's going to jump out his window!" The boy excitedly explained.

Even though Tim lived next door to Neil, they had never met. Neil couldn't believe it.

"What the @%?&$! are you guys talking about!"

"No, dude, he says he is going to jump out his window!"

Becoming a believer, Neil had mixed feelings. Because of everything he had endured, Neil had a big heart. His friends at times called him a sucker. He would fall for any sob story. On the other hand, he had no sympathy for those who were weak. He had overcome great obstacles and he couldn't tolerate those who folded at the first sign of trouble.

Each dorm room had two large, double windows. Below the window was the air conditioning unit. Tim had opened his windows, removed the screens and was standing on the air conditioner, threatening to jump.

Neil didn't know why Tim was contemplating such drastic action. As Neil listened, the spectacle continued. People were begging Tim to climb down and Tim was threatening to jump. Nothing was changing. Neil was drunk and tired. He wanted to go to sleep. As long as this sideshow continued, he knew he would not get any sleep. So he decided to end it.

Pushing his way through the crowd, Neil demanded, "Let me through, @%?&$!

When he finally broke through, Neil walked straight to Tim, grabbed him by the waist and legs, picked him up and started to push him out the window, yelling, "Tim, you want to jump dude? You want to go out the window! Let me help you! Let me help you out! Go ahead and jump! You want to jump? Go! I'll help you! I'll even go down and pick up the pieces!"

While he was talking, Neil pushed Tim further out the window. The crowd stood in stunned silence, thinking Neil was crazy; fearing he was going to push Tim to his death. Tim, overcoming his initial shock at Neil's ranting and raving, suddenly realized he didn't want to jump and started to fight back. Hitting and kicking, he screamed, "Get the @%?&$! away from me! What the @%?&$! are you doing? Let me down, @%?&$!, let me down!"

Neil then helped him down from the window. Recognizing the excitement was over, the crowd quickly dispersed.

"Are you okay? Neil asked with concern in his voice.

"What were you thinking, dude? Pushing me out the window like that!" Tim asked, still incensed by Neil's actions.

"I wanted to show you what it was really like. You were never in any real danger. I had a tight grip on you."

"Dude, you are crazy!"

"It worked. You aren't thinking about jumping anymore," Neil explained.

His adrenalin rush over, Tim calmed down. Recognizing what Neil had done, he thanked him, "Hey dude, I owe you. I still think you're insane, but thanks. I don't know what I was thinking."

That night, Neil never went to sleep. Tim and Neil spent the entire night talking. From that moment on, they became close friends.

# The Fight

Neil's freshman year was rapidly coming to a close. In the last weeks of school, the parties were more frequent and much wilder. It was a Thursday night, one of Neil's regular party nights. The list of parties for that night was unusually long. Chris was working, so Art and Neil planned to go together. Jodie invited them to join her and several of her girl friends. They all squeezed into two cars. Neil and Art did not complain.

Upon arriving at the first party, they exited the cars. Neil led the way. He knew he would be the hero of the party. Any guy who brought eleven women to a party was always welcome. The house was large, with a front porch that wrapped around one side. Upon climbing the stairs, Jodie recognized some friends and started talking to them. The porch was crowded, so Neil, Art and the other girl's hung out, talking with some of the crowd.

Suddenly, without any warning, a young man came out of the house and yelled, "Everybody, either get the @%?&$! out of here or get in the house!"

Together with the girls, Neil walked to the front door. When he got to the door, Neil started into the house. Before he could take his first step, the man, who had screamed the order, stretched his arm across Neil's chest, blocking his path. He was an imposing figure, standing over six feet and weighing 220 pounds.

"It's five dollars to get in the door," he demanded.

"We've brought our own beer," Neil replied.

"It's five dollars," the self-appointed sentry repeated.

"Man I'm bringing all these good looking chicks. We just bought all this beer. We've got eleven women with us. C'mon dude, be cool and let us in," Neil explained.

"Get the @%?&$! out of here!" he ordered, pushing Neil.

"Don't get all bent out of shape. It's not that big a deal. I've got all these women. We just wanted to party . . ."

Before Neil completed his explanation, the doorman pushed him again and demanded, "Get the @%?&$! out of here!"

"Okay. Cool your jets. There are plenty of other parties. We'll leave."

Then the doorman repeatedly pushed Neil in the chest, while repeating his demand,

"Get the @%?&$! out of here!"

Neil, holding his ground, issued a warning, "Dude, don't you touch me again!" Ignoring Neil's threat, he again pushed Neil.

Responding by grabbing his shirt, Neil shoved him through the front door. Knocking the door off its hinges, he fell through the door on his back. Neil, still holding his shirt, fell on top of him. Instinctively, Neil started rapidly punching him in the face. Suddenly, someone grabbed Neil's hair from behind and jerked him to his feet. Neil immediately turned and swung, planning to hit him in the face. To Neil's surprise, his fist landed in his chest, knocking him back onto the porch. Neil knew he was in trouble. Based on where his punch had landed, he knew his new opponent was a big boy, standing well over six feet tall. Neil grabbed him around his waist, holding him close. This would prevent him from being able to throw any punches. Unbeknownst to Neil, while they were wrestling, the doorman had managed to regain his feet and bum rushed Neil from behind, hitting him in the back of the head. Neil grabbed him with his free arm, frantically trying to avoid the punches being thrown by his two foes. Then, out of sheer desperation, marshalling all of his strength, Neil pushed forward. All three broke through the porch railing and fell the four feet to the ground. Neil immediately got to his feet.

"Let's get the @%?&$! out of here!" Art yelled, grabbing Neil and leading him to the car.

By this time, the people in the house had spilled into the yard. There were people everywhere. Neil's two foes quickly arose and gave chase, only to be blocked by Jodie and her friends. There was total chaos. Everybody was yelling, shouting threats and calling names. When Neil reached the car, he suddenly stopped. Through the din of the crowd, he heard a familiar voice, "You let go of me, you son of a @%?&$! Don't you ever touch me again!"

It was his cousin Jodie. Neil immediately spun around and returned to the crowd, struggling to reach Jodie. Art was holding him back and the girls were yelling for him to leave, but he still tried to reach Jodie. Finally, Art got Neil in the car. Shortly thereafter, Jodie and the other girls joined them. After dropping the girls off at their apartment, Art and Neil drove back to the dorm.

Once there, Art related the events of the evening to a crowd, which had gathered around Neil's room. In the room next to Neil, lived Bob, who was a starting defensive tackle for the school's football team. He stood six foot four and weighed 260 pounds. Upon hearing the story, he was furious. He wanted to take Neil back to the house. He couldn't believe two guys, both larger than Neil, would take on a blind man, two against one. Neil finally calmed him down and went to bed.

The next morning, when he awoke, he could hardly move. The side of his head was skinned up, and his hand was swollen from the punches he had landed. His whole body ached. When he opened the door to go to the shower, there was a sign on his door, which read, "Neil Halford, the Muhammed Ali of Manor Hall."

# Driving Blind

"Do you want to go to a party at the trailer courts tonight, Neil? Jason's driving," Art asked, standing in the doorway to Neil's room.

Jason was Art's roommate. The three of them had been to many parties together. Chris was working that night. This was the first offer Neil had received all day. Fearing he might spend a Friday night alone, he decided to take Art up on his offer. The trailer courts were located two miles from the campus on the west side of town. Some of the wildest parties he'd attended were at the trailer courts.

"Sounds good, Art. When are we leaving?" Neil queried.

"Ten o'clock," Art answered, heading back to his room.

Neil wasn't surprised, and in fact he was pleased. Most parties began between 9:00 and 10:00 p.m. and lasted well into the early morning hours. This would give him enough time to take a quick shower and get dressed for another night on the prowl.

The party turned out to be a drag. The ratio of men to women was poor, and the women who were there did nothing for Neil. His hopes for the evening had been quickly dashed. What made matters worse was he couldn't even drown his sorrows in beer. Upon arriving, both Art and Jason had hit the keg hard, quickly becoming drunk. Neil didn't know how they were going to get home, but he knew someone had to stay sober. By default, he became the designated driver.

He had wanted to leave for some time and finally convinced Art, at 2:30 a.m., that they should call it quits. The only problem was transportation. Jason, even though he was drunk, had been hitting on this one girl for most of the night. He had no intention of leaving. Jason had other plans for the night.

"Jason, Neil and I are ready to leave, dude. Let us take your car. You can get a ride back with your girl in the morning, or give me a call and I'll come get you," Art suggested. Jason, locked in an embrace with his lady of choice, did not respond. Without looking, he tossed his car keys to Art.

As Art escorted Neil to the car, it was obvious he was seriously intoxicated. Though Art was leading the way, Neil was holding him, keeping him from falling. Art was more stumbling than walking to the car. "Art, are you okay?" Neil asked.

"Duuude, I am so hammered. I don't know howwww . . . we're getting home. There isss no way I can dribe," Art stated the obvious, struggling to speak.

"I can drive, but I'll need your help." Neil suggested.

"Youuuu can dribe? Noooo way!" Art slurred his words of disbelief.

"I can either drive with your help, or we sleep in the car," Neil explained.

When they finally arrived at the car, Neil put Art in the passenger's seat and slid in behind the steering wheel. Jason's car was a beat-up 1984 Datsun. It was a manual transmission, but that didn't bother Neil. This was not the first time Neil had driven.

Upon falling into the passenger seat, Art instantly fell asleep. Neil decided to let him take a quick nap, hoping he would be more alert after a short rest. Sitting in the car listening to Art snore, Neil reflected back on his driving experiences.

His Dad taught him on the country roads around Fort Calhoun. He would man the gas, brakes and gearshift and his Dad, as the passenger, would steer. His brother Ryan taught Neil how to shift a manual transmission, letting him drive his Bronco II. Many of his friends allowed Neil to drive during high school.

Neil's first recollection was one of his most memorable driving experiences. It happened during the spring of his junior year in high school. A friend of his, Jeremy, had been hangin' at Neil's house. Neil left a book he needed at school so Jeremy was going to drive him to school to get it. As they approached Jeremy's small Toyota pickup truck, Neil suggested, "Jeremy, do you want to shock the track team. They're practicing right now. Let me drive. When they see me driving, they'll go crazy."

"Dude, that's an awesome idea!" Jeremy agreed. "Let's do it!"

They quickly reached the school intersection. Neil skillfully executed the left turn onto the road that ran past the school's football field and the track that encircled it, en route to the school's entrance. Slowly driving by the field, Jeremy started laughing,

"Dude, you should see their faces! Everyone is looking at you. They can't believe this."

Suddenly, Jeremy's mood changed. He swore, "Oh, @%?&$!, it's a cop!"

"Where! Where is he!" Neil asked, with panic in his voice.

"He's pulling out of the school's parking lot, heading right for us."

"Well, there sure as @%?&$! isn't anything we can do about it now. We might as well relax and enjoy it."

The driver's side window was rolled down. Neil could hear the engine of the police car approaching. When the car was alongside, Neil turned toward the deputy and waved. In a reflex action, the deputy waved back. Then, suddenly recognizing Neil, he slammed on his brakes and took a second look. He couldn't believe his eyes. By the time he realized what was happening, Neil had turned the car into the school parking lot. Considering the fact that no harm had been done and that Neil's Dad was the mayor, the deputy proceeded with his patrol. Roaring with laughter, Jeremy exclaimed, "Dude, I can't believe you waved at him! You've got balls! You should have seen his face!"

The next day, Neil was the talk of the school.

Laughing to himself, he then recalled his most frightening driving experience, which occurred during the spring of his senior year. Chris had driven his old Ford pickup out to his mother's house. He needed to get some of his clothes for a school dance that night. Neil rode with him. When they got ready to leave, Neil asked if he could drive. Chris had allowed Neil to drive his truck many times. Even though it had a powerful 351 cubic inch engine and was a four speed manual transmission, Neil handled it with ease. So, Chris didn't hesitate to give him the keys.

Chris hung his clothes on the gun rack that was mounted on the rear window. It was a warm day, so both windows were rolled down. The wind created by the speed of the truck, whipped the hanging clothes, eventually blowing Chris' shirt out the window. Chris reacted without thinking. He took his hand off the steering wheel to catch the shirt, which was flying out the window. Neil, unaware that Chris had released the steering wheel, kept driving. The truck veered to the left, across the road and headed for the ditch and the trees that lined the road. Neil reacted by letting off the accelerator and slowly braking. Chris reacted immediately, grabbing the wheel and gradually steering it away from the impending danger and back onto the road. When Neil felt the safety of the road, he stopped and queried Chris, "What the @%?&$! were you doing?"

"My shirt blew out the window, so I let go of the wheel to catch it," Chris calmly explained.

"You mean we almost crashed because of your shirt?" Neil chastised.

"Dude, chill out. You were great. You didn't panic. You the man! I saved my shirt and we missed the trees. We make a great team!"

After giving each other a high five, Neil proceeded to drive to his house. During the remainder of the trip, neither one spoke. They both knew they had just escaped a potential disaster.

Neil started the Datsun and shifted into first gear. Art was still slumped down in the seat, with his eyes closed. Shaking him, Neil yelled, "Art, wake up!"

Art opened his eyes and squinted at Neil. "You are at least going to have to steer. I can do everything else, but I'm not steering. You have to do that! " Neil loudly explained, bringing Art back to life.

Art leaned over, propping his shoulder against the driver's seat and grabbed the steering wheel. "Let's go, Mario."

When Neil slowly released the clutch and the car lurched forward, gradually accelerating. "This clutch is shot!" Neil complained.

With Art barely awake and Neil struggling with the clutch, they slowly drove down 25th Street, one of Kearney's main streets. They stopped at 2nd Avenue and 25th Street, the main intersection in Kearney, waiting for the light to change. Holding the clutch to the floor, Neil revved the engine, trying to warm the car and keep the engine running. Neil had already killed the engine at two other lights. Art informed Neil, "The light is green."

In response, Neil popped the clutch, slammed it into first gear and floored the accelerator. The tires spun, the car whipped around, did a 180 degree turn and stalled. There they sat, a blind driver and a drunken guide, stalled at the town's busiest intersection, at 2:30 in the morning facing the oncoming traffic. Neil, knowing the situation required immediate action, pressed the clutch to the floor, gave it all the gas he could, and turned the key. The car started. Neil instantly slammed it in gear, dropped the clutch, and stomped on the accelerator. The car responded by doing another 180 and Neil proceeded to calmly drive the remaining half-mile to the campus.

"Neil, we are @%?&$! Someone had to have seen us!" Art exclaimed, with panic in his voice.

"Relax, Art, here's the dorm. We're home free," Neil assured him.

Pulling into the parking lot of Manor Hall, they were greeted by the entire dorm standing outside. Someone had pulled the fire alarm. There were two hundred witnesses to their driving escapades.

# One Lonely Night

During Neil's freshman year, a number of the fraternities joined together and rented the county fair grounds for a giant, "bring your own beer," party. They charged a $5 cover charge. There were several bands and a crowd that numbered in the hundreds. The fraternities made money and the students had a great time.

Because of Neil's notoriety during high school, he was well known. Though he didn't know that many students, almost all of them knew about Neil. At these large parties, Neil was in the height of his glory. Neil would work the party, talking to everyone, on the hunt.

This night, Neil and Chris went together. Once at the party, they became separated. Neil was talking to a group, when Teraisa cut in, hugged Neil and started dancing. Teraisa was a roommate with Susie, a student whom Chris was dating. Neil met her through Chris. She was pretty, but not gorgeous. Neil enjoyed talking with her. That night, Neil, was not interested in conversation. He wanted some action. Teraisa would not be his first choice. As they danced, Teraisa started kissing Neil. He didn't mind, but the party was young. He wanted to work the crowd. Someone in the crowd called Neil's name. Neil turned and abruptly left, leaving Teraisa standing alone.

About fifteen minutes later, Teraisa reappeared, hugging and kissing Neil. Once again, Neil made an excuse and left. This continued for over an hour. Neil would escape and about every fifteen minutes, Teraisa would find him and immediately rekindle her amorous advances. Her persistence finally paid off. Neil could no longer resist. He took her into his arms and they began to dance. The affection quickly reached a fever pitch. Neil whispered, "Let's go to my place."

Teraisa smiled, and whispered back, "Lead the way."

She had her conquest for the night.

They quickly returned to the dorm. Once in Neil's room, he turned on the romantic music of Air Supply. Within seconds, they were on the bed, wrapped in the rapture of their caress. Things heated up very quickly, when suddenly, Teraisa started sobbing. For no apparent reason, Teraisa jumped up and ran from the room. Neil decided he would not chase her. He heard her run down the stairs and then heard her car leave the parking lot.

About fifteen minutes later, Neil's phone rang, "Hello."

"I'm sorry. I never told you I had a boyfriend."

It was Teraisa, tearfully offering an explanation, "He's back home in Milford."

I shouldn't have been doing this. I don't know what got into me. I'm going back to Milford tonight. I need to see my boyfriend."

Exasperated by the entire affair, Neil was not very sympathetic. He responded, "Whatever you think is best. Drive carefully."

He was angry. Neil had only been at the party for an hour, when he had succumbed to Teraisa's advances. Now it was only eleven o'clock and he was stuck in his room, alone. No one was in the dorm. Everyone else was out enjoying themselves except him. Neil decided he would not spend the rest of the night at the dorm. He started walking down the hall, knocking on every door, hoping to find someone home.

Finally, someone answered. It was Neil's newfound friend, Tim. After some persuasion, Tim got out of bed, got dressed and joined Neil at the party. Though he worked the crowd, Neil was not successful. At 3:00 a.m. he returned to his room and his lonely bed.

# Creative Writing

It was Tuesday, August 26, 1993. Neil woke up early that morning, with a sense of dread. It had been a long night of fitful sleep. Slowly gaining his senses, he realized why he hadn't slept. Today was the start of classes. He thought to himself, "Oh, @&?*$! I'm not ready for this."

Rising from his bed, Neil searched for his class schedule. After several unsuccessful minutes, he finally found it stuffed in his desk. Though he didn't feel like it this morning, Neil loved morning classes.

Neil entered Chris' bedroom and was greeted by the usual roar of him snoring. "Chris, wake up." Neil ordered.

After several tries, Chris slowly rolled over and looking at Neil through squinting eyes, asked, "What the @%?&$! do you want?"

"I need you to look at my schedule and tell me what classes I have today."

Begrudgingly, Chris took the schedule. Almost instantly, he began to laugh. "Dude, you are @%?&$! Your first class is English 101, Creative Writing, at nine this morning."

He forgot he had registered for that class. It was a required course. Chris and several of Neil's fraternity brothers had taken it last year. In fact, several of them had barely passed the class. They all unanimously agreed it was the most difficult of all the entry-level classes. For that very reason, Neil waited until his sophomore year to take it.

When it came to research papers, Neil was an excellent writer. However, he hadn't written any stories, which would be the subject of this class. Neil remembered, more than once, watching Chris pull an all-nighter to complete a story, only to bring it home to rewrite. Professor Clayton tore it apart, gave him a D and required that he rewrite the story. Neil was not prepared for all of the time and effort this class would require.

Slowly, unenthusiastically, Neil showered, dressed, and with Max leading, walked to Thomas Hall, the location of his first class. Neil, seated in his customary seat in the front row, politely listened to Professor Clayton review the syllabus. He learned he would have to write seven stories that semester, which averaged one every two weeks.

Unlike Chris, Neil quickly became enthralled with the class. Professor Clayton was an excellent teacher, who had a real love for writing. She brought a sense of enthusiasm and dedication, which was infectious. Before long, Neil's original dread evaporated and he became excited about the class. They reviewed different types of writing, different writing styles and the various techniques used to bring a story to life.

Several weeks into the class, the first writing assignment was due. Neil, in his usual style, waited until the night before the due date, to begin writing. He sat in front of his lap top computer, which was equipped with a special program called JAWS. This allowed the computer, upon Neil's command to read back anything he wrote. Staring at his computer, his mind was a blank. He couldn't decide on a suitable topic. So, he started to reminisce about the past. Like many times before, his mind drifted back to his days at NSVH. It was a very traumatic, lonely time for Neil but it was also a very good time. That period in his life always brought back vivid memories. It was like it happened yesterday, not fifteen years earlier. Recalling those times, he began to write. Before he knew it, several hours had passed and his first story was complete. It was a story about his first wrestling tournament, The Candy Bar Tournament. To his surprise, he received an A for the story.

From that point forward, this class became his favorite. He eagerly waited for the next assignment. He fell in love with writing. It was a love that would never die. Each story came as easily as the one before, with the same result, a grade of A.

The last assignment for the class, the final exam, was to write a story about a personal experience. The grade for this assignment would account for twenty-five percent of the total grade given for the class.

Neil was excited about the assignment. From the moment he learned about it, he knew exactly what story he would write. The very first night, after the class, Neil sat before his computer and immediately began. He did not stop to eat, drink or do anything else until he completed the story, three hours later. The story was entitled,

### The Blizzard

*On a cold January night, Linda was laying on the sofa, in the basement family room, listening to the late night news. Her oldest boy, Ryan, who was eight-years old, was already asleep. She was anxiously awaiting the weather report. Finally, her worst fears were confirmed. The reporter announced that a major frontal system would be passing through eastern Nebraska that coming Friday. With it, would come blizzard conditions and two feet of snow. The storm was expected to last two days.*

*Linda's thoughts immediately turned to her youngest son, Neil. When he was two-years old, he had been kicked in the face by a horse and was blinded for life. To assist him in adapting to his blindness, Neil attended the Nebraska School for the Visually Handicapped. Located in Nebraska City, which was ninety miles from his home, it was a residential program. Most of the students lived there for the entire semester, only returning home on the holidays. Neil did not. Without fail, every Friday afternoon, he would be picked up and driven home by his parents, or a family friend, only to be returned the following Sunday night. Those two days were precious to both Neil and his family. For the first time in two years, it now looked like the weather would keep Neil from coming home.*

*Turning off the television, Linda slowly walked upstairs. Walking down the hall toward her bedroom, she stopped to look in on Ryan. She quietly tiptoed to his bed, tucked him in and gave him a kiss on his fat little cheek. When she turned to go, Ryan opened his eyes and whispered, "I love you, Mommy."*

*In response, Linda returned to his bedside. "Mommy, look what I made for Neil." Ryan whispered, pulling a picture out from under his covers.*

*Linda looked at it. Ryan, instead of being asleep, as he should have been, had colored a picture of Neil and him climbing the tree in their back yard. To Linda's constant dismay, it was one of their favorite things to do. The first time she found Neil high up in the tree, she was frightened and immediately ordered him down. Now, he had done it so many times, she didn't think twice about it.*

*Even though he couldn't see, Ryan often made pictures for Neil. Linda, and her husband Larry, loved to watch Ryan meticulously describe every detail and color to Neil. It was one of their favorite times as a family.*

*"Can I give it to Neil this weekend, when he comes home?" Ryan excitedly asked.*

*Linda, fighting back her tears, didn't want to tell Ryan that Neil wouldn't be coming home. "Sure, honey. It's beautiful. I know Neil will like it a lot. You have school tomorrow, and it's way past your bedtime. So go to sleep." Linda affectionately ordered, kissing him one last time.*

*Linda closed the door and continued down the hall. She stopped by Neil's room. Whenever Neil was away, she would spend a moment in his bedroom each night, to say good night to him. Scanning the room, she smiled to herself. Neil was very much like her, a neat freak. Each Sunday, before he returned to NSVH, he would put all of his toys away. Each toy had a special place, where he always left them, in the same spot, at the same angle. All of his Star Wars space ships were lined up along the top of his toy box. The large Death Starship sat on the floor at the foot of Neil's bed with the Star Wars characters standing in their assigned spots. His record player sat next to the toy box with his records stacked in a specific order on the shelf of his toy box. It was as if his toys were waiting, in anticipation of Neil's return.*

*Looking at his empty bed, Linda sat down on its edge, as she would do if she were tucking him in. Her thoughts turned to Neil, alone in his tiny bed at NSVH. Suddenly, overwhelmed by the emotion of the moment, she placed her head in her hands and began to sob. Every minute, of every hour, of every day that Neil was away Linda was in pain. Though, for the most part, she controlled her emotions the pain was always there. The only remedy was to hold her baby boy in her arms. Now, a blizzard would keep her son from her arms.*

*Lost in her sorrow, she didn't hear Larry enter the room. When he sat down next to her, she collapsed in his arms. After several minutes of holding her, silently supporting her, Larry asked, "Linda, what is wrong."*

*"Larry, I miss him so much. I just can't bear the thought of him not coming home this weekend,"* Linda replied, slowly gaining her composure.

*"What do you mean, he's not coming home?"* Larry asked.

*"We're expecting a blizzard with two feet of snow. It will be impossible to get him back and forth to Nebraska City,"* Linda whispered her explanation.

Taking Linda's shoulders and turning her to face him, Larry, with a determined look in his eyes, said, *"Linda; that will not happen! I promised Neil he would come home every weekend and I meant it. I need my little "Doot" here as much as you. No little snowstorm is going to stop me! I don't want you to cry about it any more. I will bring him home!"* Linda and Larry, wrapped in each other's arms, silently walked to their room.

At 4:00 that Thursday afternoon, Neil and his fellow students were in the gym. An hour earlier, snow had begun to fall. Paul, a student adviser, was playing football with Neil. They had played this game many times. It was Neil's favorite game. He would always get lost in the spirit of the game, imagining he was the former quarterback for the Corn Huskers, Jerry Tagge.

However, this afternoon, Neil was distracted. Earlier in the day, he overheard some of the teachers talking about the impending blizzard. Neil was worried he would not be able to go home. There was no way his parents could drive through two feet of snow. It was only Thursday evening and it was already snowing hard.

His Dad had promised he would be home every weekend and for a year and a half, that had been true. Now, Neil thought he would miss his first weekend at home. Engrossed in his thoughts, Neil felt the football hit his chest and fall to the floor. As if on cue, he began to cry.

Paul, who was only two feet from Neil when he threw the ball, knelt down next to him and asked, in a concerned tone, *"Neil, what's wrong? You're not hurt are you?"*

Hesitantly, Neil finally answered, *"No, I'm not hurt. I'm sad, because I can't go home tomorrow."*

*"Why can't you go home?"* Paul questioned, taking Neil into his arms.

*"Because of the blizzard. My Daddy can't drive in a blizzard."* Neil explained.

Wiping Neil's tears away, Paul tried to encourage him. Giving Neil a reassuring hug, he said, *"Neil, the weather man is very often wrong. We might not get that much snow. You never know. Let's wait and see what tomorrow brings."*

Then, unexpectedly, a voice came over the intercom and announced, *"Neil Halford, please report to the Dorm!"*

This had never happened before. Neil was not only surprised but also afraid. He immediately thought he had done something wrong. Neil obediently and anxiously ran out of the gym, up the stairs and down the hall to the boy's dormitory. He was met by Mrs. Blevins, his housemother.

*"Mrs. Blevins, why did you call me up here?"* Neil nervously asked.

*"Neil, I have a surprise for you."* She excitedly explained.

*Neil was taken aback. Thinking to himself, he didn't understand. Why would she have a surprise for him and no one else? In fact, he had never had a surprise before. They didn't give surprises at this school. For a moment, his concern about not going home for the weekend had been replaced by the anticipation of a surprise. Finally, with his excitement overcoming his doubt, he asked, "Where is my surprise?"*

*"It's in your room." Mrs. Blevins answered, leading Neil to his bedroom. At the door, Mrs. Blevins stepped aside and let Neil walk into his room. He was instantly greeted by the familiar voice of his father, "Hey, Doot. How you doin'?"*

*Neil stopped dead in his tracks and tears began to swell in his eyes. "What are you doin' here, Dad?"*

*"I'm here to pick you up, son. I knew the snowstorm was coming and I didn't want you to be stuck here for the weekend. I'm here to take you home." Larry explained.*

*Neil ran into his Dad's arms, relieved he would be going home. Hugging his Dad, a sly smile came across his face. He knew he was doubly lucky. Not only was he going home, but he was also going to miss a day of school. Now he was happy about the blizzard.*

*The drive home was long and tedious. The snow was thick, the wind was strong, and the roads were slick. Normally the drive took a little over an hour. That night it took three hours. Sitting there, next to his Dad, watching his Dad fight the storm he felt so loved. In spite of his young age, for the first time he knew it was as important to his parents as it was to him that he be home on the weekends. Neil laid his head on his father's lap and fell asleep comforted by the love of his family.*

During the last class for the Creative Writing Course, all of the other students received their final story, with their grade. Neil did not. Professor Clayton asked Neil to stay after class. Of course, this concerned Neil. Because it accounted for such a large part of his final grade, he was worried she hadn't liked his story.

Sitting behind her desk, she addressed him, "Neil, I want to talk about your paper."

Holding his breath, Neil expected the worst. Professor Clayton continued, "First of all, I want you to know I gave you an A+ on this assignment." With a sigh of relief, Neil's emotions instantly turned from anxiety to exaltation. No professor ever gave out an A+.

"This story was very, very moving for me. I think this story has the potential to be published. There are a few things that would need to be changed, but they are minor. With your permission, I would like to submit it to some magazines for publication."

Neil was dumbfounded. He only spent three hours writing the story. It was just another assignment to him and she wanted to publish it.

Professor Clayton continued to explain, "Neil, your story really hit home. Several years ago, my son was in a terrible automobile accident. As a result of a severe brain injury, he was paralyzed and must live in an institution where he can receive proper care. Like your parents, my husband and I visit our son every weekend without fail. One time there was a severe ice storm. In spite of the weather, even though it was a struggle, we managed to visit him. I personally know how important those visits are to both the child and the parents. I want to thank you for writing this story, for the way it touched me."

The discussion continued for several minutes more. They agreed Professor Clayton would make some inquiries and then contact Neil. A week later, Neil received a letter from the professor informing him her husband had experienced a severe heart attack and that unfortunately, she would not be able to assist him in getting the story published.

That night Neil lay in bed thinking about the story. He had felt so inspired by the fact one of his stories had truly touched someone. Lying there, he thought to himself, "One day, I will write my story."

# The Fastest Skier on the Mountain

"John Elway Celebrity Ski Race" read the sign over the starting gate. It was April 7, 1995. Copper Mountain, was a world-renowned ski resort located in Summit County, Colorado, which was home to four of Colorado's major resorts. With an altitude of 12,500 feet above sea level, it provided some of Colorado's best skiing and most panoramic views. The weather was warm, with the temperature at forty-five degrees. There was five inches of fresh powder; spring skiing at its best.

Every year, John Elway, the all-pro quarterback for the Denver Broncos, held a celebrity ski race. His foundation used the proceeds from this event to help families and children in need. Frank Starr, a family friend, had purchased two spots in the race. Frank took one and invited Neil to take the other.

After discussing it with his parents, Neil agreed. He was excited. Frank wasn't sure if he was more excited about racing or about meeting John Elway and other Denver Broncos. Either way, he was definitely pumped.

While Neil and Frank rode the chairlift to the top of the mountain, Frank described the slalom racecourse. Situated on a "Blue", which stood for intermediate skiing, slope, the course looked steep and difficult. "It looks really fast, Neil. There are two courses, both extremely tight with thirty gates. The gates are very close. There is no room for any mistakes."

Frank had known Neil since birth. Though he hadn't told him, Neil had served as a source of inspiration. From the first time he saw Neil in the hospital after his accident, tubes and wires covering every part of his body, he knew Neil was special. Though in great pain, scared and confused, he never complained. He accepted his blindness and almost immediately went on with his life.

Neil was fearless and confident. Whatever the challenge, he would try anything. He chose not to consider himself handicapped. He competed in the world of the sighted, showing disdain for any competition that made an exception for his blindness. Frank had seen Neil snow ski, water ski, wrestle, play football, climb trees and climb mountains. You name it. Neil did it.

Though Neil was a very good skier, this course worried Frank. It was Neil's first time on a slalom course. This course was difficult. Frank was to be Neil's guide. He would ski behind Neil and signal when to turn. They'd worked out a system. The louder Frank's voice, the sharper Neil would turn.

Sensing Frank's concern, Neil joked, "Just don't confuse your left and right, and I'll bust this course." They both laughed. The first time Frank taught Neil how to ski, he told him to turn right, when he meant left. As a result, Neil unknowingly skied into the woods. Frank couldn't believe that Neil remembered that incident. It'd happened many years before.

Exiting the chairlift, they skied to the starting gate. There were two parallel courses; a blue course and an orange course, the Bronco's colors. This was to be the first of two practice runs. Each racer was allowed one practice run on each course. Frank had already taken his two runs, so he was familiar with the courses. Standing in the gate, Frank explained the course to Neil,

"When you start, there is a sharp drop for about five feet. This helps you gain speed. Then you need to make a sharp right turn. I'll be waiting for you at the first turn."

"What was your best time?" Neil asked.

"I didn't do very well. On my first run, I tried to go too fast and missed a gate. My time on the blue course was seventy-four seconds."

"I don't want to hear any excuses. You tried to be a stud and blew it," Neil laughed.

"Okay. I can't wait to see how you do, Mr. Expert. Just remember, a lot of people have already skied the course. The powder has been skied off the turns. They are very icy. When I call for a sharp turn, you really need to stand on your edges. Cut those turns."

Linda and Larry didn't ski. So, they walked up the mountain to watch Neil practice. They stood by the fence, which surrounded the course, at the mid-way point. The only spectators, they anxiously awaited Neil's run.

Standing in the starting gate, waiting for Frank's signal, Neil was apprehensive. He was having second thoughts about his decision to participate in the race. Judging from the times being announced over the loud speaker at the finish line, there were some excellent skiers in the race. This combined with the fact that he hadn't skied in five years, made him worry he would not be able to complete the course.

"Go!" Frank yelled, signaling the start of the run. Neil, instantly overcame his doubt, and pushed off with his two poles, his legs tripping the timer when he exited the starting gate. When Neil made the first turn, Frank skied behind him, shouting the directions. On several turns, Neil slid, almost losing control. Each time, he was forced to stop, to regain control and stay on the course.

"Go Neil! You're doing great." Larry and Linda shouted encouragement when Neil passed the mid point. They then turned and walked toward the finish line, watching Neil's every turn.

"He's really struggling, fighting the course," Larry expressed his concern to Linda.

"It's his first time. What do you expect?" Linda replied, giving Larry a signal not to be too hard on Neil.

"Tuck Neil! Tuck!" Frank shouted after Neil had negotiated the last turn. This was the signal that there were no more turns; that Neil should maximize his speed to the finish.

"Stop!" Frank yelled, when Neil passed the finish line. Neil obediently slid to a parallel stop. "What's my time?" Neil immediately asked.

As Frank began to answer, he was interrupted by people applauding and yelling words of support. Looking back up the course for the source of this unexpected support, Frank was totally taken by surprise. While running the course, he was unaware that the fence, once only occupied by Neil's parents, was now lined with skiers who stopped to watch Neil.

"What's all the noise?" Neil asked.

"Unbelievable!" Frank explained. "You butchered the course. Your time was four minutes thirty-four seconds and still you have a fan club.

"Any hot girls?" Neil asked, breaking into a confident smile.

"Based upon your time, I think you need to concentrate on the skiing. Save the girls for tonight," Frank replied, shaking his head in amazement.

The second run was better, with Neil trimming his time by more than a minute to three minutes thirty-six seconds. Like his first run, he finished to the roar of the crowd.

"Let's break for lunch." Frank stated, signaling they needed to ski to the base area. At lunch, the teams were chosen. Each team had six members, one from each of six brackets, based upon each skiers practice times. Each team would be ranked based upon the total time of all team members. The team with the lowest combined total, over four runs, would win. Frank and Neil were on different teams.

"You know, Neil, I have to do everything I can to help my team win. So if you go too fast, I just might get my directions confused. The woods are very close to the blue course," Frank joked.

"Based upon your practice runs, I don't think your team will be close to winning, so it shouldn't be a problem," Neil replied, with his usual caustic humor.

"We'll see. You never know," Frank retorted, trying to put some doubt in Neil's mind. Neil wasn't worried. He knew he could always rely on Frank.

While eating lunch, several of Neil's teammates stopped to tell him they were excited to have him on their team and that they looked forward to skiing with him. Upon finishing lunch, Larry asked Neil if he wanted to meet some of the celebrities. Of course, his answer was yes.

Larry, not bashful and definitely not intimidated by celebrity, led Neil to each table. Neil met John Elway, who offered some great words of encouragement. He also met several retired Broncos, including Karl Mecklenberg. Some of the current team who were present, such as Steve Atwater and Steve Watson introduced themselves. They were there to support the charity. However, they could not participate in the racing. Their contracts prohibited skiing.

The last celebrity Neil met was Rick Neuheisel, the young coach of the University of Colorado football team. Wearing the sweatshirt of Neil's favorite team, the Nebraska Corn Huskers, Neil introduced himself. Rick, apparently offended by the show of support for the Big Red, sarcastically commented, "You're from Nebraska. Oh, I'm sorry." He then abruptly turned and walked away.

"Boy, he's a bad loser," Neil commented, unaffected by the rude conduct of a "celebrity."

On the other hand, Larry was incensed. He had not asked for nor expected any special treatment for Neil. He also wouldn't tolerate or allow anyone to disrespect Neil. Sensing his Dad's anger, Neil whispered, "A guy like that will never beat Nebraska."

"You got that right, son," Larry concurred, leading Neil back to their table. That afternoon, each member raced twice, once on each course. Neil raced last each time. During his runs, spectators lined the fence. Even the other competitors stopped to watch. The cheering was so loud that Frank had to ski dangerously close to Neil, to ensure he could hear the directions. Several times, unbeknownst to Neil, their skis almost became entangled. Each time, Neil improved. His first run was three minutes, twenty-five seconds. On his second run, he broke three minutes, with a time of two minutes, fifty-four seconds.

That night there was a dinner and party. Karl Mecklenberg, his wife, and two young boys were seated with the Halfords. Karl's boys, ages 10 and 12 were also racing. They were totally enthralled by Neil and sat next to him at dinner. For the remainder of the night, Neil and the boys were inseparable.

Karl, watching his boys with Neil, turned to Larry and expressed his admiration, "Your son is very impressive. You and your wife have to be very special people to have raised such an incredible son. I am so glad that my boys had the opportunity to meet Neil and to watch him ski. It is a great lesson in life. He is a walking inspiration and I am honored to have met him. Playing professional football, I thought I had to overcome many challenges, but my accomplishments pale when compared to your son."

"Thank you." Larry replied. "Coming from someone as successful as you, it means a lot. I am so close to Neil that his accomplishments seem ordinary, expected. I sometimes forget how great he really is." Larry and Karl then spent much of the evening talking about raising boys, the challenges and joys.

The next day, while they rode the lift, Frank was pleased to see that it had snowed about six inches overnight. The new snow would make it easier for Neil to negotiate the turns. A race was scheduled for the morning, with the last run to begin right after lunch. Neil's times improved with each run. His first time was two minutes, sixteen seconds. On the last try he broke two minutes, with a time of one minute, fifty-eight seconds. Upon seeing Neil's time, the crowd went crazy, cheering and applauding. You would have thought he won the race, rather than being the slowest skier.

Later that afternoon, there was an awards ceremony. The winning team and the fastest skier were honored with trophies and prizes of substantial value. Neither Frank's nor Neil's team won. The fastest skier was a young man, in his early twenties, named Dave Masters. He was an incredible skier. His fastest time was thirty-six seconds. After receiving his prizes, John Elway presented him with a trophy, engraved with the words, "Fastest Skier on the Mountain."

Upon receiving the trophy, Dave asked Neil to join him on the stage. Standing side by side, Dave turned to Neil. Handing the trophy to Neil, he proclaimed, "There is only one person with the balls to be called 'The Fastest Skier on the Mountain' and that's you Neil." The entire room stood, giving Neil a standing ovation, worthy of a champion.

Neil returned to the table, trophy in hand. Frank, once again in awe of Neil's charisma, put the exclamation on the day, "Neil, you are amazing. I bring you to a celebrity ski race and you end up being the celebrity."

## POSTSCRIPT — CHAPTER FIVE

*The day after graduation, while I packed my belongings, for the trip back to Fort Calhoun, I was in an unusually melancholy mood. It was a bittersweet moment. For the first time in eight years, Chris and I would be separated. He decided to remain in Kearney. Two years earlier, he dropped out of college. He was working as a campus security guard. Chris liked his job, and he loved the campus life. However, I was worried about him. He seemed to have no ambition, no sense of direction.*

*Overriding my concern for Chris was my love for Carrie. For three years, we struggled with a long distance relationship. That was finally coming to an end. In one week, we would be together forever.*

*Also, I was ready to end my college years. I obtained a Bachelor's Degree in Sports Administration. This past four years had been great. They were, fun and exciting, but also very tedious. I was fed up with the studying. For more than a year, I had been retired as a party animal. I didn't think that day would come, but, to my surprise, I just lost interest. Ready for a new life, I wanted to move on, to marry Carrie, to have a family, and to start a career.*

# Chapter Six

## INTRODUCTION

*This chapter is not about my life, but the lives of Mr. and Mrs. Halford, Neil and Carrie. A week after graduation, on May 11, 1996 Carrie and I were married.*

*We were both mature for our age; she was twenty and I was twenty-one. We wanted to start to build our life together. Not just husband and wife, we were best friends. Our first home was a small, two-bedroom apartment in Fort Calhoun about five blocks from my parent's house. Carrie's parents also lived in town. Carrie and I planned for both of us to work for a couple of years before starting our family.*

*Unfortunately, plans and reality are not always the same. For the first time in my life I came face to face with the harsh reality of life. Until then, I did not understand how protected, how charmed a life I actually lived. I was a college graduate, with an excellent scholastic record. My communication skills were above average. Everyone complimented me on my job interviews. Regardless of my qualifications and skills, every application I filed was rejected. After eight months and hundreds of applications, I was still unemployed.*

*In my mind, there was only one reason. I was blind. People could not look past my handicap, and judge me on an equal basis with sighted applicants. Never before had I experienced such obvious prejudice. I was devastated. It was the most difficult time of my life. We were struggling financially and I was fighting depression, trying to stay positive, trying to marshal the determination, which had helped me succeed so many times before.*

*Finally, I was hired as a business-to-business account executive for Sloan Marketing. Basically, I was a glorified telemarketer. I was working next to people without college degrees. Some didn't even have a high school diploma. I was earning $9.50 per hour, annually grossing less than $20,000. My professional life, my inability to obtain a challenging job, which would offer me a future career, has been my biggest disappointment in life. In spite of this, with the help of my family and the love of my wife, we have a beautiful family and a happy life.*

# *Carrie*

It was the night of December 1, 2000. Neil sat in the rocking chair, next to his wife's hospital bed. Asleep in his arms was his newborn son, Cole Raymon Halford. He was less than six hours old. On the bed, asleep with Carrie, was their three-year old daughter, Emily Sue Halford. He couldn't remember a time when he was more content. Neil and his wife had known each other for ten years and had been married four years. Though they were now a happy family, it wasn't always that way. Neil closed his eyes and reflected on their rocky road to happiness.

The very first time Neil heard the name Carrie Conradson was on Friday, September 22, 1990. It was after school, during his junior year. Chris and he were standing outside the school's front door, discussing the impending homecoming festivities.

"Dude, you better hurry up and get a date for homecoming. It's only a week away," Chris admonished.

"Heck, dude, I don't know who to take."

Suddenly, a girl came running out of the school rushing toward the parking lot. As she passed the two boys, she yelled, "Hey Chris."

"Hey, Carrie, how you doing?" Chris responded.

"Hey, dude, why don't you ask her?" Chris suggested to Neil.

"Who?"

"The chick, who just said hi to us."

"She didn't say hi to us. She said hi to you. I don't even know who the heck she is!"

"Oh, you do too. That's Carrie!"

"Carrie who?" Neil retorted. He was becoming annoyed with Chris.

"Carrie Conradson."

"Who the heck is Carrie Conradson?" Neil replied, raising his voice.

He couldn't get Chris to understand he didn't know any Carrie Conradson.

"Carrie Conradson. Dude, she's in choir with you. She's on the track team. You should know her," Chris replied in disbelief. He couldn't believe that in such a small school, Neil didn't know her. Neil knew everybody.

"Dude, I don't have a clue who she is. I've never even heard of her."

"Well, she doesn't really hang around in our kind of crowd."

"Then how do you know her?"

"Oh, she goes to the same church as my Mom. I've seen her at our church's youth group, Student Venture."

"I don't go to your church. How do you expect me to know her."

"Well, just ask her!" Chris demanded, tired of Neil's excuses.

"I ain't asking her!" Neil exclaimed.

"Well, why not?"

"I'm not going to homecoming with some chick I don't even know!"

"Alright, whatever, dude. Then, you won't find a date," Chris declared, ending the conversation. Chris proved to be correct. Neil went to homecoming with some friends, without a date.

It was nearly a year later before Neil met Carrie. It was a warm June afternoon. Neil's parents were out of town at an auto show. Chris and Jesse Irwin were staying with Neil. They had spent the day relaxing by the pool. When night arrived, they decided to go up town and check out the action.

Passing the grade school, they saw two girls jogging. It was Carrie and her friend Janel. They all knew Janel. She would sometimes hang out with their group. Chris and Jesse knew Carrie. They stopped and talked for a while. Eventually, they convinced the girls to ride around town with them. Sometime later, they all returned to Neil's house. There they hung out, talked and listened to music.

Neil looked down at Cole and smiled. That was the first time he met Carrie. Even now, he remembered he instantly liked her. She was outspoken and opinionated. Talkative, friendly and energetic, she was definitely an extravert. Yet, Carrie had this sense of reserve, a sense of vulnerability about her. She had constructed a protective wall around herself. She didn't let anyone get too close to her. She did not date. From the beginning, Neil decided he would be the one to break down her wall, to really get to know her.

Though she'd attended school in Fort Calhoun since fifth grade, she did not know Neil, or that he was blind. She was one year behind Neil in school. Active in school, she participated in track, cross-country, student council, the student newspaper, both choirs and the Fellowship of Christian Athletes.

Carrie enjoyed that first night at Neil's. She liked Neil. Music was their first love. Both of them enjoyed all types of different music. They were both gifted with beautiful voices and sang in the school's various vocal groups. For many hours each day, they would just sit and talk. They loved to debate. It was not an emotional argument, but an intellectual discussion of differing views.

As the summer passed, Carrie and her friends would frequent the Halford pool, especially on weekends. Carrie enjoyed the informal and friendly atmosphere and began to loosen up, to open up to Neil.

Neil was concerned that when school started, they would drift apart. They had become close friends. Before Carrie, Neil was not open and honest about his feelings with a girl. He cherished their friendship and didn't want to lose it. Neil wanted the relationship to develop beyond being just good friends, but Carrie showed no such interest. Though it bothered Neil, he didn't push it. He didn't want to ruin their close friendship.

Through the early months of school, their friendship continued. They saw each other frequently during school and they would hang together on weekends. Their first date was homecoming.

Tracy was Carrie's best friend. She came from a troubled home and was spending the school year at Carrie's house. She did not have a date for home-coming, so she joined Carrie and Neil.

Finally, in early November, Neil and Carrie started dating, regularly. Carrie did not want to date. She enjoyed their friendship and was satisfied with the current status. However, Neil was not. Neil wanted their relationship to grow beyond friendship. Frustrated with the situation, Neil finally gave Carrie an ultimatum, date me or we can't continue to be friends. Carrie enjoyed being with Neil but was not ready for a serious relationship. She did not want the pressure and obligations that came with a relationship. Eventually, Carrie re-luctantly acquiesced to Neil's demand and they officially became boyfriend and girlfriend.

Most of Neil's time was occupied with wrestling. In the early part of the wrestling season, Neil was struggling. All of his free time he spent with Carrie. Then, on the Saturday before Christmas, Neil had a poor performance in a local wrestling tournament. That evening, Carrie and Neil planned to go to the school's Christmas prom. Neither of them felt like going, so they went out for a late dinner. They talked late into the night. When it was time for Carrie to leave, Neil kissed her, their first kiss. Neil could tell this was probably her first real kiss. She was awkward and embarrassed. To this point, Neil was pleased with their relationship. He felt he was finally starting to chisel away Carries protective wall. Neil often called her the "Ice Queen," because she would hide her emotions. On the other hand, Carrie wasn't happy. She did not like the pressure of "being a couple." Though she liked Neil, she was not ready to spend all of her time with him. Neil was always with a crowd, always at a party. They spent little time alone. Carrie occasionally enjoyed a party, but longed for her special time to herself, when she could read and meditate.

Two weeks later, during the school's Christmas break, there was a basketball game at the high school. Neil met Carrie there. Just before the game ended, Carrie leaned over and whispered to Neil, "Let's go outside and talk."

Arm in arm, they walked outside the school. Ironically, they stopped in the exact location where Neil and Chris were standing, those many months earlier, when Carrie went running by, shouting to Chris. Neil was very apprehensive. For the last few weeks, Carrie had become distant. She was not as open and honest about her feelings. Carrie decided she did not want to continue dat-ing Neil. She didn't want to date anybody else; she simply didn't want to date. She wanted their relationship to revert back to the friendship of the pre-vious summer.

Releasing her hold on Neil's arm, Carrie bluntly announced, "Neil, I want to break up with you."

"Why?" Neil asked, shocked by her declaration.

"Well, I just . . . don't want to go out anymore. I just want to be friends," she hesitantly explained.

"Well, why? There's got to be a reason!" Neil asked, raising his voice in frustration.

Pressed for an answer, which she didn't have, Carrie blurted out, "I think I can find somebody better."

"Well, fine! Go @%?&$! find someone better! Take off then!" Neil yelled in anger.

"No, No. That's not what I meant. I didn't mean it like that," Carrie responded, realizing she'd hurt Neil, something she didn't want to do.

She took Neil's hand to try and calm him down.

"Hey, @%?&$! you. If that's the way you feel, then go find someone better," Neil yelled, pulling his hand away.

At that moment, Chris and some of Neil's other friends were walking by. Neil grabbed Chris' arm, gave him a shove in the back and said, "Dude, let's get out of here." Chris, realizing Neil was angry, obeyed, without saying a word. They hopped in Chris' truck and drove away. Neil was irate. He had a lot of pride and Carrie had hurt him deeply.

Through the month of January, they didn't talk. At school, they both avoided each other. Neil had one class with Carrie and her best friend, Tracy. At this time, she was still living with Carrie. Tracy was friendly and cute. She was also eccentric. Tracy and Neil started talking frequently. Tracy was acting as the go-between for Neil and Carrie. During this time, Tracy started emulating Carrie. She bought blue contacts, she dyed her hair blonde, wore it like Carrie, and often wore Carrie's clothes. This bothered Carrie. Their relationship was becoming strained. Eventually, Tracy moved back to her uncle's home to live with him.

Then, it changed. Neil and Tracy started flirting with each other. Neil still liked Carrie, but he still remained upset about her remarks. He felt she rejected him because he was blind. Neil was vindictive and wanted to hurt her, for what she said. He hoped giving Tracy his attention would accomplish that.

One afternoon, Tracy asked Neil out. That evening, Neil called Carrie. They started talking as they had before they dated. Carrie would complain about her family and Neil would listen sympathetically. After a while, Neil revealed the real reason for his call,

"Tracy has asked me out. I like Tracy. She is a nice person. I wouldn't mind going out with her, but I would rather be dating you. Basically, I am giving you an ultimatum. Carrie, either you go out with me or I'm going to start dating Tracy."

"Okay, just go ahead and date Tracy." Coldly, with no emotion, Carrie replied.

She was irate, but she didn't yell. Once again she became the "Ice Queen."

This was not the answer Neil wanted. He could tell Carrie was fuming. Still hurt from Carries earlier rebuke, he angrily replied, "Alright, I will. I'll go out with Tracy." Without another word, Carrie hung up the telephone.

Neil immediately called Tracy and made arrangements for a date on the upcoming weekend. Instantly they were boyfriend and girlfriend, and began dating regularly. It wasn't serious. They dated once a week. However, Neil spent more time with his buddies than with her. She was also emotional, dramatic and volatile. Neil was always uneasy when he was with her. Her drastic mood swings made Neil feel like he was constantly riding an emotional roller coaster.

Carrie and Neil continued to be annoyed with each other. Whenever they were in the same room, you could feel the tension. Neil was purposely flaunting his relationship with Tracy, being spiteful to Carrie. At school, Carrie made it clear that she and Tracy were no longer friends, telling everyone they had to choose, either Tracy or her, but not both. Most students chose Carrie.

A few weeks before graduation, Neil broke up with Tracy. He just could not handle it any more. In the fall, he would be going to college. He had no intention of having a girlfriend. The night he broke it off with Tracy, Neil went to a party with some of his friends. Carrie was there. Neil started flirting with Carrie. Before he knew it, they were alone. Neil and Carrie started talking and began to re-establish their friendship.

The next night found them both at another party. That night, Neil once again professed his desire to be together. They talked for several hours, before Carrie left for home. Neil was encouraged. He felt she was once again warming to his advances, but was still unsure about their future.

Carrie was confused and frustrated. She liked Neil and longed for their intimate friendship. Yet, every time they talked, he pressured her for more. He wanted them to date. She was still not prepared for that. Yet, when Neil dated Tracy, she couldn't help but be angry.

The next day, Sunday afternoon, Tracy begged for Neil to take her back. Neil agreed and they once again began to date. He wanted to be with Carrie, but she remained noncommittal about their future. Neil hoped that by dating Tracy again, it would force Carrie to make a decision. She did. Carrie was infuriated. One night Neil talks to her about getting back together and the next night he dates Tracy. In Carrie's mind, it was over. Carrie made it clear to the entire school that she hated Neil and never wanted to see him again. In June, Neil and Tracy parted company for good. He spent the month of July in Michigan, at the Leader Dog School, getting to know Max.

Neil returned in August, departed for Kearney and started college, without once seeing Carrie. While Neil was at college, Carrie was enjoying her senior year in high school. She often thought about Neil. She missed him, but didn't try to contact him. She was deeply hurt. In her mind, he would have to make the first move. Throughout Neil's freshman year, about every eight weeks, he would visit home. Near Christmas, Chris had a party at his mother's house. Carrie was there. After some conversation, they once again found themselves alone. The night passed quickly, as they reminisced about the past.

Neil went back to college without talking to Carrie. For the next two months, they had no communication. Then, while Neil was back in Fort Calhoun, they ran into each other at a party. Again, they ended the night together. This continued throughout the remaining months of Neil's freshman year.

After Neil returned home for the summer, without an invitation, he went to Carrie's graduation party. He only stayed long enough to give her a card. Later that night, they both planned to attend the same graduation party. Jenny Grove was having a large senior party for everyone. Neil had decided he really liked Carrie and wanted to have a relationship with her, if she was willing. When he was filled with enough liquid courage, Neil corralled her and led her to a quiet room. Alone, he put his arm around her and explained his feel-

ings, "Carrie, I really like you. I know I have been a real @%?&$!. I've treated
you badly. You hurt me and I tried to get even by using Tracy. I was wrong. I
was being vindictive. I know it. I'm so sorry. Carrie, I want to see you, to be
with you and no one else. If you would be willing to make a commitment to
me and enter into a relationship with me, I will make the same commitment.
I promise I will be faithful. I want to make this work."

Carrie also missed Neil. She was ready to move their relationship to the next
level. Though still concerned about Neil's past indiscretions, she had strong
feelings for him. She did not like the way Neil tried to rush their relationship.
Carrie wanted their friendship. If it grew into something more, fine, but if not,
she was content to be friends. Neil was not. He was always pushing, wanting
a commitment from her for an exclusive relationship.

Neil went on for forty-five minutes, revealing his deepest feelings to her.
Carrie would cry periodically, as they discussed the past. Throughout this time,
Carrie seemed distant. She listened and talked, but was rigid and stoic. Never
once, did she look at Neil. Hoping to break the "Ice Queen," Neil gave her a
long hug and kissed her. After some more tears and conversation, Carrie
agreed to give him another chance.

That summer was great. Carrie and Neil were inseparable. Occasionally Neil
would party with his friends, but most of his time was dedicated to Carrie.
They both loved movies. They spent many nights at the theatres. Their relationship was fun, caring and loving.

When fall arrived, neither was ready to part. Neil had to return to college
and Carrie had a job in Omaha. They were unprepared for the emotional strain
of a long distance relationship. Initially, they called each other every night.
After the first telephone bill, that stopped. Neither one had enough money
to continue. They both realized it wasn't working. Without the constant contact, their relationship was becoming strained. Neil couldn't and didn't want
to return home every weekend and Carrie couldn't afford the trips to Kearney.

On the weekends when they could not be together, Neil would party with
his fraternity brothers, while he expected Carrie to stay home. Carrie didn't
feel it was right. So, in Neil's absence, Carrie started hanging with Jay Weeks,
one of Neil's best friends, and one of Jay's friends from Omaha, Daryl. Daryl
and Carrie instantly hit it off and started spending time together.

Neil returned home in October, unaware of Carrie's new friend. The first
night home, Carrie came to see Neil. Neil was working in his Dad's garage,
when she arrived. Immediately, he knew something was wrong. It was the "Ice
Queen" who was standing before him. Carrie, in her usual, matter-of-fact manner, told him, "Neil, this is just not working. I can't deal with the long sepa-
rations. We never see each other. I want to break it off."

Carrie's former comment, "I think I can find someone better," immediately
returned to Neil's thoughts. He knew she felt something was missing. Until
she met Neil, Carrie led a very sheltered life. Neil was her first kiss. Neil was her
first love. Neil was her first boyfriend. On the other hand, Neil lived life with
gusto and daring. Now, he was ready to settle down and she wasn't. Carrie was
just beginning "to sow her wild oats." Neil realized that until she had completed

her search, they could never really be together, she would never be totally committed. Without any protest, without the anger of the past, Neil gave Carrie a hug and wished her well.

When she departed, Neil slammed the garage door shut and began cussing, as he threw tools against the wall. The Eagles song, "Lying Eyes" was playing on the radio. He thought it was unusually appropriate. Neil was hurt and angry. Upon his return to college, he enthusiastically rejoined the party scene, trying to drown his sorrows.

Though not serious about Daryl, Carrie did not feel Neil was ready for a committed relationship, and she knew she wasn't. She still cared about Neil, but wanted to be free to enjoy life. He was, why shouldn't she.

A month later, Neil returned home for the Thanksgiving break. The night after Thanksgiving, Carrie was singing at the Red Barn in a big country music contest. The winner would receive a recording contract. Neil surprised her by attending. She had no idea he was coming. Carrie was cool, but pleasant. Carrie placed third. After the contest was over, Neil asked if he could ride home with her. She agreed.

Upon arriving home, Neil invited her in. They began to talk. Carrie was sitting on the couch. Neil laid on the couch, putting his head in her lap. Holding her hands, he once again confessed his love for her and his desire to have a committed relationship.

After a lengthy, emotional discussion, Carrie succumbed to Neil's pleas. She agreed to give it one more chance. That night they reaffirmed their love for each other and never broke up again. There were some rocky times for the remainder of that school year, but they managed to work through them. Neil made a concerted effort to return home more often. Over the Christmas break, they spent much of their time together, alone at Neil's Kearney apartment.

The following summer, they were inseparable. They spent every day of the summer together. When they weren't together, they were on the telephone. It was a summer of love and fun. They had grown close. What made their relationship special was the fact they had been close friends, before they became lovers. They knew each other like a book, every page, every word.

Departing was very bittersweet. Upon his return to college for his junior year, they were constantly on the phone. Many a lonely night, Neil would play their favorite Carpenter CD and drink a six-pack of beer. He would literally cry in his beer. Carrie would visit Neil frequently. She did not have a car, so Neil's parents would let her use one of their cars, often paying for the gas.

In late October, Neil called his father at work. He had made a decision, which he knew would concern his parents. Neil had decided to ask Carrie to marry him. He wanted to reassure his Dad that he would complete college. Also, he would need his Dad's help. His father was known for his choice of jewelry. Family and friends often asked for his help, when purchasing some jewelry for their special lady. More importantly, Neil would need help financially. He did not have the money or the credit for such a purchase. Nervously, he announced, "Dad, I want to ask Carrie to marry me. This is going to be a long engagement. I plan to finish college before we get married. I want to surprise her and ask her, this Christmas."

"Oh, my God. I can't believe it. Jeez, are you sure this is what you want to do?" Larry teasingly asked.

"Yes, Dad, I am sure." Neil strongly affirmed.

"Well, good. If this is what you want, then we'll do it." Larry said, offering Neil his encouragement and support.

"Let's keep it a secret. We won't tell anyone. Boy, we'll do this up right." Larry planned, becoming more excited than Neil.

During the Thanksgiving school break, Larry and Neil searched for a ring. Finally, they bought one at Borsheim's, regarded as the top jewelry store in Omaha. Neil didn't have much money. Larry helped Neil establish a charge account. This allowed him to buy a nice ring and also to begin to establish his credit. The ring had a center diamond of a half-carat, surrounded by smaller diamonds totaling a half-carat.

For the next month, Larry and Neil kept their secret. Even Linda didn't know. Neil told Carrie that for Christmas, he wanted to get them a hotel suite on December 23rd. She agreed. The morning of the 23rd, Larry and Neil rented the suite. They checked in, set some candles around the suite and placed a bottle of Champagne in a cooler next to the sofa. That evening, just before Neil and Carrie were scheduled to arrive, Larry returned to the room and lit all of the candles.

First, Neil and Carrie had dinner at Scot's restaurant, which was one of their favorite places to eat. The entire time, Neil had the ring box in his pocket. They went to the room and sat down on the couch. Carrie was pleasantly surprised, by the candles and the romantic atmosphere they created. She gave Neil his Christmas present, which was a beautiful sweater. Neil then announced, "Carrie, I have a big present for you. It's in a big box in the bathroom. You have to give me a minute to get it out. So, stay on the couch and close your eyes."

Neil then opened the bathroom door. Returning to Carrie, he pulled the ring from his pocket, and cautioned her, "Now, Carrie, keep your eyes closed."

Neil knelt in front of her, opened the box, sat it on her lap, and said, "Open your eyes."

Carrie obeyed, as Neil took her hands and asked, "Carrie, will you marry me?"

She immediately started shaking, and expressed her surprise, "Oh my God! Oh my God! Oh my God!"

She caught her breath and then, staring into Neil's eyes, answered, "Yes, of course I will marry you."

Neil placed the ring on her finger. Then, he popped the cork on the Champagne and poured them each a glass. After a personal toast, they fell into each other's arms. The next morning, Neil took the ring back and made Carrie promise not to tell anyone until the family Christmas gatherings. Neil wanted to surprise everyone. Carrie agreed.

Christmas day, the Halford family Christmas was held at Linda's younger sister, Marla's, house. After the meal, Larry explained he had a surprise and asked everyone to adjourn to the basement. Everyone waited in anticipation. Larry walked into the basement, followed by Neil and Carrie. Neil announced,

"My Dad doesn't really have a surprise, I do. I want to tell you that two nights ago, I asked Carrie to marry me, and Carrie and I are now engaged."

Then Neil took the ring out of his pocket, and in front of everyone, placed it on Carrie's finger. Everyone was shocked. It was mayhem. All the women cried and rushed to congratulate Carrie. The men crowded around Neil, shaking his hand and joking about his loss of freedom.

An hour later, they drove to Omaha, to join Carrie's family Christmas celebration. Carrie did not want to be so dramatic with her family. They made no announcement. They just sat down and joined the conversation. No one seemed to notice. Finally, Carrie's Mom saw her ring. At first her Mom was in shock, as Carrie announced her Christmas gift. Then the excitement commenced. Her mom and sisters were ecstatic.

From that point on, things became serious. Shortly after Neil returned to school, they realized they could not stand to be apart. Every other weekend, they saw each other. The following summer, they prepared for the wedding, especially Carrie. She spent long hours with both her Mom and Linda, finalizing the plans. Neil was a typical fiancé, trying to avoid the countless decisions. He became proficient at the standard phrase, "Whatever you want, honey. That's fine with me."

His senior year was strenuous. The costs of travel and telephone calls were staggering, but somehow they made it through the year. The week before Neil's graduation, they moved into their apartment. They rented an apartment in Fort Calhoun, about five blocks from Neil's parents' house. However, Neil refused to live there, until after the wedding. He lived at his parent's until they were married.

One week after Neil's graduation, they were married at Morning Star Lutheran Church in Omaha, Nebraska. The wedding went smoothly, until Neil knelt next to Carrie, at the altar. Suddenly, everyone started laughing. They were quiet, trying to refrain from chuckling, but they couldn't. Neil and Carrie looked at each other, puzzled by the crowd's reaction. They did not find out until after the ceremony that Neil's brother had painted the words, "God Help Me," on the soles of his shoes.

The wedding reception was held at the Fort Calhoun Community Center. It was a fun reception. However, Neil was somewhat melancholy. All of his good friends were having a good time, and he was stuck doing all of the required duties of the groom, pictures, dances, and the reception line. Finally, Carrie released him. Then, the party really started. Neil and his friends spent the night reliving the past glories of Neil's single life. Carrie and her friends reveled in the excitement of her life to be.

When it was time to leave, Neil said his farewells to all of his friends, but one. He couldn't find Chris anywhere. When they exited through the door, he found Chris. He was sitting on the ground, bawling his eyes out. Sobbing because he felt he was losing his best friend. He and Neil had been inseparable for the last eight years. Carrie knew when she married Neil that the deal included Chris. She leaned over, kissed Chris on his cheek and assured him he would always be welcome in their home.

Neil's thoughts returned to the hospital room. Looking at his family, it was hard to believe such a volatile courtship had ended so ideally. They now lived in a new house in Fort Calhoun, on the lot next to Neil's parents. They loved the security and serenity of a small town life and wanted their children to have the same opportunities they had experienced. Neil couldn't leave his parents and the wonderland in which he had been raised.

He marveled at how much his life had changed, yet had still remained the same. "I still bounce on the trampoline. However, I no longer pile drive my friends, now I wrestle with my children. I still play Marco Polo in the pool, but now I always lose to the three loves of my life."

# *Max*

After a restless night, Neil awoke at 6:30 a.m. This was unusual for him, especially on a day off from work. He often slept in on the few days off he was allowed. However, this was not going to be a usual day off. It was a day he had dreaded, a day he had postponed several times, a day he would always remember. Friday, August 7, 2003 was one of the most difficult days of his life. It was to mark the end of an eleven-year friendship.

Max heard Neil moving about in the bed. He arose from his position at the foot of the bed and walked to Neil. This was the signal he wanted his usual morning hello, a combination of petting and scratching. Neil obliged him.

After breakfast, it was time. Neil hesitantly announced to Carrie, "I think we should go."

Carrie, tears immediately coming to her eyes, suggested, "There has to be something we can do. Shouldn't we try the new diet or the medication that the vet recommended?"

Neil understood this was also difficult for Carrie. She had known Max for nine years. He had been part of the family for the seven years of their marriage. Yet, he knew there was no plausible alternative. Physically, Max was in excellent shape, but mentally, he was deteriorating. Max was such a good dog. Neil considered him his best friend. He could not bear to watch him suffer.

"Honey, you know Jeri said those treatments probably wouldn't help, because of Max's age. He's suffering every day. I can't stand to have him suffer anymore. We have no choice," Neil explained, taking Carrie into his arms.

Together they stood, holding each other, crying and trying to find the strength to do what they knew was right.

While Carrie took Emily next door to stay with a neighbor, Neil took Max for one last walk. He was as active as ever, eager to lead Neil. Neil released him from his leash, and he ran after a rabbit. Even at thirteen years old, Max was still spry.

Carrie drove, with Cole in his safety seat. Neil sat with Max in the rear of his father's truck, which they borrowed for the day. They arrived at Jeri Welchert's office, which was located on the north side of town. She had been Max's veterinarian for all of the eleven years he had been with Neil. Knowing how traumatic this would be for Neil, she made sure that no one else would be at the office. Though she didn't want to admit it, this was going to be very difficult for her, also.

Greeting them at the door, she asked, "Neil, do you want me to take him?"

"No. We've done everything else together. I need to do this with him as well. I could never let him face this alone."

Neil led him to the operating room. At Jeri's request, Neil lifted Max onto the table. He held Max's head, so he would be looking at him. Scratching behind his ears and under his front legs, Neil tried to make him feel as comfortable as possible. Jeri administered the shot. After ten seconds, his head started to get heavy. Neil could tell Max wanted to lie down. So, he gently placed Max's head on the table. Neil continued to pet Max until he was gone.

"What do you want to do with Max? I can take care of him for you, if you'd like," Jeri asked in a reverent tone.

"No, I want to take him. I'm going to bury him, in the backyard, near the creek, where he always liked to play." Neil replied, in a halting voice.

"While you get the grave dug, I'll prepare him and keep him here for you. It won't be any problem," she tried to reassure him.

On the way home, Neil remembered his uncle, Dave Romans, had taken the day off. He had Carrie stop by his house. Dave was in the driveway, working on his car.

"Hey, Dave. When you get a chance, could you stop by the house and help me with something for a minute," Neil asked.

"I don't know. I'm pretty busy today. I've got to finish this car. Then, I have to jump in the shower and afterward go to Omaha. I'll stop over on my way to Omaha."

Dave replied, not really wanting to take the time.

"Don't bother showering before you come over. I was wondering if you would help me dig a grave for Max. I just had him put to sleep," Neil explained hesitantly.

Dave stopped and looked at Neil in shock. Like everyone in the family, he loved Max. For as long as he could remember, Neil and Max had been inseparable. He could not imagine one without the other. Realizing how difficult this was for Neil, he replied, "I'll be right over."

Dave dropped everything he was doing and followed Carrie to their house. Neil showed him where he wanted the grave dug. Dave responded, "I'll take care of digging the grave. You and Carrie go ahead and get Max. Everything will be ready when you get back."

"Thanks, Dave," Neil replied, thankful he did not have to dig the grave.

Upon returning to Jeri's office, she explained that Max's body was ready. She had placed him in a body bag.

"Would you mind carrying him out to the truck?" Neil asked. Neil wanted to remember Max the way he had been, when Neil held him for his last breaths. He did not want his last memory of Max to be in a body bag.

Jeri obliged, carefully placing him in the back of the truck. Upon arriving at the house, at Neil's request, Dave carried Max to his grave. After Dave had covered the grave, Neil and Carrie stood together, saying their prayerful goodbyes.

Carrie started to lead Neil away. Neil hesitated and then explained, "I want to be alone with Max for a while." Without saying a word, Carrie gave Neil a hug and quietly departed. Neil sat on the ground next to Max's grave. Tearfully, he began to reminisce about his eleven years with Max.

It all began the summer after his high school graduation. That fall Neil would be going to college. He knew he could no longer rely on his friends to get around. A cane was not an acceptable alternative for Neil. So earlier that year, Neil's parents worked with the area Lion's clubs to arrange for Neil to attend a Leader Dog School in Rochester, Michigan. One of the requirements of the school was that every student be a minimum of eighteen-years old. Neil was seventeen. After learning of Neil's college plans, the school waived the age restriction for Neil. At the school, he would be trained with his new leader dog. The total cost was $12,000. Like they had, ever since Neil's accident, the community responded. They held several fund raising events until the necessary funds were collected.

Though Neil realized he needed the dog, he did not want to go. This was the summer after his high school graduation. He and his girlfriend of six months had just broken up. It was to be a summer of freedom and parties. When he learned the school was four weeks long, he was frustrated. He would spend the best part of his summer following some dog around. Neil was scheduled to leave on Sunday, July 5. The night before, the Fourth of July, there were parties all over town. Neil, knowing it would be the last time to party for several weeks, made the best of it. Finally, about 3:00 a.m., he staggered to bed. That morning, at 6:00 a.m., Larry dragged Neil out of bed and drove him to the Omaha airport.

At the Detroit airport, a representative of the school met Neil. Neil did not know what to expect. He knew very little about leader dogs and even less about the school. After a two-hour ride in a van, they arrived at the school. The main building consisted of two wings, which were the dormitories, a nice center lounge and a large dining room. To his surprise, the food was excellent. Behind the school was a large building where they housed the animals and an outstanding veterinarian clinic. There was also a walking course, set up like a small town block.

That evening, there was an organizational meeting, at which time the training schedule was explained. There were twenty-two students in Neil's class. Each class was divided into groups of four or five, which were then assigned a teacher.

Each of the dogs, as a puppy, was assigned to a 4-H family. They treated the dog like a normal puppy for the first year. Once the dog was twelve months to two-years old, the dog was taken from the family and trained at the school. Each trainer was assigned five to ten dogs, which they trained over a period of three months. They paid special attention to the personality of each dog and how the dog performed. Once a dog passed the required tests, the dog was ready to be paired with a student.

For the first five days, Neil walked around with his trainer, who acted as the dog. Three times a day, Neil would work with the trainer, learning how to use a dog. Neil was trained in leash commands. He learned that when he held the leash, the dog was not to lead. Neil was to lead the dog. Anytime Neil would pick up the harness, it meant the dog was to take the lead. He would hold the harness in his left hand and use his right hand to signal the appropriate command, such as forward, left, right, faster, etc. In addition to the training, during this time, the trainer was also getting to know Neil. To match Neil with the right dog, it was important the trainer know his personality and his habits, such as how fast he walks and his confidence level.

In addition to the commands, Neil was taught how to care for the dog. The dog had a tightly regimented schedule, which Neil was told should never change. He was to brush the dog three times a day, for fifteen minutes each time. The dog was to be fed only once a day, using a specified portion of the same food, Purina Dog Chow. His bathroom schedule was at 7 a.m., 11 a.m., 4 p.m., and 8 p.m. Neil was to give him water only twice a day. When the dog is in the harness, no one is allowed to pet him. The dog must stay focused.

He was also told that these dogs tend to be insecure. Having been raised by the same family for over a year, the dog is suddenly taken from its home. Then it spends three months at the training center, assigned to a specific trainer and then it is moved again. Basically, the dog has three masters in six months. Neil was told to expect to initially be shunned by the dog and to also be tested. The dog would try to determine how strict his new master would be.

Though the training was interesting, the nightlife was nonexistent. Neil was not allowed to leave the school. He was relegated to watching television or listening to books on tape. For an active teenager, this was boring, a waste of a great summer. Though frustrated, Neil accepted his plight and worked diligently.

On the sixth day, all of the students gathered in the lounge. One by one, each trainer introduced a dog to its new master. After what seemed to Neil an eternity, his name was finally called. He followed his trainer, Gary, to his room, where he was instructed to wait. Neil anxiously obeyed. He knew this was the moment when he would meet his dog. It would be a German Shepard, a Golden Retriever, a Black Labrador, or a mix of these breeds. These were the primary breeds used in the program.

Sitting on his bed, waiting, Neil hoped it would be a female. He'd always had female dogs for pets and felt they were more laid back than male dogs. Then, suddenly, the door opened, and Gary announced, "Neil, I would like to introduce you to your leader dog, Max."

Gary then brought Max to Neil and handed Neil the leash. Neil began to pet Max and to talk to him. Gary left immediately, to allow Neil and Max time to get to know each other. Max was a Black Labrador and German Shepard mix breed. He was a little smaller than a Lab, a little thinner, a little longer in the face, and his ears were slightly smaller and sat up. He was in great shape, weighing sixty-two pounds. At first, as Neil had been told, Max was not affectionate. In fact, it was almost two months, before Max ever wagged his tail.

Initially, Neil was disappointed. He had expressed to Gary his preference for a female dog, yet he ended up with a male. Gary later explained why he had selected Max. He felt their personalities were compatible. In addition, Neil possessed confidence and an extraordinary assurance of his surroundings. As a result, he was an extremely fast walker. Max was one of the few dogs who could keep up with Neil's pace. The years would prove Max was the perfect choice.

At first, Neil was strict with Max. He wanted to make sure Max knew who was the boss. Subsequently, Max never really tested Neil. Some of the other students were not so fortunate. Their dogs would purposely lead them into a tree, or escape their master's grasp.

For the next several days, Neil and Max spent hours on the practice course. Then, when the trainer felt they were ready, they were taken into the town and walked the actual city streets. After a week of practice, they began testing. They would give Neil a route to walk and then observe him. This testing took two weeks.

During this period, while getting to know Max, Neil learned several new things about his dog and his required behavior. Max was taught to pay attention to what was in front of him, where he was going, and also to watch for any overhang. He was also trained to stop at curbs.

Neil entered the program with several misconceptions about leader dogs. Dogs are color blind. They have no way of knowing when to cross the street. The dog does not know where you are going. He cannot lead you to a specific destination. The dog is there to keep you on the straight path, to follow his master's commands and to ensure his master doesn't run into anything.

Max was also taught not to react to toys. Neil was not allowed to give Max any toys. Max was only allowed a nylon bone. If Max became accustomed to chasing balls, and while leading Neil he saw a ball, he would probably take Neil on a wild chase.

After successfully completing the required tests, Max and Neil flew back to Omaha. Upon landing, they were greeted by Neil's extremely excited parents. That night, Chris threw a big party to welcome Neil home. Neil took Max to the party. Max was an instant hit. From that point on, Max became part of Neil's family.

During Neil's four years at college, Max proved invaluable, in more than one way. Neil quickly realized that Max was a chick magnet. While in class, Max would always sit under Neil's desk. Neil soon learned it was impossible to prevent people from petting Max. He allowed people to pet Max, especially if they were women. Max proved to be a great icebreaker.

During his freshman year, Neil lived in Manor Hall. Max was instantly adopted as the dormitory mascot. He would roam the halls enjoying the special attention. One of the frustrating parts of living with Max was his early morning walk. The school had emphasized the importance of maintaining a strict schedule. Neil didn't understand how difficult that would be, especially on the mornings after a late-night party. There was many an early morning when Neil would wake to the alarm clock. Still inebriated and suffering from a blinding headache, he would put on a tee shirt over his boxer shorts, descend the three flights of stairs, let Max do his business and then rapidly return to bed.

From the very beginning, Neil was worried Max would do something in class to embarrass him. Nothing happened until the last class of the last day of Neil's freshman year. Neil was sitting in the front row, next to Chris. About ten minutes before the class was to end, without any warning, Max threw up all over the floor. Chris ran to the bathroom and got some paper towels. They cleaned up the mess, to the laughter of their fellow students.

Chris quickly grew to love Max. Whenever Neil was gone and Max needed to be fed, walked, or groomed, Chris would do it. As far as Chris was concerned, Max was as much his as he was Neil's. There were many times Neil would come home and find Max lying in bed with Chris.

Max was an extremely smart dog. Neil and Chris would often leave Max locked in their room. Max was always looking for food. Somehow, he found a way to reach the pantry shelves and get down a big box of Saltine crackers. He would get into the container and eat the contents. Another time he managed to get a hold of a loaf of bread. Each time, he would never knock anything over. The only way they knew Max had raided the pantry was when they found the empty containers on the floor.

Neil rarely took Max to a college party, because there were just too many people. Many nights, before Neil and Chris would leave for a party, they would drink a few beers to get primed. Max became extremely proficient at waiting until one of them went to the bathroom. When they returned, they would find Max lapping up the floor, where he had purposely spilled the beer.

After college, Max made the move back to Fort Calhoun and the move from Chris to Carrie, with Neil. Carrie and Neil's two children grew to love Max. Max became protective of Emily and Cole. There were many times when Neil would be wrestling with his children, and Max would suddenly start to growl. It was his way of telling Neil he was getting too rough.

Max went to work with Neil every day for five years. Neil finally had to stop taking him, because he was growing increasingly restless. He could no longer sit on the hard floors for long hours. It was a difficult decision. Every morning, up to that last day, when Neil left for work, Max would meet him at the door, wanting to join him.

This was when his decline began. For the last year of his life, Max was suffering. The problem was his hearing. Anytime he would hear a loud noise, such as a hammer or a saw, he would go crazy. He would run to a corner and dig at the walls and the carpet. If Neil let him outside alone, he wouldn't leave the porch but scratched at the door, trying to get back inside.

One night, the family returned home after one of Emily's baseball games to find the kitchen and laundry room flooded with water. Max had chewed through the water return for the toilet. A few weeks later, they returned home and found Max chewing on the water return in the master bath. It was at the point where even the noise of the children would disturb Max. Neil and Carrie were growing concerned about the safety of their children. That is when Neil made the decision to end Max's suffering.

Neil wiped his eyes, as his thoughts returned to the present. Standing, he pulled a paper from his pocket. Whispering, he read his final goodbye,

"You became my eyes and lead the way,
though you were forever destined to walk in my shadow.

You chose this road without complaint,
and never allowed jealousy to deter you from your duty.

There were many obstacles which the two of us faced,
yet you always tread forward undaunted by the course.
Your attention never wavered as you walked with head held high,
though the distractions were many and the enticements plentiful.

In your younger days, you were the leader,
as you made sure each step was taken with care.
In later years you became father,
as you watched over my children.

I hope that we may learn from the life that you have lived,
may we show the same restraint and discipline which you so often showed.
May we show the same loyalty to our family and friends,
which you always gave to me and mine.

I hope that the decision I made did not destroy the trust,
which we forged over those many years of companionship.
We traveled all roads together walking side by side,
and this is why I chose to hold you when your final minutes came.

You will forever walk beside me down all the paths of life,
and I pray that the sound of your footsteps will guide me along the way.
And I hope that you will wait,
to guide me through the streets of gold."

# Conclusion

With the spring of 2004 upon us, I find myself writing the closing to what has been one of the most rewarding and happiest periods of my life. I have long since left the worries of my childhood and the carefree years of my teens behind. I have a lovely wife, and have fallen easily into the role of father, as I struggle to pass on years of lessons to my two children. What I enjoy most is the innocence of my children. To my children, I am just Daddy. They are not amazed by the fact I spend hours with them swimming in the pool, jumping on the trampoline, or climbing on the playground equipment at the park. These are all things they have just come to expect from their father. Often, on warm summer nights, I walk the streets of Fort Calhoun hand in hand with my six-year old daughter. It is on these occasions I have found myself to be most content. She is unaware of the level of trust, which she holds in her tiny hand, acting as my guide. Yet, she has never failed me.

As the father of two beautiful children, I now realize many of the sacrifices my parents made during those crucial years following my accident. The decisions they made, to assure my future success, must have been some of the most difficult choices of their lives. To their credit, they didn't falter, no matter the sacrifice. I would like to thank them for their constant support, and most of all for giving me opportunities. My parents didn't hold me back and didn't allow anyone else to keep me from growing and learning. They always gave me the chance to fail or succeed, knowing there were lessons to be learned from both.

Professionally, I feel I am at somewhat of a crossroads in my life. I have a good paying job selling travel insurance for a company in Omaha, but I still find myself longing for something more. Unlike my family life, in the work place, I find myself still having to prove my abilities and overcome the challenges of people's prejudices. At night, as I lay in bed waiting for sleep, I dream of a time when I can use my abilities to have a positive impact on the lives of others.

There are several questions, which I am frequently asked.

**Do you remember being able to see? Can you see anything?** The doctors told my parents that because of my young age, I would never remember seeing. They were correct. I have no memory of sight. I cannot remember what anyone or anything looked like. I cannot see anything.

**How do you visualize? When someone talks about something, or when you watch a movie or television, what do you visualize?** It is difficult to describe. My sense of touch is my sight. I visualize by how the various objects feel. With frequent contact, I am able to visualize the shape of an object. Many times my concept of objects have been determined by the childhood toys with which I played, such as cars, trucks, spaceships, etc. My toys taught me their shapes, but I can visualize them on a larger scale. I have no concept of color.

**What exactly is braille?** Most people think braille is just typing with raised symbols. That is not true. Braille is a system of short hand composed of six sets of dots and spaces, which combine to make symbols, each of which represents a word or group of words. It is time consuming and difficult to learn. With the improvement in computers, I have rarely used braille since high school.

**Why and how did your sense of hearing develop to such an acute state?** I really don't know and the doctors don't know. Personally, I feel it is because, unlike many other blind children, I was not protected or isolated from the real world. I was allowed to live and compete in the sighted world, without any special treatment. In many situations, I was at a distinct disadvantage. I feel my body naturally, instinctively developed my hearing. I had to rely almost totally on my hearing. It's like a muscle, the more you use it, the bigger and stronger it gets.

For several years my parents thought I had some sight, that I was at least able to see shadows. They would periodically take me to the doctor to have my sight checked. Each time they got the same answer. I was completely blind.

My mobility was further enhanced by my memory. I have the ability to walk through a house, a building, or a room and instantly memorize the floor plan. This combined with my hearing ability, makes it appear to people, who do not know me, that I can see.

I hope my story will serve to both educate and inspire people. The lessons I hope you will take from my life are:

**Never Ask "WHY?"** I have noticed that individuals, when faced with a tragedy in their lives, often ask "why me?" It has always been a silent sense of pride for me that I have never asked why God allowed this to happen to me. It is my belief there is no future in seeking answers of the past. The question for me has not been why, but rather what. What will I achieve in my life? On that summer day in July of 1977, I had something taken from me, which has impacted my entire life. I sincerely believe what was taken from me on that day is nothing compared to the gifts I have received. I have been blessed with a beautiful and loving family, five of the best friends anyone could possibly have, and the caring support of an entire community. All of these individuals, who have touched my life in so many ways over the years, make the challenges of each day worth facing. I have tried to focus my attention and resources on finding solutions rather than dwelling on problems. My parents' positive approach to life taught me this lesson.

**No matter how difficult your problems, with the love and support of your family and friends, you can overcome any challenge.** I have been fortunate. First, I have a tremendous family. My parents worked diligently to provide me with the same opportunities as any other child. In addition, I was privileged to live in a small town. During my life, the people in the town of Fort Calhoun supported me. Some helped in big ways and some in small, but each one played a part in my ultimate success. I hope that anyone who feels overwhelmed by his or her problems, who feels all alone, will realize there is someone who will help. No matter how terrible your situation, do not hesitate to ask for help.

**Life should be fun.** No matter what your situation, you only live once. Try to find the humor in your life. Enjoy life, both the little moments and the exciting experiences.

**Take chances.** Life should be an adventure. Do not approach life with fear, but rather with enthusiasm and daring.

Recently, at work, while conversing with one of my co-workers, in the break room, I commented that my friend Jason and I removed the transmission from my 1971 Cutlass Convertible. The co-worker responded, "Neil, you absolutely amaze me."

In response, I asked, "Why?"

"There are very few sighted people who can remove a transmission," she explained.

"That's because they don't try," I answered.

My point is that much of my success has been due to the fact that I am not afraid to try. If you try, you may fail, but if you never try, you will definitely not succeed.

I want to direct the following words to the established blind community, to those who determine the education, socialization and living plans for blind people. I think you are doing it all wrong! I do not profess to know of all the programs, which are available. My observations are based upon my association with other blind people. I have had only limited contact; primarily at camps I attended, at the Leader Dog School and at the Nebraska School for the Visually Handicapped. In most cases, the blind clients have very limited socialization skills, especially when interacting with the sighted world. They thought, acted and lived like they were handicapped. They were limited in their view of life, they were limited in their skills, and they were limited in their ability to deal with the sighted world. I feel strongly that if you think you are handicapped, you are. If you believe you can do anything, then, no matter your weaknesses, you are not handicapped. You choose to teach them to live with their handicaps. My parents taught me to overcome my handicap.

In parting, I would like to thank my family, my friends and the community of Fort Calhoun, for their love and support. You provided me with boundless opportunities and made my life an adventure, which I will never forget.

# Halford Family Pictures

Neil at three months old.

Ryan, 5, and Neil, 2.

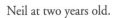

Neil at two years old.

Ryan, 7, and Neil, 3,
after the accident.

Neil wrestling at a high school tournament.

Neil after winning a match at the Nebraska High School
State Wrestling Tournament.

Carrie and Neil on their wedding day.

The Halford Family: Carrie, Neil, Annie, Ryan (standing)
Linda, Larry, Emily (sitting)

Neil and Carrie with their children, Emily, 7, and Cole, 3.